PQ
7081
.J26

80-00679/1299

DATE DUE			
~~--~~		NOV 1 7 2005	
~~--~~			
~~-15-~~			
~~6-15-99~~			
DEC 1 9 2005			

TEXAS WOMAN'S UNIVERSITY
LIBRARY
DENTON, TEXAS

The Black Image
in Latin American Literature

The Black Image in Latin American Literature

Richard L. Jackson

UNIVERSITY OF NEW MEXICO PRESS

Albuquerque

Library of Congress Cataloging in Publication Data

Jackson, Richard L.   1937-
　　　The Black Image in Latin American Literature.

　　　Bibliography: p. 155
　　　Includes index.
　　　1. Spanish American literature—History and criticism.
　　　2. Blacks in literature.　I. Title.
PQ7081.J26　　　860'.9　　　76-21539
ISBN 0-8263-0421-4

© 1976 by the University of New Mexico Press. All rights reserved.
Manufactured in the United States of America
Library of Congress Catalog Card Number 76-21539
International Standard Book Number 0-8263-0421-4
First Edition

TEXAS WOMAN'S UNIVERSITY LIBRARY

PQ
7081
.J26

For my children
Chris, Didi, Shaw, Charley

1299

80-00679

In blackness there is great virtue,
if you will but observe its beauty.
                                    Antar

Contents

Preface

Blacks have participated integrally throughout the literary history of Latin America both as characters and as authors. This book, though dealing in part with Afro-Latin-American literary expression, centers for the most part on black themes, primarily in the imaginative literature of non-black Latin-American writers of this century, to determine the image of black people these authors have projected in their writings. A subsequent volume will enlarge on the black experience as recorded in the literature of socially and aesthetically committed writers of African descent in Spanish America.

It became apparent to me some years ago that black themes and characters in Latin-American literature do possess the originality, the dramatic impact, and the thematic richness of the Indian. Indeed, the black experience in the Hispanic world is as momentous a subject as the indigenous one. An examination of the literary reflection, for example, of the racist attitudes toward black people in Latin America not only throws some light on the problem of color in that part of the world but gives some insight as well into the Afro-Latin-American's awareness of his place and role in the worldwide resurgence of the black race. Although the struggle for racial equality and social justice currently is epitomized in the demands made in the United States by black people for first-class citizenship, neither racism nor the fight against it in this hemisphere has been confined to Anglo-America.

I would like to thank the editors of the journals in which the following articles were first published for permission to incorporate these earlier versions in parts of this book: "Mestizaje vs. Black Identity: The Color Crisis in Latin America," *Black World* 24, No. 2 (July 1975); "Black Phobia and the White Aesthetic in Spanish American Literature," *Hispania* 58, No. 3 (September 1975); "A Reply to Louis Nesbit," *Hispania* 59 (March 1976); and "Black Song without Color: The Black Experience and the Negritude of Synthesis in Afro-Spanish American Literature," *Inter-American Review of Bibliography* (Summer 1976).

I am also grateful for feedback from students and colleagues, who over the years have reacted to ideas first developed and expressed in courses at Carleton University and in lectures and papers given in Birmingham, Alabama, Madrid, Spain, and at Brown University and Michigan State University. And I wish to thank Rita Lindner and Eleanor McSheffrey in particular, whose first drafts of translations made my revisions easier than they might have been.

I owe a special indebtedness to the late Professor Robert Mitchell for making many helpful suggestions on an early draft and to the late Professor James A. Hamlett, a solid example to all who knew him, especially to those of us who are his former students. The support of these two friends was constant right up to their untimely deaths.

I am grateful to Carl Mora, Managing Editor of the University of New Mexico Press for his expert editorial assistance. And I acknowledge with gratitude the financial assistance received at various stages of this work from the Canada Council, the Carleton University Arts Faculty Research Fund, the Andrew Mellon Foundation, and the American Philosophical Society. Without these grants and fellowships this study would not have been possible, certainly not at this time.

Finally, thanks above all to my wife Lillian, whose assistance and support in every capacity are indispensable.

Introduction

> . . . it is becoming more apparent that, despite
> comparatively harmonious relations between blacks
> and whites in Latin America, racial, cultural and
> class prejudices and attitudes have been significantly
> detrimental to black people both during and after
> slavery.
>
> Robert Conrad

Several years ago I wrote[1] that a study of black themes in
Spanish-American literature would correspond to a steadily increasing
interest in race relations in Latin America on the one hand and in race
mixture on the other, an interest that crystallized in the early sixties in
the publication of such briefs as Juan Comas's *Relaciones inter-
raciales en América Latina: 1940-60* (Mexico City: U.N.A.M., 1961),
which he also published in English in the UNESCO series on race
relations,[2] and Instituto Panamericano de Geografía e Historia, *El
mestizaje en la historia de Iberoamérica* (Mexico City: Editorial
Cultura, 1961), later the subject of a book in English by Magnus
Mörner,[3] a major contributor to this second volume. The first brief, I
pointed out, reevaluated and questioned the heretofore accepted
generalization that in Latin America racial prejudice does not exist, nor
has it ever existed at any time; the other brought up to date the problem
of *mestizaje,* or race mixture, with due emphasis given to the African
element in the countries outside of the Caribbean.

These two questions, race prejudice and race mixture, have
undergone increased reevaluation during the later sixties and early
seventies in attempts to bring into proper perspective the problem of
color in Latin America. The result has been that few responsible
scholars today accept without question the myth of a racial paradise in
that part of the world worthy of emulation by the United States and
other countries, where racial harmony seems, at times, to be a distant
reality. The current trend, now that this myth has been laid to rest,

leans toward determining the nature of race relations and the kind of prejudice prevalent in Latin America, usually by subjecting the area to a comparative analysis of historical and current patterns of race relations in the Americas, with particular emphasis on the United States and the West Indies.

Especially relevant in this regard is the work of Mauricio Solaún and Sidney Kronus, *Discrimination without Violence: Miscegenation and Racial Conflict in Latin America* (New York: John Wiley and Sons, 1973), and particularly the work of Harmannus Hoetink whose recent book, *Slavery and Race Relations in the Americas* (New York: Harper and Row, 1973), builds on earlier studies in which he develops his theory of the "somatic norm image," which he defines as

> the complex of physical (somatic) characteristics which are accepted by a group as its norm and ideal. . . . The somatic norm image is the yardstick of aesthetic evaluation and ideal of the somatic characteristics of the members of the group.[4]

Solaún and Kronus elaborate:

> This esthetic preference normally corresponds with the physical characteristics of the dominant group. This leads, then, to maximize racial discrimination against those groups who deviate the most from the norm. The acceptance of these esthetic standards produces those practices common in Latin America and the United States by which individuals seek to "whiten" themselves (p. 79).

As a logical corollary of the concept of "somatic norm image," Hoetink introduced the concept of "somatic distance," which he defines as

> the degree to which the difference between two somatic norm images (or rather, between one's own somatic norm image and another physical type) is subjectively experienced.[5]

Solaún and Kronus in supporting Hoetink's physical or somatic interpretation of race relations in Latin America go on to underline one of the basic points that have served as inspiration for my study, namely, the critical difference between Latin American and United States race relations, which lies in the more favorable attitudes in Latin America toward the mulatto, that is, toward the group that is somatically closer to whites. To my mind, Latin-American literature, characterized by black phobia and the white aesthetic, abundantly illustrates that in Latin America racial attitudes and the somatic distance are even more unfavorable toward black people than we are ordinarily led to believe.

It has become clearer in recent years that the somatic distance, conditioned by archetypal images of color and corresponding racial myths, has had an enormous impact on the pattern of race relations in Latin America. The white aesthetic, there as elsewhere, has taken a strong foothold in the consciousness of Latin Americans of all colors. The association of the color black with ugliness, sin, darkness, immorality, Manichaean metaphor, with the inferior, the archetype of the lowest order, and the color white with the opposite of these qualities partly explains the racist preconceptions and negative images of the black man projected—at times despite the author's good intentions—in much of the literature of the area.

Addison Gayle, Jr.[6] recently called attention to the necessity of a comprehensive study of the white aesthetic from its early origins onwards, encompassing all the nations and cultures of the world where the basic formula, in spite of various changes from culture to culture and from nation to nation, defines superior and inferior according to the amount of whiteness one has, where the concept of beauty has been measured in terms of light and dark, essential characteristics, Gayle reminds us, of a white and black aesthetic. These basic ingredients, symptomatic of racist societies, are noticeably present in Latin America, and the impact of white racism is clearly reflected in the literature.

The history of racism and racist writers in Latin America has not yet been fully explored. Magnus Mörner,[7] commenting in 1971 on the need for more research on race relations in Latin America, points specifically to the dearth of studies on Latin American racist writers, a category, he tells us, that has lingered on until very recent days. Mörner writes, too, that although one or another of the Latin-American racist writers has attracted the critical attention of modern students (Martin Stabb, for example), a comprehensive study of this interesting aspect of Latin-American thought remains to be written.

Such studies would be consistent with a recent action of the Modern Language Association Delegate Assembly whose concern with lingering racist ideas and materials are expressed in the following resolutions passed on December 28, 1973:

Whereas new studies claiming to demonstrate "scientifically" the old notion that black people are inferior have been rapidly spreading in professional literature, texts, and respectable popular magazines and are now being taught as fact in classrooms across the country although decisive evidence to the contrary has been continually presented by the scientific community, Be it resolved that MLA urges the academic community to organize and support activities to eliminate racist practices and repudiate racist ideas. It specifically urges the following: that educational institutions take steps to prevent classroom racism; that scholars expose the anti-humanist and unscientific character of racist materials, thereby denying them academic legitimacy; and that professional organizations, academic departments, and scholarly journals take seriously their responsibility to repudiate racist ideas.[8]

Roger Bastide,[9] Gregory Rabassa,[10] Richard A. Prêto-Rodas,[11] and David T. Haberly,[12] among others, have shown that racial stereotypes and expressions of prejudice and racial insult are common themes in the literature of Brazil. Racism and the white aesthetic exist in Spanish America, as in Brazil and the non-Hispanic Caribbean, as controlling factors in the lives of black people. Indeed, a cult of whiteness and a corresponding fear of blackness, whether ethnic, political, or social, are part of a tradition dramatized in Hispanic literature from Lope de Rueda's *Eufemia* (1576) to Francisco Arriví's *Máscara puertorriqueña* (1971), with numerous examples to be found in between and after. This white aesthetic leads not only to curious acts in literature that reflect a heritage of white racial consciousness but also to the distortion of the black man's literary image. This heritage of white racial consciousness, transmitted from generation to generation by the white "collective unconscious" where black is equated with negative qualities, is defined by Fanon as "purely and simply the sum of prejudices, myths, and collective attitudes of a given group,"[13] and has been inherited in Latin America not only by some white writers but by a number of writers of African descent as well, particularly in past centuries.

In this study I concentrate on some of the mainly twentieth-century literary manifestations of this heritage in the Spanish-speaking areas of Latin America to determine the impact it has had on some of the authors that expose as well as on some that propagate, at times unintentionally, racist attitudes and negative images of blacks. I focus especially on the literature of the Spanish-American mainland, where research on black themes, scarce until now, finally is beginning to gain momentum.[14]

By singling out racism and the white aesthetic, two of the most fundamental, though largely disregarded and therefore unstudied, aspects of black themes in Latin-American literature, for discussion, I hope to add another dimension to the on-going debate regarding the nature of race relations and the kind of prejudice prevalent in Latin America. Further, I hope to show that despite the somatic distance and associated racist obstacles, the process of *mestizaje*, though of questionable value to the development of black identity, is, nevertheless, an indisputable fact of the black experience in Latin America. An experience that is considered by some black writers to be an inescapable point of departure toward a better and more realistic appreciation and understanding not only of the concept of negritude as it has developed in Latin America but also of the black contribution to the human and cultural environment in the New World.

I should add that in choosing works projecting or reflecting racist images of black people I have had to survey not only some literature with high artistic value critically accepted as landmarks outside their immediate locale but also works with little to offer artistically; even "bad" books can reflect or strike a racist cord in the reading public, especially if that public shares an author's views and is ready to respond, to associate emotionally with them even if the book itself does not bear transplanting geographically, morally, and ideologically to another more "universal" locale or clientele. Artistic achievement, though partly responsible for the universality and permanence of a work, is not always responsible for the popularity some literature enjoys. Shared interest and not intellectual demands can make a work "interesting" to a reader even if not successful artistically.

This survey hardly represents the end point of criticism of these works. As a starting point, however, for literary criticism, awareness of the impact of racism and the white aesthetic in some of the literature of Latin America could lead to reevaluation and a closer examination of literature on black themes in an attempt to discover not only its artistic merit, but, perhaps more importantly insofar as the black man and his literary image are concerned, its credibility as well.

Among the several studies appearing in recent years on black themes in Hispanic literature I would like to call special attention to three publications: L. Johnson, *The Devil, the Gargoyle and the Buffoon: The Negro as Metaphor in Western Literature* (Port Washington, N.Y.: Kennikat Press, 1969, 1971); Isabelo Zenón Cruz, *Narciso descubre su trasero (El negro en la cultura puertorriqueña)* Vol. 1 (Humacao, Puerto Rico: Editorial Furidi, 1974); and Adalberto Ortiz, "La negritud en la cultura latinoamericana," *Expresiones culturales del Ecuador,* No. 1 (June 1972): 10-18. L. Johnson questions the credibility of much of the literature in the Western world by examining the "malignant and benign literary caricatures" through which English, French, and Hispanic writers attempted to accommodate to the idea of blackness in human form. Professor Johnson's comparative study forms an appropriate backdrop to parts of mine; whereas he carries his examination through to the negrophilisms of the twenties and thirties, my exploration of the impact of racism and the white aesthetic in the literature of Latin America uses these decades largely as a point of departure. Furthermore, unlike Professor Johnson, whose Spanish-American examples, limited to the first decades of this century, are selected from the Caribbean (Puerto Rico and Cuba) in general and Palés Matos and Nicolás Guillén in particular, I hope to show the continuing pervasiveness of the Hispanic tradition of literary caricature and racial insult beyond that earlier period and outside of the Caribbean area as well. My study, I believe, benefits from Professor Johnson's fine work and enlarges upon his pioneering discussions of negative reactions to blackness in human form in Hispanic literature manifested by white authors in their at times one-dimensional portrayals of black people, whether because of ignorant prejudice, incompetent sympathy, pseudoscientific exaggeration, or pathological malice. The massive work by Professor Zenón Cruz, an even more detailed analysis (exposé) of racism and racist authors in Puerto Rico than Professor Johnson's, questions the credibility of much "black" literature by white Puerto Rican authors and promises to become the standard reference for years to come on black themes in the literature of that country.

During a recent trip to Quito, I had the good fortune of meeting Manuel Zapata Olivella, the leading Afro-Colombian writer, and Adalberto Ortiz, the Afro-Ecuadorian author of *Juyungo,* perhaps the best known "black" novel in Latin America. One of the purposes of my trip was to ask of these distinguished men of letters what their present position was on negritude in Latin America, a subject on which, I learned, Ortiz was writing an essay. I benefited greatly from these contacts, and I was particularly happy to discover that Ortiz had just published his essay and that it was available in *Expresiones Culturales del Ecuador,* a publication of the Centro Andino de la Universidad de New Mexico in Quito, and that my impressions of the developing concept of negritude in Latin America were not unlike those he expressed in his article, particularly insofar as the importance of the relationship between negritude and *mestizaje,* both cultural and ethnic, is concerned.

Backdrop to Literature: Racism, *mestizaje*, and the Crisis of Black Identity

> *Racial identities are important in the face of today's realities if our intent is interracial understanding and closing the gap of human divisiveness.*
>
> *Martha K. Cobb*

In discussing the development of Afro-Latin-American cultural patterns from the early days of the Spanish colonial empire to the Afro-Cuban Movement in this century, Martha K. Cobb emphasizes that research on the Spanish-speaking Americas would add another dimension to black people's awareness of themselves and their common identity by confirming what has long been suspected, namely that there is a pattern in the African contact with Western civilization that, despite differences of language and life style, can be traced wherever black men and women have been situated.[1] This pattern, characterized largely by white racism, slavery, and racial oppression, has had a great impact on the ethnic survival of black people in Latin America, where another pattern, equally traceable, has emerged on a wide scale to threaten their ethnic and cultural identity. This second pattern is embodied in the concept of miscegenation or *mestizaje,* a process that, while loosely defined as ethnic and cultural fusion, is often understood to mean the physical, spiritual, and cultural rape of black people.

Ethnic Lynching, or *Mestizaje* Properly Seen

Despite artistic expressions of black themes, blacks in Latin America have had to wage a constant battle against extinction through cultural fusion or acculturation and particularly through racial amalgamation. The strong process of miscegenation running throughout the history of Latin America would seem to refute the existence of a pattern of racial conflict in that part of the world. The two phenomena, however, are not mutually exclusive, especially if there is any truth in the assertion, put in its bluntest form, that whites try to get rid of blacks in the United States through extermination (and birth control) and in Latin America through racial amalgamation or *linchamiento étnico* ("ethnic or white lynching"), as the process has been called.[2] Just as cultural fusion and in some instances government pressures have not encouraged the development and existence of a separate black cultural heritage, the process of racial bleaching denies the Latin-American black the recognizable African characteristics of his physical features and thus his black identity.

Black people existed in some areas in Latin America and even predominated in others where today they are hardly visible. Although statistics vary, blacks outnumbered whites, for example, in Lima, Peru, in the latter half of the sixteenth century. And until the mid-eighteenth century the ratio of slaves to Spaniards in Mexico City was two or three to one. In 1810, more than half of the population of Venezuela was made up of blacks. And black people were important elements in the population of Argentina and Uruguay in colonial and early republican days. But blacks have been absorbed in many of these places and others, such as Chile, primarily through the process of "ethnic lynching." The non-white population even in Puerto Rico and Cuba has steadily decreased during the past two centuries, dropping from more than half the population to approximately one fourth in both countries. Black Brazilians too are being "forced to acculturate, assimilate, to enter the world of whiteness."[3]

This process of "becoming whiter" is especially acute in the Dominican Republic, where the "improvement" of the caucasoid element in the population is cited as one of the motives of Dominican immigration policy, designed there, as elsewhere in Latin America, to welcome whites and to exclude blacks.[4] It has been reported that ethnic lynching has worked so well in the Dominican Republic that white Dominicans often depict their "own" blacks as being racially less "pure" and therefore aesthetically more attractive than those, for example, from Cuba, Haiti, or the Virgin Islands.[5] In short, ethnic lynching, rapidly taking place in the Dominican Republic, is, broadly speaking, characteristic of all of the Spanish and Portuguese-speaking societies in Latin America, where the problem of color, some hope, can be erased by erasing the black race.

Although racist intellectuals advanced the idea of ethnic lynching in the late nineteenth century perhaps more clearly than at any other time, illustrious advocates of this process date back to the seventeenth century, for example, when Fray Alonso de Sandoval,[6] an early Spanish defender of blacks in America and perhaps Spanish America's first Africanist, paradoxically, wanted to curtail further importation of African slaves so that the process of *blanqueamiento* ("whitening") could get underway. And in 1835 the Cuban historian and authority on slavery, José Antonio Saco, anxious to restore whiteness to Cuba, wrote: "The only remedy for making us respectable is whitening, whitening."[7]

Ethnic lynching, the process of restoring whiteness by bleaching out black people, then, has long been accepted in Latin America as a means of solving social and racial problems, a solution that rests on the expectation that the biological superiority of the white race, augmented in number through European immigration, would impose itself on the nonwhite races.

H. Hoetink recently described in some detail the process of whitening taking place in Latin America. He realized, nevertheless, that he is by no means the first to describe it.[8] As early as 1942 Preston James drew attention to this "whitening out", and T. Lynn Smith analyzed what he called the "bleaching" process in Brazil,[9] while Richard Pattee had written in 1944 that "one of the most interesting cases of the Negro in Latin America is the Negro that no longer exists."[10]

More important, however, than recognizing or describing the process is understanding its relationship to white racism and black identity in Latin America. It should be emphasized, for example, that racial amalgamation is not necessarily a sign of racial harmony. Juan Comas[11] has advanced the interesting theory that the idea of cross breeding condemns prejudice only in appearance, since in fact the individual white hopes that the "bleaching" process will be achieved through the efforts of other whites, but not of his own. If each step toward whiteness can be considered a step toward the elimination of blacks, it is not inconceivable that prejudice could have actually accelerated the miscegenation with its bleaching process that is so characteristic of Latin American societies. Put another way, the "virtually universal tendency" in the Latin countries toward *blanqueamiento* represents for Hoetink and for Bonilla Seda, upon whom he based his arguments, "a somatic preference that would be inconceivable in an environment devoid of any racial prejudice."[12] This likelihood is further supported by the remarks of a black writer from Jamaica whose on-the-spot research in Cuba reveals a kind of private racism there best illustrated in the words of a black Cuban, who, in an interview, related how her white boy friend and his father, an active revolutionary, approved of her because they believed the coupling would "improve the race": their hope, of course, was that their children would be whiter than she.[13]

Widespread miscegenation in Latin America, therefore, is a dubious sign of racial tolerance. Racial blending does not necessarily mean an absence of racial prejudice. More precisely: "It is an open question whether a society that sees every addition of white blood as a step toward purification is more, or less, prejudiced than a society that sees any appreciable trace of Negro blood as a mark of degradation."[14] In Latin America, then, where ethnic lynching can be considered "a manifestation of latent or camouflaged prejudice against Blacks,"[15] racial mixing goes in the direction of a gradual whitening of the population and a corresponding reduction of "black" blood until it becomes an infinitesimal drop. The expectation that ethnic lynching will eventually lead to the disappearance of blacks presupposes the superiority of white over black and as such is a form of white racism.[16]

Aesthetic Prejudice and the Spectrum of Racial Color

Ethnic lynching with its implied acceptance of white superiority suggests that aesthetic prejudice lies at the heart of the crisis of black identity in Latin America. Aesthetic prejudice and the premium it places on whiteness is partly responsible for the fact that African features decrease chances for racial acceptance and ascent in Latin America. The argument that aesthetic prejudice in Latin America favors those who most approximate whiteness is advanced even by a young Japanese in Brazil, who said: "In my opinion race prejudice does not exist in Brazil; there exists an aesthetic prejudice. The Japanese who most resembles individuals of the white race—for example, one who has less elongated eyes—is better accepted."[17] Hoetink, who reported this remark, adds: "This also applies outside Brazil."[18]

While antiblack prejudice is practiced both in Anglo and in Latin America, the singling out of black people almost exclusively as special targets for racist treatment in Latin America indicates that the antiblack aesthetic is perhaps the most obvious, though the least stressed, factor that differentiates the nature of the color problem in Latin America from the race issue in the United States. Anti-African prejudice is a common denominator in race relations on both sides of the border. But whereas in the United States color or race prejudice is directed not only toward all obviously black people, but toward all people with "black" blood as well, regardless of skin shade, in Latin America we have a color spectrum, and racist attitudes there are directed largely toward those colored people closer to the black end of this spectrum. This is so even in Cuba, a fact Gil Green had to admit in his book *Revolution Cuban Style,* even though his intent was to present Cuba as a place "Where Black and White Unite."[19]

This spectrum of racial color is a holdover from the colonial period's "pigmentocracy"—a social hierarchy based primarily on skin color. Since then many not-so-pure-blooded Africans have declared themselves "white," thus making a farce of the rigid colonial social structure as far as the mixed bloods were concerned. But today, a very high premium is still placed on belonging to the white end of this spectrum or on getting as close to it as one can. Therefore, when we speak of the black in Latin America we must also speak of the mulatto, and I use this term to cover a wide range of black-white interracial mixture, not just to apply to the person who is precisely half white and half black. When we speak of race relations in Latin America we must speak of black, brown, and white relations. In the United States we can use the term "Negro" or reject it, as the case may be. We can use black, or Afro-American, or any of the other terms in a collective sense to include those people, regardless of how white they may appear, who have the proverbial drop of "black" blood. Thus, the simple black-white polarity. Either one is "black" or one is "white". But not so in Latin America, where racial appearance, including color, and not the drop of blood, determines one's status, where a black, once he becomes mixed, ceases to be rigidly classified with black people as long as he possesses some "white" features, as long as he moves away, in appearance, from the black end of the color spectrum.

This distinction between physical appearance and ancestry was crystallized by the Brazilian sociologist Oracy Nogueira[20] into the terms "prejudice of stamp or color ('marca' or 'cor')" in Brazil and "prejudice of origin" in the United States. Juan Comas[21] has remarked, appropriately, that this distinction seems of great value as a means of arriving at a better understanding of the scope of racial discrimination not only in Brazil but possibly in the rest of Latin America as well. Unlike in the United States, this distinction in Latin America has built into it a tacit acceptance of the mulatto and a corresponding rejection of the black man. In other words, "the crucial difference between North American and Latin American prejudice is not, then, that one is racial and the other social but that the social definition of who are acceptable as whites is different in both areas . . ."[22]

In many cases the mulatto in Latin America forms a buffer zone between whites and blacks. There is no such barrier erected between mulattoes and blacks in the United States. In fact, the term mulatto is hardly, if ever, used here any more. It has been said often that in the United States whoever is not one hundred percent pure-blooded white is black. No one, however, has said it better than Malcolm X, who once reminded colored people in the United States that we are all black, just different shades, meaning that no matter how white an Afro-American is in appearance, he will still "catch just as much hell" from the white man as his blackest brother. Many people, using the favorable position of the mulatto in measuring the degree of racial progress, forget this paradox of a racial situation in Latin America where discrimination and aesthetic prejudice vary in direct proportion to the blackness of one's skin, or to possession of other African features. Once this fact of the black experience is realized, the common adage in colonial Brazil that the land is a paradise for mulattoes and a hell for blacks takes on new meaning, especially when applied, as well, to the Spanish countries in Latin America.

During the period following the abolition of slavery the social status of the mulattoes, however, was far from being paradisiacal. "Because of their stigmas of slavery and illegitimacy," Mörner writes, "the *pardos* were subjected to forms of social discrimination beyond that already imposed by law."[23] Over the years things have changed for the mulatto closer to the white end of the color spectrum but not for the black man because to the white Latin American, blacks are still not as pleasing aesthetically as the mulatto. Whites, in short, have come to accept the mulatto when he most closely approximates the whites themselves. This acceptance of the colored man as more aesthetically pleasing the closer he resembles the white man is, of course, a form of white racism, again stemming from the belief in the aesthetic superiority of white over black.

For some Latin Americans, then, the "black" drop of blood does not pollute or contaminate even though in some cases, as in the past when the early immigrants—the "old Christians"—from Spain and Portugal placed great importance on racial "purity" or unpolluted whiteness, there are pathological reactions to a "touch of the tarbrush." People with brown skin are now aesthetically pleasing to the Latin American eye, even preferred as an aesthetic ideal. The preference for the *morena,* a brown-skinned woman, at least as an ideal sexual partner, is almost legendary in Brazil, where one of the hit songs back in the late forties was called "A Mulata é a tal," which means "the mulatto girl is tops." Even the "somatic norm image," Hoetink[24] has shown, is darker in the Latin countries than in the non-Latin countries. But blackness is still a badge, a stigma, just as much, if not more, in Latin America as in the United States, especially when accompanied with other African characteristics and features further separating blacks and whites in appearance. When Oracy Nogueira speaks of the disadvantages of being black or of the "defect" of blackness in Brazil one cannot help but think of the racial mores in the United States: "From the start it is impressed upon the white child's mind that negroid characteristics make its bearer ugly and undesirable for marriage."[25] Further on he tells how sorry people feel for a dark child when he is born of mixed parents. And he tells how adult people frequently tease a white boy that when he grows up he will marry a black:

> Black boys are teasingly called "negrinho" ("little black"), "urbu" ("black vulture"), "anu" ("a small black bird"), etc., by their own playmates and adults. They frequently hear remarks that "blacks are not people." In all situations of this kind, in the guise of teasing, the concept of the inferiority of the blacks and the undesirability of negroid features is impressed upon the white as well as the black child's mind, although the speaker may not be aware of the effect.[26]

Language concepts in Latin America, as the foregoing passage illustrates, have propagated, as in the United States, stereotyped thinking about black people. The lack of aesthetic appreciation for blacks and their physical characteristics is seen in the many derogatory expressions, such as the above for African features, designed to instill the concept of inferiority. Hair, especially, is a criterion as important as skin color, particularly in Puerto Rico, where reference to "bad" hair as *pasa* (frizzy) and *grifo* (kinky) has divided mulattoes into two groups according to the degree of kinkiness of their hair. Recall the racist overtones and the popularity of *Tuntún de pasa y grifería,* the book of "black" poetry by the white Puerto Rican poet Luis Palés Matos.

Ann Cook,[27] one of the many blacks from the United States who have traveled through Latin America only to return disillusioned with the reluctance to identify with blackness there, encountered much anti-black consciousness reflected in directly translatable phrases that are so much a part of the culture in the United States. Whether the language of the countries she visited was English, French, Spanish, Dutch, or Portuguese, she found that there were phrases for "good hair," or for "marrying light to improve the race," and others we would recognize immediately.

She tells the story of the very prominent black man in Panama who confessed his heartbreak when the mother of the girl he wanted to marry prohibited the arrangement, chiding the girl for not having any "ambition." This man, she tells us, was rejected not because he was a bum but because he was too dark. She writes too of the extreme color consciousness she found in Brazil where Euro-Brazilians, like many Caucasian Latin Americans, claim to be color-blind. In Brazil she found that the more caucasoid a person looks the more readily he will boast to a black foreigner of his black blood. Especially relevant in this regard is the amusing experience she had when visiting a prominent Brazilian scholar and his wife in their home:

> In the course of that inevitable discussion about the race problem in this country the Brazilian turned to me with his face beaming pride. "Ann," he said, "I'm going to tell you something that will surprise you." I waited. "MY GRANDMOTHER WAS A NEGRO!" His face and gestures were saying to me, "Now what do you think of that!" I looked at him warmly and said, "Oh that doesn't surprise me at all. It shows in your features." He panicked! "No, no, no!" he shouted, shaking his head furiously. "I don't have a single Negro feature." By now his entire body was in contortions. Shaking his finger in rhythm with the other movements, he assured me, "not one!" And, of course, he had measured his skull, and his nose and his lips as so many in the

twilight zone do. He hurriedly began to pull his sleeves as he said, ''Of course, we Latins—the sun—you know—we get tanned.'' I never said a word.[28]

The author recounts other manifestations of this anti-African, or antiblack, complex in Brazil where the crisis of black identity is compounded by those who try to minimize African features. Among her accounts is the story of the obviously negroid woman who for four months lay in the hospital after seriously burning her skin trying to bleach herself with a soda solution. This woman, a brilliant young economist with very black skin, ordered a car completely white inside and out. She now goes around, Cook tells us, wearing a blond wig and with her face powdered white.[29]

Racism and the Mask of Whiteness: the White Aesthetic and the Dramatization of Racial Shame

The ''bleaching'' episode recounted by Ann Cook is a classic representation of the emphasis on racial appearance as opposed to purity of racial origins in the manner of the distinction made by Oracy Nogueira. The other Ann Cook episode, however, it should be emphasized, suggests not only a manifestation of the antiblack complex in Brazil but also a tendency to admit black blood but only so long as it is not readily visible; in other words, a tendency toward a conditional admission of black blood.

The yearning for an unconditional, racially pure, white ancestry completely beyond suspicion is not totally foreign to Latin America. In Puerto Rico, for example, where the ''touch of the tarbrush'' is only reluctantly tolerated, at times even vehemently denied, we have a crucial development forcefully dramatized in the late fifties in a significant series of plays by Francisco Arriví, the Puerto Rican playwright whose trilogy *Máscara Puertorriqueña* (Río Piedras, P.R.: Editorial Cultural, 1971) focuses, in effect, on the emphasis on appearance which results at times in attempts to bleach out blackness, as well as an emphasis on racial origin manifested in a reluctance to identify with blackness or admit even conditionally a black heritage. Persons in the second category live in constant fear of their black ancestry being discovered, much like those involved in the phenomenon of ''passing'' in the United States.

These two tendencies have great bearing on the crisis of black identity in Latin America. Even though artistically Arriví's work now is widely acclaimed as pace-setting in so far as stage techniques, dramatic presentation, and the creation of dialogue are concerned, his powerful trilogy, based on a premise designed to have a cathartic effect on the Puerto Rican public and to counter an increasing tendency toward denying the African heritage as shameful, had a less than enthusiastic initial reception. This premise, which presupposes a pervasive influence on white racism in Puerto Rican society, traces the psychological or emotional effects of racism by effectively dramatizing its pathological influence on the minds of racially insecure people who go to extreme lengths to wear a "mask of whiteness," that is, to pretend, even at the risk of great emotional trauma, a semblance of a racially pure white heritage. These extreme measures include forced seclusion of a black mother who is kept hidden from the public by a daughter who, though light, resorts to a turban to hide her own "black" hair. They include the use of heavy make-up, a mask of white powder, even plastic surgery to hide or remove African features. One character, who lives in constant fear of the discovery of his black heritage, peddles a bleaching soap to those who would be white. Such pathological behavior in confrontation with one's racial identity is an unhappy by-product or side effect of the sickness of white racism, and similar examples are found in Latin-American literature outside of Puerto Rico.

Arriví's dramas of racial shame raise critical choices for Puerto Rico as well as for the larger Latin-American societies. These choices seem to be either continuation of a fradulent denial of an African heritage, though running the risk of discovery, or acceptance of the African heritage, a choice that can bear positive consequences only if racism and racial shame are collectively put aside. Arriví throws the full weight of his dramatic forces behind the second choice as he admonishes his public to cast aside the mask of deception and to decondition themselves from the white superiority syndrome. A similar message is aimed at the largely mestizo and Indian society of Mexico by Celestino Gorostiza, who published *El color de nuestra piel*[30] in 1952, a play that criticizes the same white aesthetic as it is practiced, absurdly, in that country. Demetrio Aguilera Malta in Ecuador, like his fellow dramatists in Puerto Rico and Mexico, has also dramatized racial problems rooted in the heritage of white racial consciousness in Latin America, particularly in *Dientes blancos* (México, D.F., 1959) and *Sangre azul* (Washington, D.C., 1948).

Without a Backward Glance: Racism and the
Flight from Blackness

The pressures and effects of white racism in Latin America, especially as far as the man on the black end of the color spectrum is concerned, are as harsh and virulent as in the United States. The antiblack aesthetic manifested in the yearning after lightness or a racially pure (white) heritage is a direct reflection of this low status of blackness on the spectrum of racial color in Latin America, where the rush toward whiteness, widely practiced by people who even remotely qualify, had left the pure black man quite alone, his numbers and strength depleted by his colored brothers who, unlike most light-skinned blacks in the United States today, are reluctant to identify with blackness.

This reluctance to identify with blackness dates from the colonial period when as early as the sixteenth century "those who could rise did so without a backward glance."[31] The upward ascent, particularly of the free person of color, was not conducive to racial solidarity among those of African descent. "Far from it. The paradoxical nature of Spanish attitudes toward the subject of race assured that the free person of color, despised for the very mixture of bloods which coursed through his veins, was nevertheless rewarded for every step taken, both cultural and biological, which approximated the white ideal. Thus, for better or for worse, only under the most extreme circumstances did the advantaged person of color identify with those beneath him."[32] Racial solidarity was all very well, Bowser observes, but intelligent, free persons of color who had accumulated modest fortunes recognized in colonial Spanish America that whitening was the key to socioeconomic advancement.

In colonial Spanish America free persons of color had come to share the society's morbid fascination with racial classification. " 'Eager for honor,' free persons of color became extremely sensitive to racial classification and were offended when referred to by a term for darkness greater than that which they claimed."[33] In other words, light-skinned Latin Americans of African descent were easily offended if inadvertently placed too low on the spectrum of racial color, and, not too surprisingly, considering the demands and the rewards of a racist, white-oriented society, the desire to whiten themselves led many Afro-Latin Americans to forget their racial origins and identity and to seek the same whitening process advanced by those whites who expect to solve the racial problems in this manner.

Historical pressures of white racism have forced an identity crisis on black people in Latin America reminiscent of the color situation in the United States years ago when light-skinned blacks, for the most part, turned their backs on their darker brothers. Blacks generally see themselves differently now in the United States, although there are some who still resent being referred to as black. Regardless of their insistence, however, on seeing the word as a color rather than as a shared experience, a light skin in the United States is no longer significant to black people. As a result, "the de-escalation of color as an index of social standing in the Negro sub-society immeasurably strengthened and unified the factions previously contending for leadership and prestige. . . . Today, education, wealth, high social status, and leadership are distributed fairly evenly across the color spectrum of the Negro community."[34] And again in the United States, in direct contrast to the way things were developing in Latin America:

> If anything, the light-skinned Negro is at a disadvantage. In the old days color meant (at least nominal) privilege, for it bespoke the presence of the master's blood. Today, as the Negro develops an increasing appreciation of his own accomplishments and shares vicariously the accomplishments of other non-whites, the premium on "the master's blood" is signally diminished. Anyone whose light skin color is thought to be of recent derivation is exposed to a degree of censure and disapproval not known in former times.[35]

The following comments by Janet Foucher, a former *Ebony* fashion model often mistaken for white, reflect this recent popularity of darker-skinned blacks, this time in the fashion world. "Today, if you haven't got a Black skin, you can't make it. Black is really beautiful. . . . Once the light-skinned girls were the most accepted. . . . Now, even downtown modeling agencies are on the lookout for only black skinned girls and Blacks seem to emphasize only blackness of skin."[36] Or in the world of entertainment: "Once the 'pretty' black men were the Adam Clayton Powell types 'blessed' with Caucasian features, light skin, 'good' hair and gray or blue eyes. But 'Black is Beautiful' changed all that. At the top of any list of gorgeous males today may be those as dark-complexioned as singer Wilson Pickett and as nappy-haired as Sidney Poitier.[37] These comments reinforce the important point, namely, that in the United States, unlike in Latin America, black truly has become beautiful since the "Black

Revolution.'' Within the colored group, then, as well as in the larger United States society, a light skin—again unlike in Latin America—is no guarantee of preferential treatment.

Pure black people allegedly can take the great leap upward in Latin America, once they meet certain requirements. According to an old saying, and to recent popular thought and theory, a black man can become white or be considered white like his light-skinned brother once he improves himself through financial, educational, or some other means that hopefully will allow him to overcome the stigma of blackness. But contrary to this belief, and on this one point many Latin American writers, both black and white, concur: that as far as the white man is concerned a black man's high rank, financial position, or superb personal qualifications do not necessarily lighten his skin, even if his wealth or power is accepted and his blackness politely ignored. More representative of this feeling toward black people in Latin America is the following popular expression which reappears often with variations in the literature of the area: ''Mono, aunque viste de seda, mono se queda'' (''A monkey, even dressed in silks, is still a monkey'').

Racism and the Fight for Blackness: Historical Reactions.

Despite the flights from blackness that have helped fragment a united black consciousness movement in the larger Latin-American societies, there have been some efforts (slave revolts, black conspiracies, civil rights movements) over the years by blacks who insisted on equal treatment socially, politically, and economically, most recently in Costa Rica, where, typical of the black areas in Central America, the fight is not only for black identity but also against the practice of considering bilingual blacks—even fourth-generation blacks—as foreigners not to be identified with the Latin countries.[38] In nineteenth-century Buenos Aires black freedmen launched protests against racial inequality. Their mouthpieces were the papers *La Raza Africana o sea el Demócrata Negro* and *El Proletario*.[39] In Uruguay black people protested against discrimination and their inferior position in society in the nineteenth century through black newspapers such as *La Conservación,* in 1872. Racial barriers still existed in Uruguay in the twentieth century when other black journals, such as *Nuestra Raza,* again voiced the same protest. Black cultural and social organizations were formed in Uruguay as well as a black political party, the Partido Autóctono Negro, which set out, with limited success, to stir the political conscience of black people in Uruguay toward racial and social equality.[40]

And in Cuba in 1912 members of a black political party, failing to get justice through politics, took up arms. Similarly, in Brazil, from the *quilombos* ("resistance strongholds"), set up by slave fugitives in the seventeenth century, to our day, black Brazilians have been demonstrating for freedom and equality. For example, black Brazilians established the Frente Negra Brasileira ("Brazilian Black Front") in 1931, designed to include all blacks in the fight against discrimination on the basis of color, a problem compounded by the influx of immigrants, especially in São Paulo. Some of these "white foreigners" and their descendants, against whom blacks and dark mulattoes had to compete economically, were prejudiced against dark-skinned people. The Frente Negra became the União Negra Brasileira, ("National Union of Black Brazilians") in 1937, reaching out even further to black people all over the country to combat racism and the white aesthetic at all levels.[41] Since then other black protest movements have been launched in Brazil, most recently the one led by Raul Santos in São Paulo aimed at facilitating the integration of blacks in a "society of Whites," as he calls it.[42]

One of the most important "civil rights" struggles against the white aesthetic in Latin America was led in the forties by the Teatro Experimental do Negro, now thought to have been the "cultural headquarters of Negritude in Brazil."[43] The director and founder of the Experimental Black Theater was Abdias do Nascimento, the black playwright and actor, now living in the United States, who for quite some time had been an advocate of black identity in his efforts to instill black pride in his people, too long the victims of the white aesthetic in Brazil. The morbid anxiety for the acquisition of "whiteness," which Nascimento correctly saw as a by-product of color prejudice, is dealt with superbly, Nascimento tells us, in *Patologia Social do "Branco" Brasileiro* (The social pathology of the Brazilian white), published in 1955 by another black Brazilian, the sociologist Guerreiro Ramos.[44]

As a countercurrent to this pathological desire for whiteness these two Afro-Brazilian intellectuals, Ramos and Nascimento, tried to foster black identity by instilling an awareness in the aesthetic value of blackness. This they attempted by publicly rejecting the opinion that white is better than black. Ramos, in his newspaper *Quilombo,* also the organ of the Experimental Black Theater, advised its black female readers against straightening their hair and powdering themselves with rice or pink powder, and demanded that little girls be given not blond and blue-eyed dolls at Christmas time, but black ones. Under the leadership of Guerreiro Ramos, one of the associations of colored Brazilians held contests, for example, where the *Rainha das Mulatas* (''Queen of Mulattoes'') was elected from competitors who were as dark as possible and most typically African, a gesture of rejection of the white models of beauty. Exhibitions of paintings were held on the theme of the *Cristo Negro* (''Black Christ'') in Rio de Janeiro, designed to increase the value of blackness.[45] This recognition of the value of blackness was used as strategy in the struggle for black identity as a bulwark against white racism in Brazil.

The Experimental Black Theater, like the Teatro y Danzas Negras of Victoria Santa Cruz in Peru, and the Afro-Colombian troupe of Manuel Zapata Olivella had done in the fifties, did much to assert the values of Afro-Latin-American culture. Abdias do Nascimento describes his work as an effort to ''give value to and exalt the contributions of the African to the growth of Brazil . . . while exposing the fraud of Brazilian whiteness: a people of colored origin who officially pretend to be white.''[46] In 1968 Nascimento established the Museum of Black Art in Rio de Janeiro, a further step in his efforts to restore the value of African culture in Brazil. Black identity is important in Brazil, he believes, because ''to call Brazil a mixed nation is not valid. We know which models, values and paragons of culture dominate, identify and personalize Brazilian society.''[47]

Similar criticism has been leveled at Cuba since the Revolution by some blacks who accuse Castro of perpetuating a racist fraud at the expense of black Cubans when he labels as counterrevolutionary anyone who wishes to identify with blackness. Cuba since Castro had fast been acquiring a reputation as the first country in the Western Hemisphere to conquer white racism not only by proclaiming itself antiracist but by recognizing as well the *mestizo* nature of its society. But dissenting voices question what appears to them to be a renewed attempt to bleach out black people and to squelch out black culture by white culture.

Some of these dissenting voices belong to Black Panthers who were disillusioned with the treatment they received in Cuba. Part of Eldridge Cleaver's disaffection with Cuba was his claim that certain racist attitudes and policies still exist there, which led him to conclude that

Cuba's leaders "in giving public support to the black liberation struggle abroad while failing to complete that aspect of their revolution at home, were guilty of a certain hyprocrisy."[48] Black militant Robert Williams, Premier-elect of the proposed secessionist New Republic of Africa, also left Cuba disappointed, accusing Fidel Castro of being basically a white racist.

Perhaps the strongest of those voices rejecting present-day Cuba as a racial utopia is that of John Clytus, author of *Black Man in Red Cuba,* published in 1970 by the University of Miami Press. His book is publicized as the first complete account of a black American's experiences in Castro's Cuba. Earlier, with Fidel Castro's triumph, Clytus began to see communism as the only true revolutionary force; but, after spending three years in the new Cuba, he returned to the United States convinced that white Cubans were using José Martí's ideal of a raceless society as an excuse to blot out black consciousness and black identity by pretending that black Cubans did not exist. Seeing the race war in Cuba in 1912 as the last militant call for an identification with blackness, Clytus was particularly concerned about the models of whiteness that still prevailed in Cuba, where whites still identified with white even though blacks were not expected or encouraged to identify with black.

It would seem by these accounts, that much like in Brazil, where African culture—when it is accepted—is accepted for its picturesque and folkloric value,[49] racial blackness in Cuba as a value beyond the limits of folklore is not recognized by the Revolution. Regarding the fear of the "cultural bosses" of the Revolution of a separatist pull toward black identity based on United States models, the following comment is relevant in that it summarizes obstacles placed by those "whose ethno-aesthetic realities remain western and 'white' "[50] in the formation of black identity in present-day Cuba:

> *They're afraid,* you hear of the Cubans with the cultural titles, *because they don't understand and because they're so far out of it themselves. There are still racists in this country. When Eugenio Hernandez's play, María Antonio, was getting ready they threatened it with closing. They didn't like the facts of life coming from a black man, the black things he was getting into. And it did well because the people wanted it. But not everything gets out. Two black poets won mentions here which should mean publication, but they weren't published because what they were writing, written by a black man, was more than just literature. If*

it was his book (pointing to a white poet) *they would have let it through.*[51]

What we have then is the problem of the ethnic survival of black identity compounded by a reluctance to accept racial blackness expressed in African culture.

This debate regarding racism in Cuba seems to be on-going and it, of course, has many sides. I return to some of them in subsequent sections of this book, particularly in my discussion, for example, of the "white problem" in Chapter Three, in my discussion of socio-negristic prose and the Cuban novel since Castro in Chapter Four, and again in Chapter Five when I deal, for example, with the antiracist message of Nicolás Guillén, Cuba's national poet. It should be stressed here, however, that the question goes deeper than the impressions gathered by outside observers even though the critical views of the disillusioned, like the contrasting ones presented in Chapter Four, are borne out, on the one hand, by such black Cuban writers as Carlos Moore, who maintains that racism exists in today's revolutionary Cuba "Cuba: the Untold Story," (*Présence Africaine* 24, no. 52 [1964]:177-229); the opposing view is provided by such institutional statements as "Racial Discrimination in Cuba" (*Cuba Resource Center Newsletter* 2 [January 1973]:6-14) by Dr. Rafael López Valdés who holds, of course, that the Revolution has swept away all vestiges of racism in Cuba. Such acts as Fidel Castro's celebrated move to Harlem a few years back during a United Nations visit and the Cuban presence in Angola today, tend to reinforce this latter position.

Continuing Obstacles to Change: The White Aesthetic and Problems of Deconditioning.

This reluctance to accept the black heritage on an equal footing with white culture is linked to other, perhaps more subtle, obstacles to a more open discussion of the continuing problem of white racism in Latin America. These obstacles are rooted in racial hyprocrisy and in the continuing official acceptance of the myth of racial tolerance recently described, effectively, as a "cosmetic myth designed to buy time until immigration, miscegenation, and the *laissez faire* genocide of sharply higher rates of poverty, malnutrition, disease and infant mortality provide a final solution to the danger of white contact with Negroes."[52]

"White Magic," or the Etiquette of Race Relations

The etiquette of race relations[53] is one of the continuing obstacles to the achievement of a real racial democracy and an impediment to the full recognition of the rights and privileges of blacks in mestizo societies. The etiquette of race relations, in effect, places a moratorium on the discussion and certainly the admission of the existence of a problem of prejudice and discrimination, often effectively camouflaged by the use of blacks who have "made it," such as Pelé the king of soccer in Brazil (now playing for a New York soccer team), to demonstrate the validity of racial democracy propaganda. Government attempts to forbid denunciation of the racial democracy myth in Brazil as well as official attempts to mask the serious problems and to silence the voices of those who would rise up to denounce racism are called "white magic"[54] by Abdias do Nascimento. It is difficult for blacks, as Quince Duncan[55] has pointed out in Costa Rica, to deny the existence of racism which they have encountered in their own experiences, even though the attitude of some whites is to deny the existence of their own prejudices, thereby foreclosing discussion.

Racial Hyprocrisy, or the Prejudice of Having no Prejudice

The hyprocrisy of the white man whose "prejudice of having no prejudice," a phrase first coined by the Brazilian scholar Professor Florestan Fernandes and later used by Samuel Betances in a two-part article in *The Rican* regarding prejudice and the issue of identity as it relates to race and color in Puerto Rico,[56] best characterizes another obstacle to the formation of a genuine racial democracy in Latin America. Professor Florestan Fernandes, commenting on the racial situation in Brazil in the preface to the United States edition of his major book, *The Negro in Brazilian Society* (New York: Columbia University Press, 1959), first published in Brazil in 1965 as *A Integração do Negro na Sociedade de Classes,* stated that the hyprocrisy of the white men, especially in São Paulo, has caused him to cling to "the prejudice of having no prejudice", limiting himself to treating the black with tolerance, maintaining the old ceremonial politeness in interracial relations, and excluding from his tolerance any truly egalitarian feeling or content. This hyprocrisy, Professor Fernandes intimates, is partly responsible for the adverse stereotypes and negative images of the black man, which the white man has created and manipulated with the utmost skill.

Although the conclusions reached in his book resulted from sociological investigations into the contact between blacks and whites in the city of São Paulo, it should be emphasized that some of the implications of Fernandes's findings are representative of the larger Latin-American society as a whole, where blacks are often victims of the same errors and hyprocrisy of racial ideology and racial utopia operable in Brazil. The hyprocrisy Professor Fernandes describes is exemplified by Carlos Beltrán, O.S.A., in another recent publication: *Brasil: tipos humanos y mestizaje* (Madrid: Ediciones Cultura Hispánica, 1970). Father Beltrán's book deserves comment as it is particularly disturbing not only because it takes the hypocritical pose of which Professor Fernandes speaks but also because having been published by the Instituto de Cultura Hispánica in Madrid its negative opinions of black people carry a certain stamp of respectability. This institution, although well known for its dedication to bringing about a better understanding of the problems and peoples in the Americas, has not furthered that goal with this publication which insults black people all over the Americas and elsewhere by conjuring up old myths and images of them long laid to rest.

To begin with, according to Father Beltrán, blacks in the United States, in Brazil, and in fact, he assures us, in any other country in the world, are docile and simple people. Further on he tells us that blacks in Brazil are and always have been resigned, faithful, obedient, timid, and contented, even as slaves. These remarkable generalizations together with other incredible statements equally insulting characterize several chapters on Brazilian black people in his book. The author, frequently confirming his prejudice of having no prejudice, is intent on convincing the reader that neither he nor Brazilians harbor color prejudices toward black people, a view he adheres to firmly despite several contradictory statements that belie his convictions.

He reports, for example, that the skin pigmentation of blacks has "improved" considerably over the years, that is, has become whiter. While dismissing black militants as abominations and exceptions to the masses of good, docile Christian blacks, Father Beltrán constantly holds out as inspiration for "bad" blacks with "black souls," the great reward of a "white soul," which blacks can possess if they are "good." After all, he tells us, the best that blacks can strive for is a "white soul" since they cannot change the color of their skin. He praises Brazil as a country where racial discrimination has never existed. He does not mention that antidiscriminatory laws had to be passed in Brazil as recently as 1951. Brazilians as a people, he tells us, welcome immigrants with open arms. He fails to mention Brazil's "white only" immigration laws designed to exclude black people from the country.

Although Father Beltrán's book is hailed as an objective and sympathetic account, the author cannot tolerate any worship, cult, or culture, Indian or black, not assimilated into the white Christian mainstream. He considers those who practice African or Afro-Brazilian religions to be barbaric, repugnant, ignorant, and blasphemous people doing the devil's work. Such liturgical practices, according to Father Beltrán, have nothing to do with civilized Brazil, the authentic (white) Brazil, where progress, he tells us, is due exclusively to white intelligence. He even likens Africans to grunting animals, an image the Puerto Rican poet Luis Palés Matos popularized in his "Black Poetry," an image Father Beltrán apparently prefers as he refers to it twice (pp. 151, 168).

Although his intentions are undoubtedly good, the author in passing off as history an imaginary world of goodness, beauty, and racial harmony, which he believes he has found in Brazil, has fallen prey to the white aesthetic, to the prejudice of having no prejudice, an unthinking acceptance of white as good and black as bad, of whiteness as a virtue, a reward, and blackness as something opposite and undesirable, associated with evil, sin, and the devil. In spite of his humanitarian views he has perpetuated, perhaps unwittingly, a variety of stereotypes, racist images, and traditional insults to black people.

The prejudice of having no prejudice that helped give rise and is helping to perpetuate the well-known myth that blacks had no problem in Brazil is equally false in Spanish America, a fact corroborated— among other sources—by the literature of the area dealing with the black experience. Some Spanish-American authors have confirmed in their writings, at times unintentionally, that this subtle prejudice of having no prejudice, together with more overt manifestations of racism, have prohibited the formation of the genuine racial democracy sincerely desired by many Afro-Latin Americans and others who, like Professor Fernandes, want nothing less than a society in which all men regardless of color are truly equal in all respects and under all circumstances.

In Latin America today the black man's biggest fight is still against racism and the white aesthetic. Central to this fight, of course, is the fact that in twentieth-century Latin America color and the somatic distance are still crucial determinants of status. In societies where biological fusion is a fact of life; in societies predominantly mestizo, or mulatto, or Indian, where much of the population is well aware of its mixed ancestry; in societies where racial discrimination is illegal, where the equality of rights of all citizens, regardless of color or race, is guaranteed by law, where segregation policies on the basis of color are considered by some to be absurd, even repugnant; in societies where the word *negrita* is used as a term of affection and endearment, the black man is not only confronted with the white aesthetic with its racist notion that "white is right," that the white man and his color are superior, but also with the expectation that he, in the interest of racial peace, will eventually disappear from those societies through the process of ethnic lynching.

Granted that racial discrimination in Latin America in some instances might present characteristics and nuances differentiating it quantitatively and qualitatively from what is observable in other parts of the world. Granted also that the traditional stigma attached to being even slightly "colored" in the United States might not be as firmly entrenched in the multi-hued societies south of the border. Yet, while the complete range of racial mores and attitudes toward race and color prevalent in the United States might not exist in Latin America, the massive "demystification" program deemed necessary in the United States of "deconditioning" people from the white-superior, black-inferior syndrome, paradoxically, would not be totally irrelevant if applied as well to Latin America, where black skin and African features continue to be handicaps, white racism and antiblack consciousness realities, and ethnic lynching a serious threat to the racial identity of black people, indeed, to their very existence as a distinct race with its own black aesthetic.[57]

2

False Tears for the Black Man:
The White Aesthetic in The
Nineteenth-Century Antislavery Novel in Cuba

*In the old age black was not counted fair,/ or if it
were, it bore not beauty's name.*

Shakespeare

Antiblack feelings were reflected even in some of the literature of
the nineteenth-century antislavery novelists, who, for the most part,
shed false tears for the black man while simultaneously distorting his
image. The black in the Cuban antislavery novel was usually cast in the
role of a propaganda object useful in the interest of abolitionist, and at
times humanitarian, ideals. These novels, designed to be instrumental
in bringing about abolition, held up the tragedy of slavery before the
reading public. Yet, their authors viewed the black from the outside,
and an air of sentimental artificiality, and at times romanticism,
surrounded their works. And, in spite of what they believed to be their
good intentions, in some cases even an actual aversion to the black
man is clearly discerned.

Unable or unwilling to escape this antislavery, antiblack paradox,
these writers often speak apologetically of the black man's color and
features. The dark people in these novels, and in others not classified
as antislavery, are often portrayed as submitting to the white aesthetic
and longing for entry into the white world in order to escape the fact of
their blackness. An apparent acceptance of blackness as inferior is
projected even in these novels as they dwell at length on the negative
qualities of the black man whom they are especially prone to portray as
docile, tranquil, resigned to his fate, and lacking a rebellious spirit. In
short, while pointing up the horror of the institution of slavery, some of
the nineteenth-century antislavery writers were reluctant to accept
blackness as being aesthetically pleasing. This reluctance, paradoxical
for abolitionists but quite understandable, however, considering the

22

nineteenth-century mentality on race, led some authors to depict "black" protagonists with white features that clearly distinguish them from other black Africans, and is especially acute in Gertrudiz Gómez de Avellaneda's *Sab,* Cirilo Villaverde's *Cecilia Valdés,* and, to a lesser extent, in *Francisco* and *El negro Francisco* by Anselmo Suárez y Romero and Antonio Zambrana, respectively.

The Problem of Avellaneda's *Sab:*
Noble Black or Romantic Uncle Tom?

The conflicting opinions advanced concerning Gómez de Avellaneda's *Sab* (1841) indicate the lack of a critical consensus about the nature of this novel. One of the first idealistic novels, *Sab* is heir to the romantic tradition. It is, of course, antislavery as well. Seldom made, however, is the connection between two reconcilable objectives of the author, namely, to write about the evils of slavery while relating the story of an unrequited love. This she does by depicting a romantic soul in bondage. To further complicate the matter, Gómez de Avellaneda did not include the novel in an edition of her complete works, a decision that implies the author thought it to be either too defective, too daring with the slave-white woman love interest, or too antislavery for the mentality of the time. Whatever the case, she withdrew it from the market, a move that has helped enliven the speculation about the novel.

Even more curious for us is the fact that Sab, a mulatto slave in love with a white girl, willingly represses his love and rejects a fortune won in a lottery, making it possible for the girl to win the fortune and attract the man of her choice. Sab, victim of an *amor imposible,* ultimately dies in true romantic fashion, of a broken heart, but all the while he is cursed by his slave status and by the darkness of his skin. Although he is a mulatto and not black we are never allowed to forget that his color is the source of his misfortune. Yet, Sab, though slave in body, has a good and noble heart capable of great sentiment, feeling, and passion, qualities very important to the romanticists. Those who possess these qualities, even slaves, are exceptional, superior, and privileged human beings. In this sense Sab is much better off than others who are not slaves but who lack these qualities. But since he is not white his fate is predictable. Since he is a slave and a romantic his fate is unavoidable.

The goodness of the noble, intelligent Sab leads the author into a protest against the evils of slavery by having the protagonist outline the terrible life of the slave:

> "It is really a terrible life," replied the peasant, glancing congenially at his interlocutor. "Under this burning sky the half-naked slave works all morning without rest, and at the terrible noon hour, overwhelmed by the weight of the firewood and cane that he carries on his back, and burned by the rays of the sun that toast his skin, the poor man arrives panting to enjoy the only pleasure he has in life: two hours of sleep and a sparing ration. . . ."
>
> "Oh! it is surely a cruel spectacle to see degraded humanity, men converted into beasts carrying the mark of slavery on their countenances and the desperation of hell in their souls."[1]

And Carlota, the white girl Sab loves, wants the slaves to be free and, in her turn, speaks out against their unfortunate state:

> "These poor unhappy people!" she exclaimed. "They are considered fortunate because they are not beaten and insulted, and eat peacefully the bread of slavery. They are considered fortunate and their children are slaves before being born, sold like irrational beasts afterwards. . . . Their children, their own flesh and blood! When I become Henry's wife," she added after a moment's silence, "no happy human being shall breathe at my side air polluted by slavery. We shall free all our black people.[2]

Sab, though a slave, is a noble character, but it is his perfection that brings about his ruin because he is too good, too considerate, too long suffering, too much like the proverbial Uncle Tom. Sab is a man so in love that he would do anything for Carlota except follow the impulses of his heart. Instead, he sobs, sighs, and dies a noble but frustrated individual. Yet Sab, paradoxically, is a strong character. Much like other mulatto characters in Spanish-American literature, Sab shares the rare honor of being a foreman in command of other slaves. Sharing this high honor further dramatizes his castration and weakness when compared with other mulatto foremen in twentieth-century Spanish-American literature set in slavery times who use their strength and superior position to greater personal advantage, especially in their relationships with the white women with whom they come in contact.

Further evidence of Sab's frustrated and submissive character is his failure to strike out, to rebel, even though he does at times speak frightening talk of rebellion. But he is not one to join a rebellion or to lead one though he thinks someone ought to avenge the oppressed black slaves. At one time he thought of rebellion and spilling white blood but only to get Carlota. He hates whites not because of slavery but for keeping her from him.

The nobility of Sab links the novel to the noble savage tradition in literature which includes such royal black slaves of heroic stature as Aphra Behn's *Oroonoko* (1688) and Hugo's *Bug-Jargal* (1826), two of Sab's most well-known predecessors. The noble black in Hispanic literature is not limited to Sab: Lope de Vega introduced some outstanding ones in the seventeenth century. His conception of the noble black "is little different from that of the Noble Moor that we see in contemporary literature, Othello, for example. He is courtly, generous and brave, possessed of refined sentiments and a code of honor worthy of the most Christian gentlemen of the Renaissance."[3]

It is probably due to Oroonoko, however, that there are so many royal slaves in literature and that such a large percentage of black slaves were kings in their native countries or sons or grandsons of kings, persons of quality and natural goodness. Aphra Behn's novel has indeed inspired many writers, and her sympathy for blacks and her outrage against the cruelties of slavery make her work a good candidate for the honor of being the first emancipation novel, even though we must remember that the degree of her humanitarian feelings are affected to a certain extent by her description of Oroonoko. We know that, though attracted by the novelty of her subject and imbued by humanitarian considerations, Behn took great pains to avoid suggesting a real negroid type in her novel. Her subject is daring but her approach is cautious and unrealistic. Though jet black, Oroonoko is given an exotic Indian-sounding name and long straight hair, a small mouth, a "noble" face, and a rising Roman nose, undoubtedly to make him a more acceptable "hero" to the reading public of her day. But she refused to accept black as beautiful: ". . . bating his colour, there could be nothing in nature more beautiful, agreeable and handsome."[4] The color black is the only aspect of the black person that is physically unattractive in the heroic tradition. Royal heritage, greatness of soul, and other virtues, however, overcome the drawback of blackness.

In physical description we see Behn's legacy in Sab, our more recent noble black. Gómez de Avellaneda, in pointing out that Sab "has none of the servility and coarse nature so common among people of his kind,'' (p. 44) rejects the negroid type by presenting Sab as a mulatto, perhaps in order to make him more acceptable to her own standards of beauty and to those of the reading public of her time. The suggestion that color is the cause of the apparent repulsion the author felt for the black man becomes even more likely when she has Sab make condescending remarks regarding his black mother who was beautiful—he says—in spite of her color. Although the royal and noble slaves are described in glowing terms according to literary tradition, an aversion to blackness usually reveals the author's true feelings toward the black. Though camouflaged by her antislavery pronouncements and by clichés inherent in the ''noble Negro'' tradition, her natural repulsion toward the black is apparent. While simultaneously going to great lengths to depict Sab as white as possible, light in color with ''good'' hair, positive attributes to match his ''white soul,'' Sab, in short, is made to share the aesthetic prejudice of whites who do not see beauty in blackness. This aesthetic prejudice, of course, is based on the aesthetic contrast between black and white, dark and light, which is ''deeply rooted in us as representing in all aspects the ethical contrast between sin and virtue. In describing the first Indians he saw, Columbus, like his successors, remarked on their physical beauty: they were not Black.''[5]

Blacks were accepted in Romanticism on humanitarian grounds as noble symbols of compassion, of greatness of soul. Victor Hugo revived the noble black as a literary figure by choosing a black slave of Santo Domingo as the hero of *Bug-Jargal,* his first novel. *Oroonoko* was very popular in eighteenth-century France and the resemblances of Hugo's novel to it are quite apparent. It would seem that Sab is related through *Bug-Jargal,* which Gómez de Avellaneda might have known, to the Oroonoko tradition, since Hugo was well known in Spanish America and since it is known that *Bug-Jargal* had reached the hands of some of the antislavery writers in Spanish America, causing one of them to remark that it is the kind of novel that should have been written by a Cuban.[6]

Although Sab does not lead a slave revolt in the manner of Bug-Jargal there are many similarities among the three novels. All three devote attention to the sad position of the slaves; there is much pity for them in these novels. Like Sab, Bug-Jargal is hopelessly in love with a white woman and would do nothing to displease her. All three black protagonists have royal ancestors though they are now slaves. All three are magnificently proportioned, tall, with powerful bodies and, of course, noble deportment. They are very strong and brave but very gentle. Though lavishly adorned and described physically, all three show some signs of being African. Like Bug-Jargal, Sab saved a white man's life and as a result should receive his freedom. All three are held in great respect by the other slaves. Like Oroonoko, Bug-Jargal was not meant to wear irons. He is superhuman, endowed with herculean strength. Educated, he spoke French and Spanish with equal facility. Sab spoke good Spanish unlike that of a slave. Both Bug-Jargal and Sab make their initial appearances in the novel singing. The white heroine in both novels is going to marry another and again in both novels the rivals meet early in the narration. Sab and Bug-Jargal saved the lives of their white rivals. Like Bug-Jargal and Oroonoko, the description of Sab makes him acceptable to the public. All three, in short, are noble and generous in every way, capable of great humanity, affection, and romantic sentiment. But Sab, in choosing to remain a slave in order to serve his master's daughter becomes a romantic Uncle Tom, who, with his sad expression, goes through the novel sobbing and sighing.

It appears, then, that although Sab is described in glowing terms according to the literary tradition of the royal and noble Negro, an aversion to blackness is still inherent in the author's feelings. Though camouflaged by clichés common to this tradition and her antislavery pronouncements, Gómez de Avellaneda's false tears are nevertheless manifest in her apologetic descriptions of other slaves and in her penchant for portraying them as being tranquil, docile, and happy with their lot, indeed, even unaware of their misfortune.

Cecilia Valdés: Literary Portraits and Ethnic Descriptions

Although hailed as a document in favor of slave liberation, Villaverde's novel *Cecilia Valdés,* a classic of nineteenth-century Cuban customs that first appeared in 1839, with part two not published until 1882, takes an equally paradoxical position toward blacks. The tears shed for the black men in this novel are clearly false because the antislavery intentions of the author are offset by a white aesthetic he apparently supports. Feelings of self-hatred by blacks and a strong desire to be white are key motivating forces for many of the characters in this novel. The plot itself concerns the preference of colored women for white men. The protagonist Cecilia has mixed blood, and her single ambition in life is to marry a white man, an ambition fortified by Seña Josefá, her grandmother, who reminds Cecilia that her blood is better because her father was a white gentleman. She also cautions Cecilia to remember that a white man, even though poor, makes the best husband. The reader is never allowed to forget that white people are of a higher social class. This fact is especially dramatized with Leonardo's ultimate rejection of Cecilia, despite her beauty, for a woman of his own race and class. Cecilia had the double disadvantage of having mixed blood and belonging to a lower social class. She could not hope to leave the social class into which she had been born or enter into a white society in a land of slaves. Thus, society had conditioned her into believing that to marry "colored" would be to lower her in esteem. She felt that she must marry "white" or do the next best thing, namely, to have an affair with a white man. Her only choice is to have a love affair with Leonardo, a decision that eventually leads to tragedy.

Although its central theme is not the depiction of the situation of African slaves in Cuba, it is undeniable that one of the objectives of the book is to provoke the reader's indignation at the institution of slavery. To this end there are antislavery pronouncements in the novel and many instances of slave mistreatment designed to arouse the reader's anger. Yet, as an antislavery document Villaverde's novel is hampered in part because of the white aesthetic, in part because it deals mainly with the position of the mulattoes and not with the black slaves. One of the most original features of *Cecilia Valdés* is the novel's concentration on portraying the psychology of the mulatto. Well known also is the elaborate description of Cuban customs of the time, which the author faithfully recorded. The novel should be lauded also for its fascinating study of race relations and of the ethnic composition of the different races in Cuba. The whole spectrum of color is represented in this novel, and the author never tires of dwelling on facial features or of stressing the cleavage between races, and within races the sharp divisions between African-born blacks and creole blacks, between free of freed and slave blacks, between blacks and mulattoes.

Indeed, the most striking impression one is left with after reading the novel, perhaps, is the painstaking care the author lends to minute detail in his creation of literary portraits of the people, especially those with mixed blood. He does not allow a single character—major or minor—to appear without pausing to focus on facial features or underscoring such predominant racial characteristics as skin tone or nose shape. He tells us that Señá Josefá, Cecilia's grandmother, is a mulatto with a Roman nose and copper skin who, because of her years, could be taken as an offspring of a mulatto and a black. Another mulatto appears with handsome head, heavy nose, expressive mouth, and thick curly hair. Another black appears with an ebony neck and white hair. He sees a sick girl in bed through a cracked door and remarks that she has a well-shaped nose, for a person of mixed race.

In chapter two we have the first description of Cecilia at the age of twelve or thirteen with copious wavy hair, straight nose, high forehead, small white teeth, perfectly arched eyebrows, black eyes, small mouth, full and voluptuous lips, full, round cheeks, and a dimple in her chin. In chapter five she is referred to as an Afro-Caucasian Venus because of the bronze tint of her skin. She is now the tall and beautiful *"virgencita de bronce."* He tells us that she could be mistaken for a sun-tanned white girl with no colored blood. In chapter ten Cecilia is referred to as nearly white, if one were to consider only her hair, eyes, nose, and lips, and to discount the color of her skin. Villaverde, throughout the novel, tries hard not to blacken his heroine or to give her African features in order to maintain his standard of white European beauty. Uribe, one of the few black characters in the novel, has African features, and Villaverde makes a point of emphasizing his flat nose, bulging eyes, and very thick lips. Pimiento, Cecilia's jealous suitor, has mixed blood, but with a preponderance of Spanish physical characteristics. The newspaper description Villaverde gives of a runaway slave with all the attention given to physical details is also typical. Furthermore, the author constantly emphasizes the distinctions within the social spectrum as well, referring to a black, for example, as an African by birth, or a Cuban mulatto.

What is the significance of Villaverde's chronic preoccupation with the physical description and social status of his characters? The crucial problem of social strata based on color is of paramount importance in this slave society, where racial purity and skin color were just as important as independence from Spain itself. For this reason the very careful attention Villaverde gives to racial appearances is a reflection of a universal desire to avoid being wrongly placed at the black or African end of the color spectrum. Herein lies a major fault with this novel as an antislavery vehicle, for this white standard is consistently in force. We see it when the author relates that all José Dolores lacks to be recognized as a gentleman anywhere is a white skin, that María de la Regla detests her curly hair, that colored girls should marry white men, that a mulatto child hates his black mother and that a mother hates her black child, both for the same reason, which is the cult of whiteness. Although the author sets out to show the horrors of slavery, such cult-of-whiteness scenes and situations permeate the work. Equally serious is the author's implied acceptance of the social cleavage based on the white aesthetic and reinforced by his references to the black race as inferior and to the white race as superior.[7]

Villaverde describes excessively the ethnic differences in people and the various stratifications and divisions of Cuban society. But his accepting them as a *fait accompli* suggests that his antislavery argument is built on a false premise, or at least one that does not attempt to contradict the hierarchy of color. And it is this tacit acceptance of the status quo, of a society patterned on a color spectrum that views black features as undesirable, of a society that rarely sheds real tears for the black man, that weakens Villaverde's antislavery argument.

Contemporary Accounts and Remembered History:
Esteban Montejo's Contrasting View

Other nineteenth-century novels were more directly and exclusively concerned with slavery than *Sab* and *Cecilia Valdés*. The two best known are *Francisco* (1839) of Anselmo Suárez y Romero and *El negro Francisco* (1873) by Antonio Zambrana. The former, which actually began the cycle of antislavery novels, depicts the life and tragic situation of the slaves in the sugar refineries. It was published in 1880 but was read earlier in literary gatherings and influenced Zambrana, who later published his novel in Chile.

Both novels weaken their antislavery potential by casting the black characters in the role of impotent, primitive, and resigned slaves. Both novels end with the suicide rather than with the rebellion of their black protagonists. Zambrana, despite having created an "*Apolo de ébano*," of having recognized the beauty and strength of Francisco, undermines the image of his creation by having him remain humble, accept slavery and commit suicide, which though seen as a form of protest, is hardly as effective or productive as taking the life of the enslaver. The sad and melancholy Francisco of Suárez y Romero, "so humble, so meek," hangs himself in despair because the girl he loves had given herself to her master. Even the author, who has the lovesick Francisco suffering unbearable punishment in silence without striking back, realized he had created a ''good Negro'' and admitted this meek, humble creature to be a major fault in his novel, despite the fact that this characterization effectively allowed the depiction of the white masters' cruelty.[8] The nineteenth-century antislavery novelists were not anxious to endow their slave characters with a rebellious spirit, therefore falsely suggesting that the slaves themselves felt no real desire for freedom, that the white people were primarily responsible for whatever movements toward manumission that existed at the time.

The authors' propensity for shedding false tears is understandable as it would have been difficult for these writers to look at slavery from the slaves' point of view. This conflict of interest was undoubtedly fortified by the deplorable fact that some of the antislavery writers themselves continued to own slaves, a practice publicly censured by Enrique Piñeyro in a nineteenth-century Cuban journal, *El Ateneo,* pointing specifically to Suárez y Romero.[9] Equally damaging to their antislavery arguments from a humanitarian viewpoint is the suspicion that the Cuban liberals who were willing to tolerate slave liberation had every expectation that the freed slaves would join them in their fight against Spain, thus suggesting that their abolition efforts should be taken with the same political grain of salt as Lincoln's Emancipation Proclamation. This same goal is shared by José Martí, but with one important difference. Unlike the antislavery novelists, José Martí looked beyond the immediate goal of a free Cuba to that larger question of nationbuilding, to a Cuba in which all of its citizens could live together as equals.

The nineteenth-century antislavery writers were just that— antislavery—and not necessarily proslave or problack, and this handicap influenced their portrayal of the black man. Their abolitionist sentiments stopped short of accepting the black on equal terms with other human beings. The mulatto Martín Morúa Delgado, dissatisfied with Villaverde's novel especially, moved to correct this literary lacuna toward the end of the nineteenth century by writing *Sofía* (1891) and *La familia Unzúaza* (1896, published 1901). The short autobiographical sketch of the slave Juan Francisco Manzano, while designed as a protest against slavery from the inside, emphasizes not the rebellious spirit of the black but rather the cruelties of the masters.

To really understand what it was like to be a slave in nineteenth-century Cuba we should turn to the autobiographical account of a former slave who told his own story, edited and published in 1966 in book form by Miguel Barnet, the Cuban poet and anthropologist. In this book, *Biografía de un cimarrón* (Havana: Instituto de Etnología y Folklore, 1966) which must be contrasted directly with the nine-teenth-century accounts of the then contemporary scene, Esteban Mon-tejo gives us a realistic picture of his own life as he lived it before and after the abolition of slavery.

Esteban tells us much about slave life and black customs not only in Cuba but in Africa as well; he tells us about slave quarters, for example, and about slave labor in the cane fields where blacks worked twenty hours a day under the watchful eyes of the overseer and his whip. Esteban tells how the strongest and healthiest males and females were made to copulate to increase the holdings of the masters. He talks about sodomy practiced among the other slaves who were deprived of women, about punishments inflicted on the slaves, about the sickness they suffered, and the suicides he witnessed. Esteban endured slavery for as long as he could, and one day, instead of taking his own life, he crushed the head of his foreman with a stone and escaped into the hills where he lived in a cave for a year and a half. Other runaway slaves lived in groups of two or more; Esteban, however, lived completely alone because he loved solitude and tranquility. He would come down from the hills and steal chickens and pigs for food; he would use herbs for medicine when he got sick. He tells of the several jobs he held after emerging from hiding following the abolition of slavery, always careful to avoid those areas where abolition had not changed things for the black. Though he never married, Esteban tells us about the many women he had, criticizing priests for not being as open and honest as blacks about their bastard children.

Esteban was a rebel, and there are many pages in this biography that underscore the rebellious spirit of this *cimarrón*. He elaborates as well on other rebellious types. He gives many reasons why he took flight, the most obvious being that he detested slavery and would prefer to try to survive in the hills than in bondage. He tells of the dogs turned on the runaway slaves by the masters who tried to recover their lost property.

Esteban gives José Martí a clean bill of health, considering him to be ''the purest man in Cuba,'' (p. 110) a good patriot and a good Christian. Throughout the course of his recollections Esteban provides some insights concerning the black in the Cuban wars of independence which he interpreted from a racial perspective. Blacks rebelled, he says, because they were deprived of things they wanted. One day he decided to go off to the war and, like many other slaves, he rode into battle armed only with a machete. He was as enthusiastic about the end of the war as he was about the end of slavery.

Esteban Montejo, the runaway slave, gives the reader a sense of immediacy and authenticity unattainable in the nineteenth-century antislavery novels by white writers. The obvious importance of Esteban's autobiography is the inside look it gives us of slavery told by a former slave who at the age of one hundred and six remarkably has a clear head about events and details transpired and lived many years ago. What results from the transcribed notes and tape-recorded conversations over a period of two years is not only a major literary achievement but a moving human experience as well, in part attributable to Barnet's skill in putting conversations on paper and in part to Esteban's talent for reliving and bringing to life that period of his existence as a slave and his subsequent flight and return after abolition to such honorable activities as field worker and revolutionary. He does this with a personal and subjective involvement unmatched by any of the antislavery novelists.

Esteban's overpowering sense of integrity and his constant search for dignity convert his observations into a human document so much in touch with the realities of his experiences as a slave, runaway, and revolutionary that it far outdistances the nineteenth-century white-oriented attempts to portray the black experience at that time. There is nothing false about Esteban nor about the experiences he narrated, nor about the respect he inspires. What we have is his truth, not the truth of the abolitionist writers who rarely, if ever, were able to get inside the man as Esteban does, a truth told with the simplicity and at times boastful nature of a man who exhibits a total avoidance of pretension and sophistication. Esteban's single-minded determination was to live an independent existence free of restraints. He tells his story in this same uninhibited spirit.

Esteban's personal and subjective account is a remarkable literary achievement that can be effectively contrasted with the image of the black found in the nineteenth-century antislavery novels in Cuba and in other novels whose authors did not consider slavery a problem. In Colombia, for example, we have notions of the black slave who longs to be white, living happily on the hacienda of his patriarchical master, as is the case in Jorge Isaac's *María* (1867). This well-known book, one of the most widely read of Latin-American novels, has many black characters, most of them contented, many of them faithful, and practically all of them to a degree removed from the evils of slavery. In addition to this "contented slave" image, Isaacs, under the influence of Chateaubriand, interpolates a sentimental story about some noble Africans whom he idealized. Consistent with the noble savage tradition, he distinguished them from other Africans by giving them "long, straight hair . . . aquiline nose."[10] These blacks with white features confused one of my students into thinking they were Indians, a logical mistake judging by their description. Concha Meléndez has summed up aptly the situation of the black slave in *María:*

> Slavery still had not been abolished in Spanish America. In Colombia, according to the novel, the children of slaves became free at the age of eighteen. Although the narrator reveals touching pity in the story of the capture and sale of Nay and Sinar, and although the black boy Choto, Emigdio's slave, runs by with his arm crippled in the sugar mill, the blacks are not a social problem in *María.* In the novel those on the plantation are well dressed and fed and are treated affectionately by their masters. Two black children are casually described: Juan Angel and Estéfana. They love María "with a fanatic affection". In the story of Nay and Sinar—a narrative with African exoticism interpolated in three chapters—the black theme is treated picturesquely and romantically. It only becomes dramatic at the end when the lovers are separated by slave traders going in different directions.[11]

The black slaves at Yolombó in the novel *La marquesa de Yolombó* (1928) are equally fortunate as the ones in *María* because they do not have a cruel and inhuman master. La Marquesa refutes the old argument that the white men brought the black out of dark Africa to teach him religion. She knows that the black was brought to the New World to work and be enslaved. She believes that the African should have been left in Africa and taught religion there, that they did not have to be enslaved for this purpose. She sincerely believes that setting the slaves free would be a grand and beautiful act of justice consistent with the obligation of every good Christian. La Marquesa is depicted as another Pedro Claver, a saint of the slaves, but *"en enaguas"* ("in skirts").

Similar to the patronizing tone in *María* is *El alferez real* (1886) by Eustaquio Palacios, another widely read Colombian novel with an idyllic colonial setting designed to show how benevolent the slave masters were to their happy, contented slaves. In Venezuela we have "Manuelote" by Eduardo Blanco, depicting a faithful slave who would rather kill his wife than permit her to betray their master to the Spaniards. Again, in the short story, "La negra", by Rafael Bolívar, a faithful slave chose to care for her penniless mistress rather than accept her freedom.

I am not saying here that such faithful, contented, and black-hating slaves did not exist, only that nineteenth-century and some twentieth-century Spanish-American writers rarely wrote about any other type of slave. All slave-holding societies have had their share of what Malcolm X would call "house Negroes" as opposed to what he would call "field Negroes." In the modern nomenclature, "Negro" in quotation marks, synomymous with Malcolm X's "house Negro," means a colored person satisfied with the way things are, and "black," synonymous with his "field Negro," denotes the revolutionary, the protester who wants to change things, through violent ways if necessary. Malcolm X tells the story of the "house Negro" who because of vested interest loved the master more than life itself because he, too, lived in and shared the comforts of the big house. If the master got sick the "house Negro," to illustrate his devotion, would run for the doctor, whereas the "field Negro" would send the doctor the other way. The "house Negro" would pamper and care for the big house, whereas the "field Negro" would burn it down, given the opportunity.

Few of the "black" or "field Negroes" gained entrance into nineteenth-century literature in Spanish America, which was characterized quite predictably and understandably by false tears and negative images.

Into the Twentieth Century: The Discovery, Use, and Abuse of Black People and Their Culture

*To demand a realistic portrayal of Blacks by Whites
is to demand the impossible, for Whites are neither
mentally nor culturally equipped for the task.*
Addison Gayle, Jr.

White Racism and the Paradox of Discovery

Negative images of blacks reflecting a nineteenth-century mentality on race, surprisingly, have not been completely discarded in the twentieth century. I say surprisingly because we expect to find such emphasis in the nineteenth century, when the climate of opinion regarding dark people was not very favorable, but not in our own supposedly more enlightened age. Negative opinions about dark-skinned peoples in the late nineteenth century were strongly influenced by European racist theories such as those in Count Gobineau's classic *Essay on the Inequality of Human Races* that coincided with the racist opinions of New World intellectuals who, inheriting the old prejudices of the colonial ruling class, were convinced of the inferiority of the darker races.

With amazing ease the European versions of racism were applied by homegrown racists to the multiracial environment of the Americas. As if to take the edge off, Magnus Mörner, commenting on the extreme racists this New World environment has produced, reminds us that two of the most influential Latin-American racists, Carlos Octavio Bunge and José Ingenieros, both Argentines, were of immigrant background.[1] A good example of this pseudoscientific racism, for example, in the Río de la Plata area, is voiced by Ingenieros, who, referring to blacks, declared that "people of the white race, even of the inferior ethnic groups, are separated by an abyss from those beings who seem to be closer to anthropoid apes than to civilized Whites.''[2] Such nonsense still finds currency in twentieth-century Latin America where some writers use Negro-ape comparisons freely, suggesting their acceptance of racist myths that dwell on bodily form and physical features as sure marks of inferiority that put blacks closer to apes than to whites. In a very aptly titled first chapter, ''The Sick Continent,'' Martin Stabb,[3] like Magnus Mörner,[4] referred in his recent book to nineteenth-century racist opinions which were popular not only in the Río de la Plata area but in Mexico, Bolivia, Chile, and Brazil as well.

Paradoxically, toward the latter half of the nineteenth century, when these racist opinions were strongly influential, the darker peoples were ''discovered'' by Africanist and *indigenista* intellectuals. *Indigenismo,* a term that identifies the social and literary process designed to integrate, uplift, and effect the Indian's twentieth-century renaissance, became the order of the day, even though, paradoxically, one of the first *indigenistas* was the Bolivian racist Alcides Arguedas. In Brazil, Afro-Brazilian studies were initiated under Nina Rodrigues—himself, paradoxically, a racist convinced of the inferiority of black people[5]—and continued with the work of Arthur Ramos and Gilberto Freyre, to name only two. And in Spanish America, it was the Cuban Fernando Ortiz, also labeled a racist in some quarters,[6] who had begun to publish his studies around the turn of the century, analyzing the African contribution to Cuban culture and society.

The dark-skinned peoples, nevertheless, were ''discovered'' in this century and together with the land became the focal point for a new outlook on life, defined as *mundonovismo* (''New Worldism''). In her important book on Latin American culture Jean Franco has written:

> After the 1914-18 war the Spanish American intellectuals began to seek in the cultures of the Indian and the Negro and in the land itself alternative values to those of a European culture which seemed on the verge of disintegration. This attempt to find roots in the native culture is related to the rejection not only of European cultural values but also of the rational, intellectual and scientific assumptions on which modern European civilization was based.[7]

With these words she begins her discussion of the artistic triad—the Indian, the Negro, and the land—that Latin-American artists were to discover in this century.

As an important member of this trilogy, the black in Latin America came to be looked upon as part of the American scene, as a homegrown constituent with distant roots in Africa, but whose destiny is inextricably involved with, indeed, has influenced, the development of his new environment. The discovery of the black in this century, however, is not an isolated phenomenon. It is, in fact, part of an overall attitude that Latin-American writers have taken toward their nations and problems. It is linked up with what Jean Franco has called a movement back to the roots, a form of cultural nationalism desirous of bringing all segments of the community into national life and arts. Authors have delved into the past and into all geographical regions in search of the historical and ethnic factors which have helped shape the courses their nations were to follow.[8] This struggle to achieve national unity, one of the most important movements in Latin America in this century, helped contribute to the discovery of the black and to his entrance into literature as a major theme.

The discovery of the black in this century in Latin America is partly a result of this search for something truly autonomous, for something as American as the native landscape, and the black, far removed from Africa, has helped provide this reorientation toward a literary Americanism. The awareness of the African's role in the destiny of America is a recognition of what the black man has contributed to the cultural nationalism of the countries to which he was forcibly taken many years ago, a recognition of his contribution to the historical and cultural processes that have helped shape Latin America; and it is this recognition of the black presence that has inspired much of the literature on black themes.

This discovery of the black, like that of the Indian, came in part from the outside, for Europeans, too, had recognized something of value in Africa and things African in the New World. Exotic native scenes had become a fashion in Europe before and after the First World War, where primitivism was the rage, where white Europeans—Frobenius, Spengler, Gide, Apollinaire, Picasso—were caught up in the Harlem and African vogue. But even though European fascination with the black helped legitimize his acceptance, we must remember that this movement was no more than a fad in Europe, a passing fancy, whereas in Cuba, for example, the white intellectuals, even if their interests were partly touristic and not social, at least saw the black as part of the Cuban mosaic.

And this movement was to a certain extent home grown. José Martí, for example, in the late nineteenth century already had discovered the importance of the black. And, though occasionally falling prey to racist stereotypes,[9] José Martí for the most part was an exception to those authors who were partly responsible for the racism and the general spirit of pessimism and resignation that pervaded much of the Latin-American essay during the waning years of the nineteenth century. Even before the "discovery" of the black in this century, José Martí had taken a uniquely modern stand in defense of blacks and the contributions they had made and would make in what Martí dreamed one day would be a free Cuba. Had he lived longer, his plans included a book on the black. Judging from the many scattered references he makes to blacks in his voluminous published works, we can conjecture that this book would have been as influential as his much-publicized views that in Cuba there are no black Cubans and no white Cubans, just Cubans, that there are no races but only a number of variations in man. Small wonder that Martí is revered in Castro's Cuba; one of the most publicized goals of the Cuban Revolution is the application of the concept of racial equality prescribed by José Martí many years ago.

Shortly after the turn of the century, Fernando Ortiz had begun to see the African elements in his country as part of the essence of *"la cubanidad,"* of what makes Cubans Cuban. Ortiz, who combined interest in anthropology, literature, and many other fields, saw that the real culture of Cuba was strongly influenced by Africa. The long and distinguished career of this Cuban humanist came to an end with his death on April 10, 1969.

In 1954 Eric Williams wrote a glowing tribute to Ortiz in an article on race relations in the Caribbean:

> And so with Cuba and Fernando Ortiz, whose humanism, historical research, assiduous contributions to the cause of racial equality, analysis of the myth of race, editing of the works of famous Cuban authors, emphasis on transculturation and on the African contributions to Cuban culture in music and folklore, make him the legitimate child of the century which gave birth to Martí. Dean of contemporary Caribbean scholars, he is the Caribbean white man at his best, and when the time comes to write the story and assess the significance of the indigenous cultural movement towards which the Caribbean area has been groping in recent years, Fernando Ortiz will have the place of honor, not only as a scholar—which would be distinction enough in communities markedly anti-intellectual, Cuba excepted—but as an enduring inspiration in liberalism in race relations.[10]

Despite this high praise of Fernando Ortiz, who, like Nina Rodrigues, had done much to foster interest in black culture in Latin America, colored intellectuals have criticized these white "discoverers" of the black and their followers for dealing with him as an exotic being largely associated with religious cults. They object to the classification of the black as an African curiosity, the target of anthropological studies, the descendant of slaves. Such characterizations, they believe, are responsible for negative connotations surrounding the modern-day black, whose human feelings and social problems in contemporary society are being ignored. They feel, perhaps, that blacks are being "put in their place" by the white man in much the same manner as the following:

> I profited perhaps by learning, at an early age when one's mind had not yet been prejudiced, that Negroes are men like ourselves . . . , I as a white man thus gained, perhaps, the possibility of always being natural with a Negro—and never, in his presence, to fall stupidly and imperceptibly into that attitude of ethnographic investigator that is still too often our unbearable manner of *putting them in their place*.[11]

The white author of the above quotation had sense enough to realize the overbearing dangers of an *africanización perpétua*,[12] which were implicit in incessantly studying the black man as an exotic or problematic subject matter; by constantly subjecting his behavior patterns to microscopic examination in books and theses with a view toward turning up a latest theory about what makes black people tick or about how they have survived or failed to survive or how they have or have not adapted, acculturated, transculturated, integrated, or miscegenated. Black intellectuals recognize, in short, that there has been a critical imbalance in the studies on black themes and black people in Latin America and would welcome a shift away from an exaggerated emphasis on the so-called black problem, an emphasis that tends to minimize the devastating role white racism and white people have played in the creation of what in part should be phrased a "white problem."

In Brazil the black intellectuals who criticized the large number of predominantly white Africanist intellectuals were for the most part associated with the Teatro Experimental do Negro.[13] This group stressed that the black was Brazilian and should be studied as such. In Cuba this same critical assessment, which was leveled at the Africanist studies of Fernando Ortiz, was associated with the views of Gastón Baquero[14] who has accused Ortiz of perpetuating anachronistic negative images of the black African as a primitive with criminal tendencies. The black Cuban poet Marcelino Arozarena has even accused Nicolás Guillén, his fellow Afro-Cuban poet, perhaps erroneously, of perpetuating similar negative images of blacks, for example, when he presents the superficial dimension of the "Negro of sex and rhythm, a Negro of the slave days and old sugar plantations."[15] When he presents the single black man or woman, the black plantation worker or the mulatto dancer, Arozarena asserts, Guillén's image of the black is retrograde and historically out of focus.[16]

False Black Poetry

Fernandez Ortiz's researches into black life and culture were preliminary to the Afro-Cuban movement where poets, using in part his findings, gave birth to poetic Negrism, a form of poetry characterized by African-sounding words, rhythms, and language. Yet, a shallow understanding of black culture by its white discoverers is partly responsible for some of the negative and, at best, one-dimensional images of black people widely perpetuated in modern Spanish-American literature and particularly in "Negro Verse."

Poetic Negrism in the Caribbean, which set the tone for the mainland, was, although seldom spoken of as such, primarily an exploitation of black culture by white writers. Generally an end in itself, poetic Negrism was easily accomplished by several good practitioners or skilled manipulators of language who tried to talk "real black talk," or *en negro de verdad,* and to beat black drums in poetry, using African-sounding words for rhythmic and musical effect. Such nonblack poets as Alejo Carpentier, Ramón Guirao, Emilio Ballagas, and Luis Palés Matos became masters of the verbal sound and play with words with or without meaning. They, like the Africanist intellectuals before them, became experts on black folklore and rituals, which they repeated aesthetically in their poetry. But since poetic Negrism was largely a movement of white intellectuals, it developed into a game played by those well-versed in the ways of black people who, largely for picturesque reasons, used African stylistic means in Spanish poetry. This literary fashion, which often relied on derogatory caricatures, has antecedents dating back to Spain's Golden Age and before, to Lope de Vega, Góngora, and to other writers who recognized the presence of the African element on Hispanic soil.[17]

Professor Lemuel Johnson[18] recently published an excellent survey of this Hispanic tradition of caricature that has made the black a literary toy, an Orphic buffoon, a bongo-beating idiot mindlessly singing and dancing his way down through the centuries, all the while speaking a "broken tongue." Professor Johnson's survey has followed the black man into the New World where he was transformed, especially in the Caribbean, into a sensuously animalistic, amoral creature. We should note the exception of Sor Juana Inés de la Cruz, however, who, in contrast to her seventeenth-century contemporaries, did take some note of the black man's suffering. She used the same deformed style of black speech as Góngora, but not for comic interest. She did not think the black man funny. Sor Juana protested against the social injustices that victimized black people, as Fernández de Lizardi did later in *El periquillo sarniento* (1816), rare actions for their time, when writers who included blacks in their literature generally considered them inferior.

The white practitioners of poetic Negrism in this century were mostly European in their outlook, and they stood in awe of the black man as a curious, exotic, and sensual subject. They made no conscientious effort to get rid of the old stereotypes and old myths of the black past. These white poets continued the Hispanic tradition of not dwelling on the black man's suffering, or the *dolor negro,* so much a part of the social drama of black people in this and past centuries. Very little protest against prejudice and racial discrimination came from the white practitioners of poetic Negrism. In fact, Luis Palés Matos typifies the paradoxical result of the "discovery" of the black man in our century by some non-black authors. One of the most skilled manipulators of African sounds, language, and rhythms, Palés Matos resorts to Negro-ape analogies in his poetry; he also dismisses the struggle for freedom and independence in Haiti as just so much concern with absurd titles. Palés Matos, Professor Johnson rightly observes, is the most famous resurrector of racist clichés that rely on one-dimensional caricatures of the black as a picturesque, sensual, or primitive buffoon, not too far removed from the jungle. Professor Johnson illustrates this view by referring to Palés Matos's "Danza Negra" where the "cro-cro-cro/pru-pru-pru" is a "picturesque, tolerant onomatopeic mockery that syncopates the Negro's engaging onomatopeic mindlessness."[19] It becomes clear that we cannot approach this poetry in a narrow formalistic way by evaluating or assessing only the musical effects, the alliteration, the rhythm, the onomatopoeia, when what we have here are racist caricatures perpetuating images of the black as a mindless primitive.

It also becomes clear that the white practitioners of poetic Negrism overlooked essential parts of black life in Latin America. These white poets did not see the black *por dentro,* or from the inside, as the expression goes. They were more interested in the black as a child of nature, and they propagated an image of him as an amoral primitive, full of song, dance, unusual rhythm, and sensuality. All they could hear were African drums and maracas. All they could see were the *ancas, nalgas,* and *grupas,* or the uninhibited rump swaying and rhythmic hip-swinging of the black *hembras* ("females"). In short, they were dazzled by the black's primitive exoticism and were given to promoting a one-dimensional image of the black as an unintellectual, sexual animal. The colored woman especially became a distorted figure not too far removed from the jungle, a figure reappearing repeatedly, as we shall see, in modern Spanish-American prose fiction as well.

Such one-dimensional images, partly a result of the *africanización perpétua* of which we have spoken, help create an impression of false black poetry as these images for the most part do not project, as it was not their intention to do so, a well-rounded vision of the modern-day black. Partly for this and for other reasons "black poetry" has been classified at one time or another as false. Fernando Ortiz[20] himself declares much of it to be "white" poetry in that, despite black themes, much of it is written in "white" language, from a "white perspective," that is, expressed in an European language though often depending on the African sound. Even this African sound that characterizes so much of black poetry together with some of the lexical items, has been rejected as unauthentic by Humberto López Morales,[21] who contends it to be no different from the language typical of Spanish spoken by whites. Rejecting in effect African influence on Cuban Spanish, Humberto López Morales on the contrary asserts that black Cubans learned to speak Spanish with characteristics of Andalusian speech.

Especially relevant to the question of false black poetry written by white poets is the point raised by Juan Ramón Jiménez in the following quotation on the question of whether whites can write authentic black poetry:

Indian, black, and gypsy from the outside make forced literature, not direct poetry. For it to be so, it is essential for the poet to be gypsy, black, or Indian, not a white man painted in whichever of the three races.[22]

A view directly opposed to this one was recently developed by Victor Franceschi, a Panamanian poet who defends the right of whites like himself, he says, to write black poetry. Franceschi, whose volume *Carbones* had been accused of the same insincere superficialities common to much of false black poetry of the white exponents of this literature, asserted: ''No sir! It is not necessary to be black or to have black blood to cultivate black art.''[23] Further, Franceschi thinks that the important thing is to write this poetry completely free from the kind of racial prejudice associated with the United States or with Adolf Hitler.

Black poetry, then, much of it false, spread over the Caribbean and the mainland, and, as in the United States and in Europe, the blacks became a center-stage attraction, where the white man—and some blacks, too—had him performing in puppet fashion, until the Cuban Regino Pedroso, a colored poet, stepped in with his famous poem, ''Hermano negro,'' and told the dancing figure, *''apaga un poco tus maracas,''* to stop playing his maracas so much, to stop grinning, dancing, and jumping about for the white man. He told his black brother to give to the world instead his voice of rebellion, his human voice.

There were black poets in Latin America before the twentieth century: José Vasconcelos (''El Negrito Poeta'') in eighteenth-century Mexico, allegedly the first colored poet in continental Spanish America; the nineteenth-century Afro-Cubans, among them Gabriel de Concepción Valdés (Plácido) and Juan Francisco Manzano; the Colombian Candelario Obeso; and, at the turn of the century, the Panamanian Gaspar Octavio Hernández, to name a few. But they, too, put no real stress on the black man's suffering. It was left to twentieth-century colored writers, such as Regino Pedroso and his fellow Cuban Nicolás Guillén, the Ecuadorians Nelson Estupiñán Bass and Adalberto Ortiz, the Colombian Jorge Artel, for example, to forcefully recognize that black life was characterized by suffering as well as rhythm. Guillén, like most Afro-Spanish-American poets who easily mastered the style of poetic Negrism, would be the last to deny the sensual, rhythmic nature of the black dance. But he would be, like Pedroso, the first to stress that there is much more to the black than sensuality, dance, and rhythm. Nicolás Guillén himself, in "¡Negra, mueve la cintura!", in *Prosa de Prisa* (Buenos Aires: Editorial Hernández, 1968), his first collection of prose writings, sums up extremely well this very important point:

> Blacks are, there is no need to deny it, ardent and sensual. Their dances share this characteristic. . . . However, blacks are far from being all dance, and dance does not represent the only contribution blacks have made in the development of our sensibility.

> We are not going to stop smiling, but we shall say now that we find it an exaggeration to attribute to the black the choreographic quality as his only spiritual one; always seeing his soul in his feet. Of course this is what his detractors would like to see, and have always wanted to see, because while he twirls about they humor him along and confuse him, the better to take advantage of his helplessness . . . without refraining from dancing and singing his music for him. (p. 22)

False Black Images: Racial Preconceptions, Misconceptions, and Stereotypes

Racial preconceptions, misconceptions, and stereotypes are not exclusive to poetry. The literary reflection of the paradoxical discovery of the African cultural heritage is evident in Latin-American fiction as well. Some Latin-American novelists, too, wittingly or unintentionally, have perpetuated similar racial myths damaging to the black man's image. Frederick Douglas, I believe, once wrote that blacks can never have impartial portraits at the hands of white artists. He believed it was next to impossible for the white man to take likenesses of black men without grossly exaggerating their distinctive features. Some modern Latin-American novelists whose visions of reality are colored by their racist views toward black people are guilty of such literary distortions.

Though well-meaning, many twentieth-century novelists are too apologetic, patronizing, and condescending. Their fascination with blacks, not too unlike the white practitioners of poetic Negrism, is aimed at the superstitious and primitive, at extolling the atavistic and the exotic. They depict the black as an inferior jungle beast, a comical provider of music. The black woman becomes a sexually uninhibited amoral animal full of sensual jungle rhythm, oozing sex through animal eyes, sensual voice, and inviting flesh. In short, like the white practitioners of poetic Negrism, some modern Latin-American novelists use, or misuse, black culture as an excuse to perpetuate one-dimensional racist images of black people, and, like some nineteenth-century novelists before them, there are twentieth-century writers who still subscribe to the myth of the docile black slave, with no rebellious spirit. Popular clichés, then, found in modern Latin-American fiction, while giving false if not one-sided images of the black, at the same time help indicate racist feelings toward black people among Latin-American authors.

In *Risaralda* (1936) by the Colombian Bernardo Arias Trujillo, animal sensuality, violence, and drunken orgies seem to sum up the author's conception of black life and customs. Arias Trujillo appears to be a fascinated onlooker to the hip-swinging spectacle of the black whom he types as a happy-go-lucky, violent, barbaric primitive, usually docile and tame until fired up with passion, alcohol, and fiestas. The sensual dance movement of the black provides some of the highlights of the novel. In the following passage, which rivals *poesía negra* for description, the author has not missed a single detail even of the movements that simulate sexual possession and surrender:

> From one end of the room they begin to dance the *currulao,* a type of *cumbia* from the Pacific that is purely African. Juancho begins by moving his whole body . . . and Rita does it with even more sensuality, as if enjoying the sensation of orgasm. She moves her hips with a sea-like rhythm because it is the dance of the coast, and she keeps on drawing closer, closer, with . . . her whole body in motion. She shakes as if offering herself for pleasure, as if urging avidly to be possessed. He, in turn, quivering with desire, moves in that excited, unrestrained way of the buck. Finally they meet; they kiss, press against each other, smell each other, hug, intertwine their legs voluptuously, feigning sexual intercourse. They separate immediately to join, back to back, . . . In this position . . . Rita's breasts, hard and pointed, stand out obscenely, as if naked under her perspiration-soaked cotton blouse. Her sensuous movement causes her savage and desirable breasts to undulate like spinning

tops, their tips lewdly firm in a phallic-like erection, inviting and exciting the male to his own erection.

Now, Rita begins to move . . . her torso, her breasts and nipples, her abdomen, her rump, her thighs . . . and all that God in His kindness gave her.[24]

There are other sensual portrayals of black dances in other novels.[25] It would be difficult, however, to find examples more explicit than the one taken from the pages of *Risaralda*.

It should be noted, however, that *Risaralda* does give us a good history of the formation of the black town of Sopinga in Colombia, located in the valley of the Risaralda and Cauca Rivers in what is now the state of Risaralda, of the first black men who built this town, and of the men and women who recall the days of slavery with songs from Africa passed down from generation to generation through which the pain and suffering of their forefathers are relived. Racial stereotypes aside, *Risaralda* is an important novel with historical, social, and aesthetic merit, crammed with details about Colombian customs, local color, and music.

The Central American novelist, Paca Navas, in *Barro* (1951) has approached black customs along the Atlantic coastal region of Honduras with similar racial preconceptions. She depicts the blacks in this area as simple, uncivilized people who reproduce like rats. While taking an interest in black life and customs, she leaves the impression that she does not really know these people through actual contact. To Paca Navas, blacks are overly superstitious and want, more than anything else, to emulate white people.

White Spanish-American novelists seem to have taken to heart Rómulo Lachatañaré's phrase ''Wherever there are blacks, witchcraft will also be found.''[26] Although witchcraft and superstition play important parts in novels about black life by many white writers in Latin America, it would be well to remember that, just as colored poets such as Nicolás Guillén and Regino Pedroso reject the one-dimensional image of black people as primitive, propagated by nonblack practitioners of poetic Negrism, black protagonists of some black novelists also reject superstitions and witchcraft. Máximo in *Corral de negros* (1963) by the Afro-Colombian Manuel Zapata Olivella, for example, believes that superstition and witchcraft in Colombia are tied to the condition of a society made up of exploiters and the exploited. Máximo, like Charles in *Los cuatro espejos* (1973) by the black Costa Rican novelist Quince Duncan, believes in doctors, medical science, and hospitals, not superstitions and witch doctor cures. He despises the barbaric rites of his people, which he believes are products of an ignorance perpetuated intentionally by leaders of the country who are reluctant to provide good educational facilities for black people. And Ascensión Lastre in *Juyungo* (1943) by the Afro-Ecuadorian Adalberto Ortíz, did not put too much stock in magic and superstition. He felt even priests took advantage of the beliefs of his people, who still lived in primitive conditions in the country and in the city. And Juan Pablo Sojo, the Afro-Venezuelan folklorist, thinks it an error to put too much emphasis on witchcraft and superstition when dealing with black culture. He cautions: "To consider all witchcraft as being of black origin is to commit a serious mistake. Superstition knows no color or race."[27] In other words, he feels that black culture should not be abused; black people should not be depicted as having a monopoly on superstition and witchcraft.

Superstition and witchcraft, then, together with the sensual portrayal of the black dance, were basic ingredients of the staple diet of black culture exalted in Latin-American prose and poetry. Other ingredients in prose as well as in poetry would include, among others, the drum—an invariable accompaniment of black dance—religious rituals, and magical incantations.

Pompeyo Amargo (1942), by the Uruguayan Dionisio Trillo Pays, is a good example of another cliché-ridden category underscored by persistent Negro-ape analogies and atavistic nonsense, that ties the black to a primitive past from which escape is difficult, if not impossible. Set in the urban environment of Montevideo in the early twentieth century, this long novel deals with the adjustment problems of a black adolescent who must come to terms with a patronizing and at times cruel society that shares the racist principles of the author. The story traces the trials and tribulations of the young Pompeyo, who lived with and was educated by a middle-class white family in Montevideo, where his struggles include facing the taunts and teasing pranks of his fellow schoolmates. The author repeatedly characterizes his black protagonist with words such as stupid, ugly, ignorant, foolish, grotesque, idiotic, as well as with the string of Negro-ape analogies.

The novel consistently suggests an assumed inferiority of the black. The author even has Pompeyo refer to himself as a senseless *"pobre negro bruto."* Even his mother, the cook for the family that housed them, believed in the *"letargo ancestral,"* or "ancestral lethargy," which weighed heavily on the shoulders of black people. One of the white members of the family literally takes Pompeyo by the hand to lead him to overcome this mark of birth, thus suggesting that a semisavage can overcome, with a guiding white hand, innate inferiority and inherited jungle tendencies.

The author devotes much of the novel to Pompeyo's early childhood and to the transformation of his character from the family buffoon, the comic Negro, to a young man with some acquired intelligence who could achieve, if properly guided. The second part of the novel finds Pompeyo about to enter the University of Montevideo around 1922, when he later quite innocently gets involved in student strikes and revolts by simply going along with the crowd. At this point in the novel the author has one of the protesters speak out in defense of the black, implying again that blacks are too stupid to chart their own course. Pompeyo eventually comes of age, moves out of the house, becomes interested in women, and comes to grips with his destiny.

Trillo Pays apparently has good intentions, but his attempts to redeem the black race smacks of a humanitarianism based not on acceptance of equality but rather on myths and theories of inherent inferiority. The author rules out Pompeyo's salvation through any means other than by the guiding hand of a white environment that turns the savage into a civilized person. Generally there is far too much psychological probing and analyzing in the novel, which relies too heavily on racial myths to account for Pompeyo's successes and failures. Black people should not despair, however, since, according to the author, they are not really to blame for their shortcomings. The culprit is that ancestral link, over which the accursed black has no control.

The Negro-ape analogy is the racist core of *Ebano* (1955) by the Nicaraguan Alberto Ordóñez Argüello. Set in the coastal area of Nicaragua, the novel narrates the absurd story of Jonathan Brown, a black who is characterized with relentless regularity as a worthless beast of burden, an ape, a savage wild animal from the jungle. The author gives him the English nickname of Ball Blue because of his small round head that is so black it looks blue. Ball Blue is extremely repulsive physically, and his background included thefts, murder, and the attempted rape of a white woman. This novel leaves the impression that blacks are primitive people whose customs are limited to drunken bouts with gin, the rhumba, tap dance, and other dances reminiscent of the jungle. But here again the black is not to blame for his shortcomings. The author tells us, like Trillo Pays in Uruguay, that atavism is responsible for the black man's inability to overcome his inherited savage traits. In *Ebano* the black has no redeeming qualities; Ordóñez Argüello apparently sees none.

Ebano, then, is another cliché-filled novel relying too heavily on racist explanations and descriptions always to the disadvantage of the black man. Furthermore, the author sees the blackness and dark deeds of Ball Blue as symbols of corruption, sin, and the forces of evil applicable to Nicaragua. The author even delves into history to substantiate his image of the black as animal and thief. And finally, as a catalyst to the action, the author has as a plot line the absurd story of Ball Blue's love for a white coquette from Louisiana, who had brought her antiblack views—which closely parallel those of the author—into Nicaragua from the southern United States. The Indian in this novel fares much better than the black. One of the white characters even falls in love with an Indian girl, marries her, and takes her to the United States to live, in the deep South.

"La piel," a long short story by the Cuban Alfonso Hernández Cata, tries to show how an intelligent black is trapped by his ancestral leanings which prevent a complete grasp of the white man's learning. What is more, Eulogio, the black intellectual, is rejected by the whites because he is black and by blacks who resent his superior learning and his tendency to move away from their ways and habits. Rejected by both sides, his fate is tragic as he dies a victim of a political plot in which his own people have participated.

Eulogio was an ex-slave given a chance at a white man's education. Although he was determined to overcome the stigma of color, Eulogio felt threatened constantly by those natural atavistic tendencies that the author attributes to the black, a race depicted as amoral, with a slave mentality tied to a "primitive" past, still manifesting itself in barbaric dances, shouts, rhythms, and native rituals. Hernández Cata only halfheartedly makes Eulogio an exception to his race; he never concedes that education can totally overcome these natural jungle tendencies. His conclusion is that the black is better off in the jungle where he would be happier in an uncivilized and uncomplicated state. Since atavism will out, and since skin color cannot be changed, the worst possible thing a black man can do, according to the author, is to take on a "white soul," that is, to become civilized.

The tragedy of the black who wills to be white perhaps reaches its maximum expression in *El negro que tenía el alma blanca* (1922), by the Cuban-born Alberto Insúa. This novel is a classic example of the theory that no matter how much wealth, culture, and position a black man manages to acquire, he is still a black. Pedro Valdés, born of slave parents in Cuba, was taken to Spain by his master's family, and in Europe he grew up to become a famous dancer who assumed the English name of Peter Wald. Whatever the magnitude of his success he was constantly weighed down by the reality of his color. He fell hopelessly in love with a white girl who had a "natural aversion" toward black people—which the author says all decent white girls harbor—and eventually died of grief.

Peter hated his color, which he tried to overcome by becoming a "civilized" person, in effect, white on the inside. But this was not enough, and he carried his flight-from-blackness tendency to an extreme by having his servant massage his nose and lips frequently with certain instruments to remove his negroid features, to make them look more caucasoid. Peter even had hopes that his industrious servant would uncover in some German books a skin-whitening process that would lighten his skin, thus making the transformation so complete as to enable him to hurdle that last and most important obstacle to success, thereby bridging the somatic distance.

Peter should have met Augusto, who had marketed a skin-lightening soap in the play *Medusas en la bahía* (1956), by the Puerto Rican playwright Francisco Arriví; or the doctor in *Sirena* (1958), by the same author, who successfully performed plastic surgery designed to minimize the negroid features of Cambucha, a mulatto mistress who wanted to whiten herself for her white employer; or Dr. George Brandon, a plastic surgeon in the short story "El negro que se pintó de negro" by the Mexican Manuel Becerra Acosta, who developed a method, as a solution to the racial problem, that transformed blacks into whites by eliminating through plastic surgery not only negroid features but black skin as well. For Peter, however, this was not to be, and his blackness continued to be a barrier. The white girl he coveted still felt that natural repugnance for him, in spite of her admiration for him as a gentleman and a dancer.

The apparent message of this novel is that there is nothing more ridiculous than a black man who has left his natural bestial ways to become civilized, cultured, and learned. Toward the end of the novel, the author has Peter long to return to the good old happy days of slavery. Insúa painted an irresistible picture of slavery and plantation life in Cuba, with wonderful masters surrounded by contented, faithful slaves. Some of his descriptions of plantation life in Cuba would make proslavery novels in the United States suffer by comparison.

All of Peter's problems started the day he left the plantation. Insúa coupled his picture of the plantation paradise in Cuba for blacks with the statement that it was in Madrid that Peter first realized the difficulty of being black. Ironically, while insisting throughout the novel on a racist atmosphere in Spain, the author seems to be unaware of the persistence of his own racial preconceptions, assumptions, and racist stereotypes, among them that the bestial soul of the black race came out when Peter danced the fox-trot, that Peter still retained his black smell regardless of the perfumes he used and the precautions he took, that slavery was so benevolent blacks wanted to remain slaves even after they had been set free, that Peter's father had improved his disposition—which means he had toned down his rebelliousness— thanks to contact with the superior white race, that Peter was deprived of the beauty of slave life in Cuba by being taken to Europe, that his mother preferred to go with the white family to serve them in Spain rather than remain in Cuba with her husband. From his perspective of white supremacy Alberta Insúa is so thoroughly convinced of his racist beliefs that he has Peter share them.

Insúa published a sequel to this novel fifteen years later, *La sombra de Peter Wald* (1937). This sequel, which he calls part two, is a Freudian attempt to explain away the guilt feelings suffered by Emma, the white girl whose rejection of Peter had led to his death. After a few pages, the author has Emma convinced that the "natural aversion" toward black people was justified; she was only responding to the imperatives of the white race.

Peter's defeatist, self-hating attitude is matched by Lolo, another black protagonist who puts a white woman on the proverbial pedestal, this time in the novel *Roquedal* ("a rocky region"), by the Mexican Ramiro Torres Septién. *Roquedal,* a fantastic account of interracial obsession, is another example of concession to the white standard. The interracial flavor of the novel is provided by the black Lolo and the white girl Toni and their enforced sojourn together on a deserted rock enclave where they end up the only survivors of an airplane crash. Toni, a Mexican girl, had always felt a repugnance for black people, and Lolo was the blackest person she had ever seen. After Lolo's many acts of kindness, however, Toni's repugnance disappeared; Lolo's blackness became beautiful, and her hate turned to love. Lolo accepted her advances reluctantly because of his feelings of inferiority, and their relationship entered a new phase. Toni became pregnant, and the fear of a black child haunted both of them, especially Lolo, whose self-hating attitude reached ludicrous proportions. Rescue became possible after the black child was born, and Lolo, in order to spare Toni the shame of having to share a life with them in the world outside, kills the child and commits suicide.

Lolo's supreme act of self-hatred is more melodramatic than tragic, at least to a black reader who could scarcely identify with this black character. But identity is not the important measure of significance of this novel. The most important fact regarding the novel, at least as far as racism and color prejudice are concerned, is the implication it carries regarding antiblack feelings in Mexico, largely a *mestizo* country. Equally important, however, is the author's acceptance and perpetuation of racial preconceptions, such as the belief that blacks judge themselves unfit to live since they are not white. W. E. B. Dubois once said, I believe, that the assumption that of all the hues of God whiteness is inherently and obviously better than brownness or tan leads to curious acts. There is no act more curious than Lolo's suicide and murder of his child to spare Toni the shame of their blackness.

The racial angle in the novel is set within a larger question the author poses: What is the difference between reality, or truth, and fiction? What is real and what is imagined? The question is raised in the novel that Toni's whole experience, marooned in that rock prison, existed only in her mind. Everyone except Toni believed that she was there for only four days. To her, the period was four years. The speculation is never really resolved, perhaps because of the fantastic nature of the novel. In working out her fantasy, however, the author has touched on a wide range of questions of racial interest, among them the subject of miscegenation.

Racism, Miscegenation, and the Mulatto Image

It has been said that racism finds one of its most obvious outlets in the field of sexual relations. As we saw in Chapter One, miscegenation and racism are joined in Latin America in a curious marriage that works, paradoxically, toward the eventual extinction of the black man. The implication is that the mulatto points to the future. Several novelists have dealt with the mulatto, and their novels reflect his favorable position and his largely positive image *vis-à-vis* the unfavorable position and the negative image of the black man in Latin-American society and literature. It is important to emphasize that most white writers who have presented a rebellious type have chosen mulattoes for their protagonists, conceivably attributing, subconsciously or intentionally, their rebelliousness to a white heritage while correspondingly casting the black man, the pure African, in a submissive role.

The well-known Venezuelan writer Arturo Uslar Pietri, for example, in *Las lanzas coloradas* (1931), has given us the proud, beautiful, and savage Presentación Campos, a mulatto slave who rebelled against his master and marched off to the independence wars in Venezuela, taking with him the slaves of the hacienda to act as his soldiers. The superiority of this mulatto over the rest of the slaves is clarified from the first as he enters the novel with a commanding air that demands their respect in spite of his obvious scorn for them. A strong, majestic mulatto, Presentación, though respected, was feared by the other slaves. To Campos there were only two kinds of people, those who are on top and those who are on the bottom. War gave him the opportunity to adjust the present system of values which had a strong man like himself enslaved by a weakling like his master, don Fernando.

Arrogant and proud, he went off to war full of self-confidence, feeling himself invincible. Before leaving he paused long enough to rape doña Inés, his master's sister, who had tried to stop the revolt and had insulted him by calling him a cowardly slave who should know better than to revolt against his natural masters. In one of the best scenes in the novel Presentación literally thumped his chest and slapped her bottom, saying, while in the process of stripping her naked, that he was not a slave, that he was as free as anyone, that this was the flesh of a man, *"carne de macho,"*[28] of a free man, and certainly not the slave of her cowardly brother.

In battle Presentación was fearless, daring, and savage. His strength and ruthlessness grew and he became a vigorous, merciless master of men possessed with the fury to kill and the desire to dominate, to assert his manhood. One could be tempted perhaps to consider him the personification of cruelty, or a person who incarnates the barbarism that dominated Venezuelan life after independence. But we do not have to look for a symbol in Presentación Campos; he does not really symbolize anything but himself. He is a courageous person who wants to demonstrate his valor and who wants to be on top whatever the price. He is a proud, arrogant flesh and blood man and one of the strongest antitheses to the faithful slave myth in Latin-American literature.

Conversely, in this same novel, the other slaves, the black people, are the objects of one of the most consistently degrading barrages of racist insults ever encountered in this literature. Rarely is there such repulsion felt toward black people as that which characterizes Uslar Pietri's mulatto protagonist. Through the eyes of Presentación Campos the author sees the black people in the novel as cowardly and frightened, wooly-headed creatures who are constantly bowing down, almost stretched out on the ground like submissive dogs. The author, through the eyes of his mulatto protagonist, sees the other slaves as bestial, dirty, repugnant people with revolting, stinking black flesh. He despised them because they were weak, worthless, submissive, abject, and defeated. And to further substantiate that the author felt the black man incapable of rebellion, he has one of them bring the news of the revolt of Presentación Campos into town to don Fernando, the owner of the hacienda, who in turn vents his anger on this black slave, choking him and accusing him of cowardice for not rebelling too. This attitude toward black people closely parallels the one superimposed on Nat Turner by William Styron in his controversial bestseller, *The Confessions of Nat Turner,* which the black author John Killens calls the confessions of Willie Styron.[29]

Another mulatto protagonist, José Manuel, in the Peruvian novel *Matalaché* (1924), by Enrique López Albújar, is depicted also as superior to the other slaves. The author tells us, in fact, in no uncertain terms, that the white blood of his intelligent mulatto protagonist was the source of his rebellious spirit. The black slaves in the novel, on the other hand, are depicted as docile and contented as long as they had a good master and enough food to eat. In *Matalaché,* María de la Luz, daughter of the hacendado, recently returned to the hacienda from college, feels a strong attraction toward the handsome mulatto slave who has a local reputation as a skillful lover. She gives herself to him in a clandestine arrangement, becomes pregnant, and unable to hide her condition, contemplates suicide. The angry father avenges his honor, forcing Matalaché into a boiling vat of soap.

A primary objective of the author in dealing with this theme during the era of slavery was to show the irresistible attraction of the sexes, regardless of the racial and social norms at the time. Yet in addition to two other concessions to white racist thought, namely, that white blood is responsible for rebellious spirit and blacks were basically content with slavery, López Albújar, though making a plea for interracial sex, nevertheless stops short by portraying his "black" lover as almost white. Physically and spiritually José Manuel is the least "black" of all the slaves at La Tina. For example, he is endowed with a Roman nose, smooth hair, and thin lips. He has a preference for white women and a desire to be considered a white man. Further, in a letter to the Spanish writer Ramiro de Maeztu, who had criticized the interracial flavor of his novel, López Albújar, in defending his creation, is very careful to point out that José Manuel is a mulatto and *not* a pure black man.[30]

A similar interracial theme involving a mulatto protagonist born in slavery and a white woman occurs in *Pobre negro* (1937) by the Venezuelan writer Rómulo Gallegos. His novel gives a sympathetic picture of black life in Venezuela before and after the abolition of slavery, with much of the action taking place during the federal wars that followed abolition. *Pobre negro,* however, carries the primary message of racial amalgamation, a theme which had found expression in an earlier novel by Gallegos, *La trepadora* (1925).

In *Pobre negro,* Ana Julia, obviously suffering from a severe case of sexual repression and frustration, was tormented by her attraction to and fear of the black. Her feelings of guilt manifested themselves in the form of *"una misteriosa fiebre."* One night she and a rebellious runaway slave, "Negro Malo," bewitched by the sensuous beat of drums, were drawn into the woods and into a sexual union "against their will." This was the origin of Pedro Miguel, who years later became the choice of Luisana, the niece of Ana Julia and her opposite in terms of attitudes. Luisana overcame the tragic sexual frustration and terror of her aunt, falling in love uninhibitedly with Pedro Miguel, an act of personal liberation from and defiance of the prejudices and customs of her day. Both women, each in her own way, came face to face with the problem of personal choice, Ana Julia in a momentary, violent, involuntary sexual act, the victim of a fear that attracts, and Luisana in an act of love, voluntary and lasting, without sexual frustration and fears.

Pedro Miguel, the mulatto protagonist torn by an inner conflict patterned on an ambivalent attitude toward white people, came to symbolize Venezuela and the country's search for a way out at a moment in history when a stabilizing factor was needed. For Gallegos this factor was racial integration. The ultimate mutual acceptance of the white Luisana and Pedro Miguel, the mulatto born in slavery, augured well for the destiny of the country that depended on the breaking down of class barriers for survival as a nation. The final symbolic scene in the novel contrasts sharply with the acute black phobia earlier harbored by Ana Julia, Luisana's aunt.

The mulatto's role in the future of Venezuela is the subject of *Cumboto* (1950), another Venezuelan novel. The author, Ramón Díaz Sánchez, makes a strong plea for better race relations by calling for a partnership between the black and white races. His theory is that each race would contribute an important aspect of human nature the other allegedly lacks. The black man is to bring intuition and primordial vitality, the white man, reason and intelligence, which, according to the author, are totally foreign to black people. Díaz Sánchez builds an impressive case in his story, set in the early twentieth century on a coconut plantation in Venezuela where blacks had comprised the work force for generations. The symbolic union involved don Federico, the last in a long line of ruling overlords, and the black girl Pascua. It was their mulatto son who returned to the plantation years later to take up an equally symbolic residence in the "Big House," before occupied only by white people and faithful servants like Natividad, who narrated the story and his part in it.

The theory of the author was first broached in the relationship between don Federico and Natividad, who had been good friends since childhood. It was Natividad who set in motion the forces brought to consummation in the relationship between the black, hot-blooded Pascua and the cold, Nordic don Federico. Natividad had grown up in the Big House and had acquired some of the white man's knowledge and reasoning power. This link with civilization, however, influenced only a small part of his mind for he still believed, for example, in witchcraft and superstitions. Don Federico, on the other hand, realized that he, too, had to become more sensitive to the black world, and he depended on Natividad to lead him into this world, alive with savage fervor and jungle madness, and into the relationship with the black girl who supposedly typified this world. Their union bore forth the messenger, their mulatto son, who brought with him a message for the future, a future which had no place for black people.

On a practical and historical level *Cumboto* relates in fiction how the mulatto came to take over the plantations and property of their white fathers. Díaz Sánchez, then, is dealing in part with history. His psychological analysis of the forces working toward racial amalgamation, together with his richly poetic renditions of folklore, sociology, and anthropology, make this an ambitious novel from an artistic point of view worthy of the honors it has received. Movingly related, for example, is the description of how the original inhabitants of the region of Cumboto (runaway slaves) preferred to risk the fury of the sea to the inhuman treatment they were receiving from their masters. The novel is puzzling, however, when we realize that the black man here again is subjected not only to extinction but to racial preconceptions and insults as well.

To Díaz Sánchez the black man is a faithful servant given to drunken sprees with parties that often end in knifings, clubbings, and broken heads. His life is one long party filled with flashy colors, irrepressible laughter, childlike behavior, singing, and constant chatter. The black is mischievous, the author tells us; he loves to play. He behaves like the mindless creatures of the forest. The author states categorically that there is no black who does not firmly believe that animals can talk. Such racial preconceptions, which we find throughout the novel, serve to substantiate the author's theory that black people can bring nothing more to an interracial partnership than primitive instincts. Ramón Díaz Sánchez leaves little doubt that the mulatto is his preference as a proper model for the future.

Racism and interracial sex in Latin-American literature are by no means limited to the favored position of the mulatto. Interracial sex has played an important part in character contact, as we have seen already in several novels. While there are no real rape and lynch sequences, there are, nevertheless, other clichés and stereotypes that recall the sexualization of racism as we know it in the United States.

Many Latin-American novelists deal with miscegenation in the twentieth century where the white woman takes on the character of redeemer, who overcomes racial prejudices, at least toward the mulatto, only to suffer the consequences. The two novels of Gallegos and López Albújar illustrate that the "New Desdemona,"[31] however, has not always been a twentieth-century woman. In addition to the redeemers, we have seen the coquettish white woman (Ordónez Argüello, *Ebano*) and the white woman whose fear of rape by black men is more desire than fear (Gallegos, *Pobre negro*). And we shall see in the next chapter instances where the black male is used sexually by the white female who rejects him afterwards (Arcocha, *Los muertos andan solos;* Granados, *Adire y el tiempo roto*) as well as novels by Joaquín Beleño C. where, among other clichés of the sexualization of racism, the white woman cries rape when her overtures are rejected by her black target. We also have in Spanish-American literature cases of the colored woman who tries to acquire whiteness through association with white men even if marriage is out of the question (Villaverde, *Cecilia Valdés;* Díaz Sánchez, *Cumboto*). This one-dimensional image is a concession to the stereotype of the black woman as an amoral sexual animal who is there for the taking, especially if the taker is white. And we have seen that old classic of racist mythology: the white father who is afraid the black man is out to get his daughter (Insúa, *El negro que tenía el alma blanca;* Ordóñez Argüello, *Ebano*). In short, in many Latin-American novels, sex, as in similar American fiction, becomes the reason for racial persecution.[32]

There are many novels deeply rooted in Hispanic tradition, however, which deal with the same problems of sex and race, that draw on similar racist clichés and solutions. Novels such as *Matalaché, Pobre negro, Cumboto,* and *Las lanzas coloradas* are important to the theme of miscegenation in Latin America. They are significant not only for the ideas they carry on the sexualization of racism but also because of the favored position they grant to the mulatto in Latin-American society *vis-à-vis* the black man, often pictured in a bad light.

Toward Racial Equality:
The Socio-Negristic Narrative,
The Black and His Literary Defenders

> *¡Aunque sea en América Hispana ser negro es ser negro!*
>
> *Joaquín Gallegos Lara*

The late W. E. B. Dubois, often referred to as the father of the Afro-American Liberation Movement, said in 1903 that "the problem of the twentieth century is the problem of the color-line—the relation of the darker to the lighter races of men in Asia and Africa, in America, and the islands of the seas."[1] This prophetic statement, which proved true in so many parts of the world, is, as we have seen, no less applicable to Latin America, where the struggle for racial equality continues. This struggle has become one of the main themes for those committed writers who have taken on the task of exposing the problems and hardships suffered by black people.

Although the problem of color in Latin America is widely documented in social science research, some of it sponsored by UNESCO,[2] the point was made recently that "our understanding of any significant movement in human affairs can hardly be said to even approach completeness until the evidence from literature is in, that literary criticism can bring to the surface what otherwise might lie buried in the culture's subconscious, and regarding the Negro specifically, that it is not just to the "objective" sociological, political, and economic accounts solely but to the literature as well in which the image of the Negro has cast its shadow that we must look if we are to find meaning that might otherwise elude us."[3] This admonition is especially relevant to Latin America where one of the most enduring clichés of modern literary criticism holds that Latin-American novels, products of an *engagé* tradition, are more reliable sources of information about the lives and problems of the people than history books and sociological tracts. In Latin America socially committed writers have exposed and condemned racism and color prejudice in their homelands, for example, by having their characters mirror existent prejudices based on skin color. Regardless of the practice of substituting "social," "class," or "economic" for "racial" when referring to discrimination, nonblack literary defenders of the Negro realize what blacks have always known, namely, that the color of a man's skin is still a significant factor in determining social acceptance in Latin America.

In previous chapters we have seen racism and the white aesthetic manifested in the racial preconceptions, misconceptions, and stereotypes propagated either wittingly or unintentionally by white authors whose approaches perpetuate racist myths damaging to the black man's image. But not all of the "white" literature on black themes takes an obviously negative approach to black people. In many novels committed writers throughout the Caribbean and the mainland reject the nineteenth-century mentality on race and attack racism and discrimination which they see as allies in the social, racial, and economic oppression of black people. In these socio-negristic novels, which are designed to carry to the reader a message of racial equality and social justice, overt expressions of prejudice come from the characters.

In short, many "liberal" nonblack writers who, in this century, have discovered the black and his African heritage have attempted to react against the heritage of white racial consciousness and have become literary defenders[4] interested in the redemption of black people as members of the proletariat. In the *engagé* literature under review some novelists unavoidably use the black as a literary social symbol of protest against a modern social phenomenon.[5] Others, however, though partly for this same purpose, take a retrospective look at black slavery.

Black Slavery in Retrospect: The Ironies of History and the Socio-Negristic Prose of Alejo Carpentier

The Caribbean, together with Brazil, perhaps has the largest percentage of blacks in Latin America. Much of this black population is found in the Spanish-speaking countries of Cuba, Puerto Rico, and the Dominican Republic, where the theme of race and color is abundantly reflected in the literature of these areas, especially Cuba whose outstanding prose stylist Alejo Carpentier provides a logical starting point.

Some of the Cuban novels by Carpentier and others written during the peak of Afro-Cubanism in the early thirties especially, while discovering slave life in retrospect, also defended the black slave against the distortions of history by rejecting the myth of docility, protraying him, instead, in well-documented prose, as rebellious and discontented. Such novels as *Caniqui* (1930) by José Antonio Ramos, *Pedro Blanco el negrero* (1932) by Lino Novás Calvo, and to a certain extent, *Ecué-Yamba-O* (1933) and later works by Alejo Carpentier give, like *Biografía de un cimarrón,* quite a different picture of slavery and the black slave.

Caniqui, whose name gives the novel its title, is the rebel slave par excellence whose legendary acts of defiance made him famous in the eyes of the other slaves. Caniqui repeatedly tells his master: *"Amárreme, mi amo, o métame en el cepo, porque si no, me juyo!"* a phrase that always signaled the determination of the slave to take flight. His words reflect a will and determination his master was unable to break. Quite obviously, the central underlying emphasis in this novel by José Antonio Ramos is the strong desire for freedom symbolized by the character Caniqui. He is a type not seen often in the nineteenth-century novel.

Pedro Blanco el negrero by Lino Novás Calvo is a novelized biography of a slaverunner. The facts of Pedro's life frame the novel, but the author is just as interested in portraying the horrors of slavery and the slaves' resistance as in narrating the life of the slaverunner himself. In contrast to the nineteenth-century antislavery novelists, Lino Novás Calvo portrays the slave as almost in a constant state of rebellion. And, in contrast to the nineteenth-century antislavery novels, *Pedro Blanco el negrero* documents the inhuman conditions to which the slave was subjected on board ship, rather than concentrating on slave activities, as for example, on plantations.

This novel further disassociates itself from those earlier abolitionist works by its notable lack of artificiality and romanticizing. There are no false tears. There are no false individual heroes. There are no artificial speeches calling for the abolition of slavery. Rather, the author makes his antislavery message apparent by recording the cold, hard facts of the cruelties of slavery as objectively as he records the facts of Pedro's life, and these facts are not pretty; they speak for themselves loudly and clearly of the slave's desperate world in his passage from freedom to slavery and to death. A historical novel with footnotes and bibliography, *Pedro Blanco el negrero,* a mixture of the real and the imagined in the manner of *Caniqui,* is one of the representative Cuban novels of the early thirties that retrospectively have as their central themes slavery and the rebellious slave.

Slavery and the rebellious slave have often provided sources of inspiration for Alejo Carpentier, one of the most outstanding writers of our time. His first novel, *Ecué-Yamba-O* (1933), in addition to documenting Afro-Cuban customs and to exposing the conditions of black people in the Cuban countryside and towns, is valuable, too, for the early indication of the author's interest in slavery and the lasting fascination he will develop in the rebellious slave. The novel is set in the twentieth century; yet, the chapter "Juan Mandinga," which reads like a long aside, a footnote to history, evokes the horrors of the slave crossing and the hard times of slavery. In this flashback Carpentier relates a slave uprising. One slave, when asked his opinion about this uprising that takes place on a neighboring plantation, replies to his master: "Cuando e río crese e porque hay lluvia,"[6] These words announce the approaching end of slavery.

In this first novel, the most ambitious example in Cuba dealing with African traditions retained by black people, Carpentier carries his early association with poetic Negrism over into prose fiction complete with photographic documentation. In addition, however, to the abundance of information concerning the customs and traditions of black people in the New World that pervade the novel, particularly in such chapters as "Fiesta," *Ecué-Yamba-O* unveils early in this century the constant presence and menace of the United States in Cuba immediately following the First World War; he shows, too, both the homegrown and Yankee-inspired racial prejudice and scorn toward blacks widespread at that time. The point is made throughout the novel that whites looked down on blacks[7] much to the dismay of the latter who considered themselves to be equal to any man, if not superior in so far as real rather than pecuniary values are concerned. In addition, then, to his use of black myths, superstitions, rituals, traditions, and cults in this first novel—as in later works—to enrich his aesthetic vision, Carpentier's interest in the ethnic significance of the Cuban black has social overtones as well.

Carpentier continues his interest in black themes and the magical world of the Caribbean black in *El reino de este mundo* (1949), his second novel, which narrates the slave insurrection in Haiti during the second half of the eighteenth century and the beginning of the nineteenth, begun under orders of the rebel slave Mackandal, precursor of his people's liberty. The author gives a fascinating account of Mackandal's flight from slavery and his use of poison to bring about a reign of terror in the white community. He had proclaimed a crusade of extermination against whites and, with the help of maids and house servants on each plantation, managed to wipe out whole families with poison.

There is an important connection between the flight of slaves and black rebellion, both actions indicative of nonpassive reactions to slavery. The desire of the runaways for freedom and escape from servitude provided models of behavior for rebel slaves throughout Latin America where blacks escaped and set up strongholds that became symbols of resistance to slavery.[8] This relationship between runaways and organized resistance to slavery is dramatically presented in Carpentier's story of Mackandal, a historical character of legendary fame who fled and established voodoo as a vehicle and force behind the rebellion in Haiti.

El reino de este mundo, highlighted by historical details and the narration of extraordinary events, projects race pride as well as race hatred in a way that allows for a subtle protest against the ways of white people, as the author, sometimes gently and at other times in a devastating manner, satirizes whites while defending black pride and the vision of reality held by the Haitian black. Black kings, for example, in the old days are described as real men, true kings, who were also warriors, hunters, judges, and priests unlike the white European monarchs draped in false hair. Whites fare badly throughout the novel and, although the conflicts drawn are not always between black and white, there is a constant offsetting of whites and blacks in this work to the disadvantage of the former. For example, in the first chapter, Ti Noel holds a wax head under his arm while thinking how much it must resemble the bald head of his master under his wig. Further on in the novel we see the Governor practicing before a mirror the signal he would give to order the death of Mackandal, the rebel leader; we see the "lady" actress, a "timid player of bit parts", insisting on using her stage name; we see M. Lenormand and his views on the inequality of races basing his beliefs on what he thought was a lack of feeling among the blacks about Mackandal's death when the reader is made to realize that it is M. Lenormand who did not understand that Mackandal still "lived" in the minds of the Haitians.

Carpentier expertly paints a picture and invites the reader to draw his own conclusions, though his choice of words, clever expressions, and telling irony and sarcasm are continually pointing up the whites' weaknesses. A commanding narrator, Carpentier in this novel, though occasionally falling prey to racist stereotypes about black sexuality, does succeed in seeing and presenting things as blacks interpret them, expressing reality in new and different ways. *El reino de este mundo* shows, in effect, how blacks like Mackandal held a strong fascination not only for other blacks but for the author as well, a fascination which helped shape Carpentier's well-known theory of *"lo real maravilloso,"* manifest, to a large degree, in the many incredible evocations of Africa in America.

The slave revolt in Haiti forms a brief backdrop to the action in *El siglo de las luces* (1959), perhaps Carpentier's most ambitious novel. The book, with its ironic title, "The Age of Enlightenment," deals with the effects of the French Revolution in the Caribbean area. One of the most consistent impressions left by Carpentier is that it really had no effect at all as far as the black was concerned because, in spite of the Haitian Revolution, the French Revolution, and the abolition of slavery, equality for blacks, whose lot was not improved by the various revolutionary decrees, was hardly a reality. To the contrary, his situation worsened as "progress" was made in the interest of "Liberty, Equality, and Fraternity." In the French territories black people had been set free and declared free citizens; yet, those who had not been forced to become soldiers or sailors were still working from sunrise to sunset in a servitude no different from what they had experienced before under the whips of their overseers. But now, as free citizens, blacks ironically had become eligible for the guillotine, and many of them paid with their lives for attempting to exercise the freedom and equality granted to them with the abolition of slavery in 1794. One of the major paradoxes of this "age of enlightenment" that Carpentier sets out to expose is the fact that so many blacks met with such injustices.

Carpentier further exemplifies the meaningless character of the abolition decree in the French colonies in an episode illustrating the misfortune of a group of slaves being transported in a Spanish vessel who had placed themselves under French protection, as it was their understanding that blacks in the French colonies were now supposedly free citizens. The French sailors, however, shackled the men and promptly carried the women off to the thickets. Some of the sailors wanted to keep their black women, and the captain promised that they would be able to do so once the women had been named, manumitted, and registered as free citizens. The French captain, however, intended to sail to a Dutch island to sell the shipload of blacks, despite the Decree of the Abolition of Slavery.

One of the biggest ironies of the age was the restoration of slavery in the French colonies. The slaves, now free citizens, refused to work as slaves. Carpentier recounts how, after slavery was reestablished, thousands of former free blacks were rounded up, run down with dogs at their heels, and returned to their compounds in chains. He tells how some of them fled into the hills and how others stole boats and canoes to make their escape. Some of the most forcefully narrated passages in the novel describe these flights from slavery. He tells how those who had not surrendered, or who were insubordinate, were whipped to death, dismembered, beheaded, and subjected to other appalling atrocities. At one point in the novel Carpentier outlines the history of black rebellions that had occurred in America since the sixteenth century, when Miguel, a black in Venezuela, led an uprising; he also mentions, among others, black rebellions in Mexico, Brazil, and Jamaica. Carpentier thus emphasizes that black people had not waited for the abolition decree; they had proclaimed themselves free countless times.

Carpentier is aware that the black problem remains. He has one character say that his grandsons will look back on these horrors as trivial episodes in the story of human sufferings, while the problem of the black will still be paramount. In this novel the author underscores the relevance of the paradoxical Age of Enlightenment to the present day. He is especially effective in pointing up the paradox when he has one of the exponents of the French Revolution demean the black, relegating him to a position of inequality and inferiority. These thoughts, which emphasize that white people are superior and black people inferior, are, of course, the heart of the race issue today. Such discussions and opinions remove the novel from the limited sphere of the Caribbean during the time of the French Revolution and show its universal relevance to the problems black people continue to face.

Carpentier wrote one major novel about the black during the Afro-Cuban Movement and then repeatedly returned to him throughout his later work. From the Cuban black he moved to the Haitian Black and from there to blacks in the whole Caribbean area, culminating with implications for the whole question of black rights and freedom. In most cases when he deals with the black he writes retrospectively, but in a way that makes the messages in his novels very contemporary.[9]

With Carpentier and other twentieth-century Cuban novelists who take slavery as a theme we are far removed from the false tears and distorted images of the black in the nineteenth-century antislavery novels. In these contemporary novels, the black portrayed in slavery is no longer the artificial self-hating, resigned object of insincere abolitionist propaganda; nor is he the picturesque primitive "discovered" by the white practitioners of poetic Negrism. In these novels the black has become the incarnation of freedom, rebellion, and human dignity.

The White Aesthetic and the Cuban Novel since Castro

The literary redeemers of the black are by no means limited to the Cuba of the early thirties or to the work of Carpentier; nor do they confine themselves to updating the image of the black slave. Some recent writers have attacked racist attitudes based on a hierarchy of color that dates in part from slavery and in part from racist thought emanating from Europe around the turn of the present century. But much of this racism, especially in pre-Castro Cuba, was imported from the United States. Indeed, one of the overriding concerns in contemporary Latin-American prose fiction is the impact of the race issue in the United States on race relations in Latin America. The white supremacist attitudes of many Americans from the United States who insist on a color bar abroad in areas where United States business interests are partially dependent on colored labor have been used by anti-Yankee writers as a weapon to criticize the "colossus" of the North. There is an obvious racial basis for many of the antiimperialist novels in the Caribbean, Central, and South America, where social protest novelists have been hard at work lambasting those responsible for the misfortunes of the colored workers. These socially committed writers realize that the ideals of racial harmony and social justice have not yet been achieved. They realize further that the United States is at least partly responsible.

Cuba vied, at one time, with Panama for the dubious honor of being the most racially prejudiced country in Latin America. It is significant that native racism in both countries at that time was strongly compounded by racism United States style. Alejo Carpentier had given us in his first novel, *Ecué-Yamba-O,* published in 1933, an early example of this influx of foreign racism immediately following the First World War, a racism that was partly responsible for the discrimination against the black that segregated him and kept him in his place—and out of sight of Yankee tourists—in pre-Castro Cuba, when the black man, as in the United States, was the last to be hired and the first to be fired.

But more recently, post-Castro novelists in Cuba would have us believe that race relations before Castro were bad and good since Castro, that there is an improved relationship between blacks and whites since the Revolution and its ban on discrimination. These novels usually deal with pre-Castro Cuba and picture white Cubans as racists, or with Cuba since Castro where we find the black faring better. Despite recent skepticism reported, for example, by John Clytus, Eldridge Cleaver, and Robert Williams, several eyewitnesses had gone to Cuba earlier and verified this good progress between the races, certainly during the early days of the new society. Harry Ring[10] wrote in 1961 that blacks in Cuba were the first of any country in the Americas to win full economic, social, and political equality. He also quoted W. Worthy, another visitor to Cuba who had observed that, compared to pre-Castro times, there is now free and unself-conscious mixing of the races and complexions, unlike before when the worst job and social discrimination, Worthy said, was practiced by the United States companies, when blacks were not permitted access to hotels and clubs because their presence would be "bad" for the tourist trade.

Against this backdrop of an improved relationship between the races in Cuba, the authors writing at the outbreak of the Revolution in the late fifties reveal, according to Seymour Menton,[11] racist attitudes in the characters that act out their roles in the period prior to the Revolution. Blacks when depicted, are shown in a bad light. A basic characteristic of these earlier novels is the depiction of protagonists who generally are not working men, *campesinos,* mestizos, mulattoes, or blacks but white and middle class or aristocratic. Blacks, however, have entered gradually in varying degrees in more recent novels often exemplifying, consistent with the Revolution, a rebellious spirit as, for example, in *Bertillón 166* (1961) by José Soler Puig where a black, one of the principal organizers of revolutionary activity, had dared *"meterse con Batista,"* overcoming with a show of bravura the distrust of his companions.

The increasing black presence is seen in *Gestos* (1963) by Severo

Sarduy, also set in Cuba during the downfall of Batista, which has as its protagonist a black woman who takes in laundry by day, sings in night clubs by night, and throws dynamite in revolutionary forays in her spare time. The song of this female revolutionary as well as that of other Havana blacks, many unemployed, is heard throughout the novel with accompanying remarks by the author:

> . . . The blacks of Havana never cease. It is right here, on this corner, where they all gather when they come from the beach. They always sing. They never stop because they have no job; therefore, they do not stop singing. They come and go at all hours, always singing, and sometimes stop to have some coffee, sometimes to jot down some numbers, and then, still singing, to wander around, from one side of the street to the other. Always singing . . . They never stop, never.[12]

Two novels that perhaps best illustrate the struggle for racial equality that faced black people in Cuba before Castro are *Los muertos andan solos* (1962) by Juan Arcocha and the prize-winning *Adire y el tiempo roto* (1967) by Manuel Granados.

Arcocha's example of racial attitudes toward blacks before Castro implies that free and unself-conscious mixing of the races was nonexistent at that time. In his novel he had Rosa, the white protagonist, solicit and sleep with a black only to rush him out of the house the next morning before daybreak to avoid discovery by her friends. Rosa realized the incompatibility of her attitude that accepted a black as lover privately while rejecting him publicly. But her actions were a sign of the times, of a society that practiced yet frowned on interracial sex where a black was involved.

To Rosa blacks were not human beings but rather instruments of pleasure, useful for satisfying a physical need. Rosa, in fact, despised black people and considered them inferior. She even justified her relationship with blacks by rationalizing to herself that no matter how debased she became as a person she would still have someone below her upon whom to look down. She conceived of the relationship in a master-slave perspective wherein she had no cause to give account to a slave. Later on in the novel, when the Revolution was under way, another white character, once having accepted the Revolution, promptly accepted the black as his brother, thus illustrating a point Cuban novelists since Castro have emphasized: that to accept the Revolution is to accept the black as an equal partner in a nonracial society.

And finally, *Adire y el tiempo roto* (1967) by Manuel Granados is perhaps the most ambitious example of a novelist's preoccupation with the relationship between race prejudice in Cuba and the Revolution. In this novel, Julián, the black protagonist, is a member of the oppressed working class who must rid himself of his self-conscious feelings of inferiority, which the racially prejudiced pre-Castro society had forced upon him. This white-dominated society had convinced him that the stigma of blackness was the worst possible disaster that could befall him. The novel, which flashes back from his death in the cause of the Revolution to his earlier life leading up to and determining his involvement, reviews some of the incidents in his life that helped ingrain those feelings of inferiority. Before his involvement in the Revolution, Julián had considered leaving Cuba because of the color prejudice he was experiencing. He had thought of going to the United States but rejected this alternative when he learned of the treatment of black people there, especially in the South.

The author dramatizes Julián's mixed feelings about race through his frequent contacts with white women. Elsa, one of the women who reached out to him, was from a white family that harbored a pathological repulsion for black people, whom they considered to be dirty, vulgar, uncivilized beggars. Elsa was to a degree a new breed, but not completely, because she still harbored vestiges of racial preconceptions. She resolved her mixed feelings when she confessed to Julián that no matter how strong her desire for racial equality was she still could not forget that he was a black. And this is really what the novel is all about: the difficulty of being black and trapped by racial preconceptions, aesthetic prejudice, and a predetermined fate from which there seemed to be no escape, that is, of course, until the Revolution. Once he became a revolutionary Julián felt free and happy. His conflict was resolved. He was no longer ashamed of his color. Life was no longer frightening. Once he became a revolutionary he felt as though he had arrived, as a black and as a man.

Much like Carpentier's *Ecué-Yamba-O,* black people in Granados's Afro-Cuban novel take refuge in African ritual, deriving strength from identification with African gods and the forces of nature. A proud past lives on in rituals and ceremonies, offsetting the inferiority complex which black people suffer in a society dominated by white racists. Like Carpentier, Granados, too, includes a glossary of Afro-Cuban terms.

The increased emphasis on racial equality in Cuba will help assure that the theme of race and color, as Coulthard[13] has predicted, for years to come will continue to constitute a rich vein of literary material in the Caribbean.

Social Protest Novels in the Dominican Republic

The theme of race and color in the Spanish Caribbean is found not only in Cuba but in the Dominican Republic and in Puerto Rico as well. In Puerto Rico the theme is perhaps best known in the poetry of Luis Palés Matos, one of the leaders of the Afro-Antillean school, and in the plays of Francisco Arriví, specifically in his *Máscara puertorriqueña*. Arriví's trilogy defends the African ethnic heritage in the racial composition of Puerto Rico while dramatizing, as we saw in chapter one, the impact of racism and the white aesthetic on the minds and behavior of several characters who are portrayed as victims of a pathological fear of blackness and a corresponding obsession with whiteness.[14]

In the Dominican Republic, which has been thought of as a mulatto country, three social protest novels that deal in part with blacks are *Caña y bueyes* (1935) by F. E. Moscoso, *Over* (1939) by Ramón Marrero Aristy, and *Los rompidos* (1963) by Sanz Lajara. In *Caña y bueyes* Moscoso portrays a North American who thinks all the local inhabitants, most of them colored, are inferior and ignorant. Mr. Moore and his wife—who is from the southern part of the United States—are racially prejudiced, the author tells us, like all North Americans. In *Over* Ramón Marrero Aristy not only comes to the defense of the exploited masses in his country but levels as well a sharp criticism toward the "Great White Father" image Britain was taking toward its black colonies. And more recently Sanz Lajara in *Los rompidos* deals with the more general question of revolutions in his native Dominican Republic but with implications not only for blacks but for the whole of Latin America.

"*Los rompidos*" ("the broken ones") are the victims who lose their lives in these revolutions. The protagonist is the mulatto López, an ambitious revolutionary who rose to the leadership of his country, a short-lived honor as he was assassinated a few moments after gaining power. López wanted to be in a position to help his people. He tried for the presidency because he was convinced that the white people who had governed his predominantly colored country previously had not done a fair job. He felt that it was now time for a nonwhite to take over to provide honest and sincere leadership. López was proud of his color, and his revolution was inspired by his desire to improve the lot of the darker elements of the population and to challenge the view that whites are the only ones qualified for positions of leadership.

Los rompidos, while focusing on the hunger, misery, frustration, and humiliation of the dark-skinned masses in Latin America has, as an additional feature, an emphasis on racial equality through race mixing. An anomaly in this novel is Bob, a blond, blue-eyed gringo who came to Latin America with a liberal attitude toward the mixture of races, fell in love with a mulatto woman, and came to believe that true love and friendship were the keys to better relations among races and countries. He felt that racial harmony was still possible in the world if only friendly hands, not gifts and money, were extended. Blue-eyed, blond-haired gringos are usually villains in the Latin-American novel of social protest. Bob is an exception.

Literary Defenders of Blacks in Mexico and Central America from Fernández de Lizardi to Joaquín Beleño C.

Literary defenders of blacks in Mexico date back, perhaps, to Sor Juana Inés de la Cruz, who showed some sympathy for them in her works, and to Fernández de Lizardi, whose *El Periquillo sarniento* (1816) has been called the first antislavery novel in America, certainly the first to denounce slavery and reject racist arguments. Together with nineteenth-century antislavery novels in Cuba, Fernández de Lizardi's novel can be called a legitimate forerunner of the social tendency that has been so much a part of Latin-American literature of this century. It is appropriate to find in this first full-fledged Spanish-American novel an attack on racism and black slavery. This hostility toward slavery and the slave trade was the direct cause of the censorship imposed on the first edition of volume four by the colonial authorities. In that edition, Fernández de Lizardi has a cultured and intelligent black defend his race in a discussion with an British official who was convinced that to be white is to belong to a superior race of people. In one of the earliest defenses of the black in Spanish-American literature, Lizardi argues that:

> If blacks are held inferior because of their customs, which you call barbarous because of their African background and their lack of European civilization, you should be aware that strange customs seem barbarous and uncivilized to every nation. A

refined European will be a barbarian in Senegal, the Congo, Cabo
Verde, etc., since he will not know their religious rites, their civil
laws, provincial customs, and, finally, their languages. Transport
a wise Parisian courtier with his intellect into such countries, and
you will see him rendered helpless, scarcely able to indicate, no
matter how many gestures he makes, that he is hungry.
Therefore, if every religion has its rites, every nation its laws,
and every province its customs, it is a very gross error to deem
stupid and savage all those that do not correspond to our way of
thinking. . . .[15]

The black component in the Mexican ethnic mosaic appears in much
of that country's literature and the writer in this century who has done
much toward presenting this diverse ethnic composition is Francisco
Rojas González, whose stories focus on the different geographical
regions. Born in Guadalajara, Rojas González studied ethnology and
anthropology and did field work and research, founding a journal of
ethnology and sociology. Preoccupied with the plight of the lower
classes, he has written many stories about the Indians of Mexico. Our
concern, however, is with his novel *La negra Angustias,* which won
for him Mexico's National Prize for Literature in 1944.

Angustias is the protagonist of the novel, one of the late examples of
the novel of the Mexican Revolution. A complex character whose
rebellious spirit is linked to color consciousness but who perhaps is
poor first and colored second, Angustias, an aggressive leader of men,
paradoxically falls in love with a timid weakling. She becomes his
submissive wife and retires from the Revolution which she had joined
partly inspired by her father's exploits as a famous bandit. She, too,
decided to take from the rich and give to the less fortunate.

The character Angustias is based, allegedly, on a real person. There
is some uncertainty, however, regarding the literary origin of the
female protagonist. Although there are several theories questioning the
originality of the author,[16] the achievements of Rojas González in his
novel are multiple. The author deviates from standard revolutionary
fare in concentrating on a central character. He also makes this
character a female, a revolutionary leader of men, a *coronela.* And to
top this, he makes her a black. Taken together Angustias is a very
special case indeed.

A very clear early defense of the black in Guatemalan literature is
found in *Los Nazarenos* (1867), a historical novel by José Milla,
''father of the Guatemalan novel'' based on the conspiracy of the

Nazarenos against the president involving the important families in the old capital of Guatemala (Antigua). The action, which takes place between 1655 and 1657, has a colonial setting. The element in the plot development involving the black Macao has been isolated, anthologized, and given the heading "El castigo y la venganza del negro Macao," a story *"entresacada al través de toda la obra."*[17] At the very beginning of the book Macao, slave of Juan de Palomeque, tries to kill his master who barely escapes the bullet aimed at him. After this unsuccessful attempt Macao does succeed in killing him later, and the author half justifies the crime because of the horrible treatment the slave had received at his master's hands. The reasons for the slave's discontent are found in this mistreatment. Juan Palomeque is depicted undoubtedly as one of the cruelest masters of all time. Milla devotes much attention in his novel to expressing this inhuman side of the slave owner. Paragraphs like the following abound:

> "Why did you not put the load on your shoulders, you despicable dog?" Palomeque answered angrily. "Do you believe that you are worth more than one of my mules?"
> After he said this, the gentleman seized the slave by the collar and, in spite of his size and strength, threw him to the ground and kicked him furiously in the back. Forthwith he took the whip used for driving the mules and beat him cruelly for more than a quarter of an hour. The pain did not draw a single moan from that unfortunate creature, on whose face anyone who had taken the trouble to examine it could have seen the unmistakable signs of intense hatred and somber despair.[18]

Thomas Gage once wrote that blacks were the only courageous people in Guatemala, where the expression *"esta es obra de negro"* meant not merely that this is a job for blacks but rather that this is a real man's job.[19] Consistent with this image of the black in Guatemala, José Milla in his novel gives a positive and vindictive side of the black slave, a notable exception to most nineteenth-century portrayals of the black in Spanish-American literature.

The Indian and the dictatorial governments, two central themes in the work of Nobel Prize winner Miguel Angel Asturias, both give way to the antiimperialist theme, primarily in his "banana trilogy." It is in this trilogy where his concern for the African element, generally thought to be completely mixed now with the Indian and the white in Guatemala despite visible racial strains and recent black immigration, is developed to some length. In *Viento fuerte* (1950), the first volume of the trilogy dealing with the exploitation of Guatemala's banana plantations by the United Fruit Company, there are blacks working as doormen, chauffeurs, maintenance men, and railroad workers. And there is the meaningful conversation Mead has with the *zambo* on the station platform where they discuss "unequal and unjust working conditions."[20]

It is in *El papa verde* (1954), the second volume of the trilogy, that a mulatto family enters and becomes increasingly important. In this volume as well as in the third and final one of the trilogy, *Juambo el Sambito,* the most visible member of the family, is the servant of the powerful Geo. Maker; he occupies a central role in these novels, a role that finds him inextricably involved in the chain of events that hold the trilogy together as a series, emerging as well as a character of stature. It is Juambo's family that: ". . . with all the children held on to the plot of land. A futile gesture."[21]

A sharp division between the haves and have-nots is drawn in the novel, and Asturias occasionally points up this difference in such scenes as the following:

> In the car, eating bananas, Juambo the "Sambito" waited while the *señores* had lunch. . . . One banana after another. . . . They, the bosses, were having lunch; he, Sambito, was eating bananas.[22]

Juambo continues to function as a link between novels, enlarging his role in the third volume of the trilogy, *Los ojos de los enterrados* (1960), in which he emerges, with his sister Anastasia, as a prominent participant in the strike that culminates the work, the strike that *"daría el jaque mate a la Compañia."*[23] His role ostensibly was to work as a fruit toter with the company and to spy in the general offices where from childhood he had been a trusted servant. But Juambo's participation in the strike has double significance for him:

> . . . He wanted to pay, to be punished to the utmost for the neglect in which he had left his parents. His father died toting fruit. For a man who had the means, who had owned the lands on the Atlantic coast which he had inherited from his forefathers, to die that way . . . to die in his own bloody vomit under the overwhelming weight of a bunch of bananas, fallen like a useless, malaria-ridden old beast, powerless to get up again, rubbing in his own blood the immense mute wound of his mouth. He had to

> pay. Juambo had to pay. He could not go down to the plantations
> to work at any job other than toting fruit . . .[24]

Juambo wanted to atone for having abandoned his father to the hard work that eventually killed him. And he intended to do this through participation in the planned strike that would cripple the company, but first he had to do penance by working there just as his father had done before him. But Juambo, no longer "the boss' flunky but another Juambo moved to join in the strike,"[25] would cooperate not only for his father "dead with his eyes open" but for all those "buried with their eyes open,"[26] buried like this because injustice still reigned in the world. The big strike would bring justice and peace and those buried with their eyes open would then be able, as the legend goes, to close them. In *Los ojos de los enterrados* Juambo el Sambito comes to the forefront and remains there as one of the best-developed characters in the novels of Asturias.[27]

Committed Central American writers:[28] in Belize, El Salvador, Honduras, Nicaragua, and particularly in Costa Rica and Panama, like Asturias in Guatemala, have written a literature of commitment that has made itself responsible for the defense of workers like Juambo, who are beset by hardships and difficulties often brought on by racial oppression. The black presence, though ambivalently approached, is a thematic constant even in the works of the Nicaraguan Rubén Darío, perhaps Latin America's foremost literary figure.

Rubén Darío, who has been referred to at times as a mulatto, admitted to having black blood—an admission not shared by his son. He had, on occasion, shown himself to be an ardent literary defender of the black race in the interest of social justice, and he admired others who did so as well. At the other extreme, however, he agreed with some racist opinions and equated the black man with the ape in many literary comparisons.* In the short story "La miss" (Vol. 4, pp. 172-78) he calls blacks *"animalitos"* who make monkey-like gestures. There are many Negro-ape analogies in his chronicles; in "París nocturno" (Vol. 4, p. 1051), for example, and again in "Los exóticos del Quartier" (Vol. 2, p. 521). His fear and suspicion of the bloody potential of the black man, especially of the "arrogant" black in the United States, is seen in the article "La raza de Cham," where he links the black to an anthropoid past, referring to him as an African

---

*The following citations are taken from Rubén Darío, *Obras completas,* 5 volumes (Madrid: Aguado, 1950-1955).

cannibal, a black animal from the jungle (Vol. 4, p. 1387). In this article Rubén Darío quotes from a black author who believes that black people are superior both physically and spiritually to whites and from white authors who have concluded the black man to be perverse, inferior, and worthy of being lynched.

Rubén Darío's sentiments are with the latter. Yet, while finding consolation in some published ideas that black people are inferior, capable only of barbarous acts, and blessed only with the gift of mimicry, he rejects, nevertheless, the un-Christian cruelties of the lynch law. His humanitarian sentiments are evident in his short story ''El linchamiento de Puck.'' He is saddened and indignant on witnessing a scene where racial insults are hurled at a black and a mulatto at a sidewalk café in Paris. On another occasion, while traveling through the United States, he reacts sarcastically to the separate facilities for blacks and whites. And he admires the humanitarian efforts of people like José Martí. In short, although Darío often shared the contempt toward black people common in Spanish America and even though some of his poems are reminiscent of racist images found in ''false black poetry,'' much of his social poetry paradoxically is a protest against the hardships suffered by black people.[29]

The defense of blacks is less ambivalently approached in social protest literature in Costa Rica and Panama where racial conflict, as elsewhere in Central and South America, often results from clashes between the West Indian immigrant worker and white supervisory antagonist from the United States. The black population in Costa Rica is relatively small. Yet, since much of the important fiction in Costa Rica deals with the exploitation of the banana workers, many of them blacks, this small black population and its problems are as a result much publicized. Costa Rica in fact is often thought of as the white country of Central America though approximately one-third of the population of Puerto Limón is black and mostly bilingual because of the heavy influx of immigrants from the West Indies.

Carlos Luis Fallas in his *Mamita Yunai* (1941) has written perhaps one of the most biting indictments of the banana companies in his description of the hard life of the Indian and black workers in Costa Rica. Often in this novel Fallas, a strong defender of the modern-day black, turns his gaze toward the downtrodden and raises such questions as the following, which is characteristic of the novel's tone:

Where were these people coming from and where were they

going to, bearing through the centuries the heavy burden of their
burnt skin? Where would they find their promised land?

They fled into the African jungle, away from the slave hunters;
they stained with their blood the irons in the deep holds of the
slave ships; they moaned under the whip of the overseer in the
endless cotton fields; they rebelled and took flight, pursued by the
owner's dogs. . . . And now the poor Costa Rican blacks, after
having enriched the banana potentates with their blood, had to
flee at night through the mountains, dragging their offspring and
household possessions. The slaveowner's dog did not pursue
them: the specter of misery did. What would await them on the
other side of the frontier? Where would they come to rest?[30]

Puerto Limón (1950) by Joaquín Gutiérrez is another Costa Rican
novel similar in tone to *Mamita Yunai* in that both novels carry a strong
denunciation of the powerful banana companies in their descriptions of
the miserable existence of the black, an important element of the work
force in Costa Rica. Related to the protest theme against the banana
companies is the short story "La mujer negra del río"[31] by Fabián
Dobles, one of Costa Rica's better-known writers, whose social protest
message is explicit in his narration of the situation of Sam Jackson, a
black who has a farm near the Reventazón River in an area that had
been abandoned by the United Fruit Company. In this story, together
with the criticism of the United States, protests against the United Fruit
Company are evident in the conversations Sam has with his friends and
in references to the acquisition of those lands by the company and the
subsequent poverty suffered there when it abandoned the area. The
black stands out in this tale because he is the only one who dares to
accept the challenge to make something out of this apparently useless
land ruined by overproduction.[32]

Thus far in our survey we have seen the black in Central America
and in the fiction of the area most associated with the banana industry,
one of two well-known enterprises that bring into contact the *gringo*
from the North with blacks in Latin America. The other is the Panama
Canal.

Although officially abolished, racial discrimination remained in
force in Panama, especially in the Canal Zone, because of the steady
influx of North Americans, many of them from the South, who came
there with their prejudices. On the theory that Southerners knew how
to handle blacks, the administrative authorities in the Canal Zone hired

its supervisory personnel largely from the South. And these Southerners in turn imposed a system of racial discrimination similar to that existing back home, establishing, in effect, a "Jim Crow" system in Panama. Many of the blacks in Panama, as in other Central American countries, are of West Indian origin who came in as laborers to work on railroad construction, on the Canal, and for the banana companies. At one time in Panama a black was a black to the Americans from the United States, regardless of his shade of color or place of birth. Thus, all of the dark people: mulattoes, blacks, native born or imports, were lumped together. This simplified approach was in keeping with their belief in the inferiority of the darker races and with their determination to keep the black in his place.[33]

At that time in Panama the mostly black Panamanian workers were paid in silver coins and the white United States supervisory personnel in gold coins. This distinction gave rise to the notorious system of "Gold Roll" and "Silver Roll," which became the symbol of racial discrimination, especially in the Zone area. Here separate facilities for blacks and whites existed, blacks were punished for drinking out of water fountains marked "white," or black-listed for violations, or laid off without pay, for example, for using the latrines marked "white." Panamanian novelists illustrate these and other injustices. They illustrate, for example, how the courts used a double standard to administer justice. And they show how various forms of discrimination were practiced even in hospitals, cemeteries, and prisons. One novelist sarcastically observed that the United States exploiters probably had heaven divided into Gold Roll and Silver Roll.

With the Gold and Silver Roll, replaced in the late forties by "U. S. Rate" and "Local Rate," as inspirations and with the abundance of racial discrimination and anti-Yankee sentiment in Panama, it comes as no surprise that Panamanian novelists have concentrated on the theme of protest, recording in effect racial conflict in the Canal Zone by outlining some of these Jim Crow practices. This is true of Panama's outstanding writer Rogelio Sinán whose contemporary techniques, especially in *Plenilunio* (1947), artistically convey the racial conflict in the Canal Zone. His short story, "La boina roja," develops a racial situation based on one of the problems blacks face in Panama, namely, their involvement with white women, usually with the latter's consent.

Similar unfortunate sexual involvements are recounted in the novels of Joaquín Beleño C. whose three best-known works, *Luna verde*

(1951), *Gamboa Road Gang* (1960)—which carries this English title though written in Spanish—and *Curundú* (1963) are representative of the critical attitudes taken in Panama toward the myth of Yankee superiority. These novels benefited from the author's own experiences in the Canal Zone, thus allowing him to present injustices committed against blacks from firsthand knowledge. In *Luna verde* he speaks of racial segregation in his country:

> From fear of contamination the American overseer does not associate with the local help. This racial division is maintained at the water fountains, in the restaurants, police station, cinemas, and in all places in which men have to live together. There are communities like La Boca, Red Tank, and Silver City for blacks and Latins, and there are white districts like Chagres, Gavilán, Miraflores, Ancón, and Balboa. Segregation here is rigid. Blacks and Latins are not allowed to live in white neighborhoods. It is a crying shame. In the Canal Zone the *gringo* is God; the Latin is his vassal and the black his slave.[34]

There are many outbursts in *Luna verde* condemning the racial attitudes of the North Americans. The author best illustrates these attitudes, however, in the form of a letter which reportedly fell into the hands of the narrator, a letter from a loving son, George, a United States soldier stationed in Panama, to his mother back in Virginia. The letter, which is an insult to Panama and to both black and white Latins, is written in English. The author provides a Spanish translation at the end of the text. The letter is effective because Beleño captures the psychology and the poor style of an ignorant Southern white man. It reads:

> Dear Mother:
>
> I dont know whats happened to me but lately I've stopped thinking about all the things that used to be near and dear to me. All this broken country and endless rain and thunder seems to have overcome me. All nature here conspires to drive white men crazy but we must fight against the tropics and win out over them to prove that we really are the masters of the situation. Now I want to tell you that I plan to get married to a Panamanian girl. I know youre going to think I've gone completely out of my head, but thats the way it is.
>
> If you go and tell everybody about what I've decided to do,

they are all going to think that Im marrying a colored girl. We
used to think that all the girls here were colored. But this girl is
Latin. She is as white as any girl who is out in the sun every day.
She is little more than a child, really. But I'm almost out of my
head and need somebody to straighten me out, and I really think
shes just what the doctor ordered.

*   *   *

If you were here going crasy, hopping from swamp to swamp,
chasing or running away from insects hiking all over the place,
pushing a crew of lasy natives who laugh about protecting our
water supply then youd understand why I need a woman—any
woman even one who is not my equal as far as race or language is
concerned. I hope you will understand what Im trying to say in
this letter.

Yours loving son,
George.[35]

One can imagine the outrage felt by the Latin narrator who had
intercepted this letter, a device the author uses to show the little regard
Americans held for Panamanians.

Beleño's second novel, *Gamboa Road Gang,* is extremely critical of
the double standard of laws for the gringo and for blacks in Panama.
He contrasts, for example, between a fifty-year sentence at hard labor
on the road gang for a black caught in a relationship with a white girl
and the brutal rape of a black girl by a group of white men who were
allowed to go unpunished. While exploring in some detail racial
problems interwoven with the black male-white female relationship in
Panama, Beleño in this second novel also traces the story of the son of
a North American soldier and a Jamaican black. The fate of such
offspring had caused him some concern in his first novel.

Curundú, though published in 1963, was conceived and sketched in
the forties when the myth of white racial superiority was rampant in
Panama. This myth and the sickness of race prejudice are captured in
the following words by the author who ties it in with the concept of
racial superiority associated with the United States:

"—I am an American citizen . . . My name, Red . . . Red
Box. The Killer . . . and you . . . negars . . . (in English).
That's why you have to obey me. I am from the States, and my
skin is white. That's why I command and you obey."[36]

Social Protest, Committed Literature, and the *Pobres Negros* of Colombia, Venezuela, and Ecuador.

Black people in continental Spanish America have been a significant element of the population since colonial times when they outnumbered whites in many areas. Though now outnumbered, next to the Caribbean, the United States, and Brazil there are nevertheless more blacks and mulattoes in the northern part of the continent, particularly in Colombia, than in any other area in the New World. The port of Cartagena on the Caribbean coast was one of the largest slave markets in America, and slavery, like black life and customs, was a popular literary theme reflected in much of nineteenth and twentieth-century Colombian literature.[37] In this century the black man in Colombia, as in Peru, has found his staunchest literary defenders from among his own ranks in the literature for example, of Jorge Artel, Arnoldo Palacios, and Manuel Zapata Olivella,[38] three of the better-known Afro-Colombian writers. Like the Afro-Peruvian Nicomedes Santa Cruz who, aside from Enrique Albújar and his *Matalaché,* is the main contributor to the black theme in Peru, these Afro-Colombians are making a formidable impact on the Colombian literary scene.

The social protest message on behalf of black people, though, is clear in *Oro y miseria* (1942) by the Colombian Antonio Arango, who narrates the injustices committed against the black worker in the gold mines of the Chocó, an area lodged between the Isthmus of Panama and Colombia. His novel, highlighted by the exploitation of the black worker by white supervisors from the United States, is another example in Latin-American literature of the presence and depiction of imported prejudice. Arango's novel is specifically concerned with the racial discrimination and injustices perpetuated by these supervisors against blacks who attempt to rebel but either are brutally repressed or manage to escape into the jungle, only to succumb to the deadly beri-beri disease. As a result, the author relates that "the mountains are nourished with the blood, flesh, sweat, and outcries of black people."[39]

The black presence in the ethnic composition of Venezuela, whose black population has always been quite large, is reflected in much of the literature of the country. Just as there are black communities in many parts of Spanish America: Cartagena in Colombia, Bluefields in Nicaragua, Puerto Limón in Costa Rica, Calidonia—"the Harlem of Panama City"—in Panama, in Venezuela it is Barlovento, the setting for much of the Venezuelan literature on black themes. The area itself has received special consideration in an essay by Oscar Rojas Jiménez: "Geografía lírica de Barlovento," in which he describes at length this "land of blacks and cocoa."[40]

The separate black community aside, Juan Pablo Sojo, a Barlovento black who has written about the exploitation there, believes that the black is integrated through racial mixing into Venezuelan society to a greater extent than in the Caribbean islands, Brazil, or other parts of America; that, on the whole, he exists in Venezuela not so much in appearance as through his beliefs and customs that are now common to all Venezuelans.[41]

Perhaps the best-known advocate of racial integration is Rómulo Gallegos, whose novel *Pobre negro* (1937), though set in Barlovento, is a study primarily of miscegenation, a theme that as was seen in Chapter Three, had found earlier expression in *La trepadora* (1925). As in Carpentier, black themes occur persistently throughout Gallegos's works. Seymour Menton[42] has written that to get a panoramic view of Venezuela one must read all of Gallegos's novels. The same is largely true of the black theme in Venezuela: Gallegos has dealt with many types in his fiction and essays as well where he has written about the *"Tambor de San Juan en las poblaciones negras del Barlovento venezolano."*[43]

Gallegos's concern for the exploitation of blacks is seen in *Canaima* (1935) where, early in the novel, a cargo of blacks destined for work in the mines appear in a scene reminiscent of the days of slavery. This novel also contains "Estampa negra," a short section which tells the unfortunate story of Ricardo and his wife Damiana, black laborers brought in to work these mines. Cabo Pisao appears in *El forastero* (1942) who, like Juan Parao in *Cantaclaro* (1934), enters telling his life story. Both at one time had resorted to banditry. The poetic and sympathetic redemption of the black Venezuelan is symbolized in *Cantaclaro,* in the person and death of Juan Parao, the misguided but loyal defender of his country and its leaders in wars not always beneficial to him. This redemption is crystallized in the following well-known eulogy:

> You poor, long-suffering, rebellious blacks are good people, good Venezuelan people! Betrayals and injustice have driven you to a life of crime. . . . Poor unfortunate people willing to die for a leader in whom to put your trust, but not finding one. . . . Who sings of the black heroism of your submission and the pure virtue

of your loyalty and the painful drama of your love of mankind
which will always betray and abandon you? Who will express,
without humiliating you, the ideal—your great ideal!—that you
pursued when you were looking for a leader? Good black man,
long-suffering and rebellious![44]

Gallegos has brought out the hopes and frustrations of Venezuelan
black people not only in the person of Juan Parao but in the
characterization of Juan Coromoto as well, who in *Pobre negro* was
indeed "the poor black, a whole people, abandoned . . ."[45] Even
Cabo Pisao represents "our people, unknown to us for a long time,"[46]
conveying in effect the same impression of a race betrayed by those in
whom he placed his faith, confidence, and expectations.

Black themes and characters are abundantly represented in
Venezuelan literature, and such major writers as Guillermo Meneses,
"known to some as the novelist of Negroes and Mulattoes,"[47] with his
better known works *(La balandra Isabel llegó esta tarde, Canción de
negros),* Ramón Díaz Sánchez *(Cumboto),* and Arturo Uslar Pietri *(Las
lanzas coloradas)* have, like Gallegos *(Pobre negro)* made major
contributions on black themes. In *Mene* (1936), however, Ramón Díaz
Sánchez develops a strong social protest theme along the lines
followed in much of the Spanish-American literature in which black
workers are depicted as being at the mercy of white supervisory
personnel largely imported from the United States, this time in the
Maracaibo oil fields. Especially tragic is the case of Narcissus, the
black who committed suicide on learning that he had been
"blacklisted" and would not be able to find work because he had dared
to use the private bathroom reserved for "whites only." *Mene* carries a
strong condemnation of the race prejudice of the North American in
Venezuela. The tone is anti-imperialist as well.

Blacks in Ecuador, located primarily in the region of Esmeraldas,
experience the same difficulties encountered by blacks elsewhere. Contemporary Ecuadorian writers, particularly the Guayaquil novelists, are,
together with such Afro-Ecuadorian writers as Adalberto Ortíz and
Nelson Estupiñán Bass, in the forefront of the literary redeemers of the
black in Latin America. In coming to his defense they have laid bare the
evils of racial prejudice, discrimination, and exploitation while portraying
the black as a proud, rebellious type not reluctant to fight for his own
social and political betterment.[48]

In 1930 Demetrio Aguilera Malta had published, with Joaquín

Gallegos Lara and Enrique Gil Gilbert, a collection of short stories entitled *Los que se van,* which dealt mostly with the Montuvio, an ethnic type whose racial strains indicate a black component. These three authors, together with José de la Cuadra and Alfredo Pareja Díez-Canseco, perhaps the two major novelists in the Guayaquil region, were in fact known as the "Group of Guayaquil."[49] All of these dedicated writers were committed to the creation of protest literature designed to expose the social evils suffered by the downtrodden, largely dark-skinned, of Ecuador.

José de la Cuadra, generally considered the most accomplished stylist of the group with his masterpiece *Los Sangurimas* (1934), focused largely on the lives and problems of the Montuvios. But Alfredo Pareja Díez Canseco created in *Baldomera* (1938) an impressive black female character. An unusual mixture of warm-hearted motherliness and uncouth drunkenness, Baldomera at all times has class and proletarian solidarity uppermost in her mind. Basically a kind person with a conscience of family, Baldomera is concerned for the underdog and is always the first to join a strike or demonstration to protest injustices committed against her people. Baldomera is a fighter, a strong person who often engaged in street battles with the police. Her actions symbolize not only the rebellious spirit of the black but of all oppressed people who must fight against injustice and exploitation.

The following imposing description of Baldomera sets the stage for her later development in the novel:

> Baldomera is still a young woman. She is barely forty. When she is seated one sees her as a middle-aged woman. But when Baldomera stands up you have to notice the difference. She seems to be almost six feet tall even though she really is not more than five-foot-six or seven. Only by considering Baldomera's slippered feet could one estimate her corpulence. Her feet are enormous. Her dress, which has faded, reaches her ankle and outlines no shape, for Baldomera lost her waistline a long time ago. She is square. Simply square. Baldomera's breasts, which hang almost to her belly, are large and fat: they are two masses of stuffed flesh.
>
>   *   *   *
>
> Furthermore, Baldomera is black.[50]

Baldomera's participation in the workers' uprising that led to the strike of November 19, 1922, in which thousands of workers were killed by government troops, is duplicated by Alfredo, the black protagonist of *Las cruces sobre las aguas* (1938) by Joaquín Gallegos Lara, who also took part in this uprising. The novel in fact is a biography of Alfredo, who, at the age of fifteen, had left home to fight in behalf of blacks. His idol was Spartacus. The novel is replete with phrases such as "the black man because he is black is overworked and kicked around. The black woman is screwed because she is black. . . . Haven't blacks ever stopped being treated as slaves?"[51] In this novel—in which blacks are poorly treated by large companies, even abandoned in their old age—Alfredo gives his life in the pursuit of freedom and a better life for his people.

Demetrio Aguilera Malta, who normally writes about the suffering of the less fortunate in his homeland, has registered in *Canal Zone* (1935) a protest not only against United States imperialism but against the racial oppression of black people in Panama as well. The novel, dedicated in part to the black in Panama, is a protest against the abuses of whites and a sincere plea for social justice and more racial understanding, a theme the author returns to in his plays,[52] with specific emphasis on the senselessness of racial inequality. *Canal Zone* narrates the story of Pedro Coorsi, a young, intelligent mulatto who, born of a black woman and a white man, was unable to advance in life because of his color. He decided to cast his lot with the exploited blacks in the country, risking imprisonment by becoming a revolutionary fighting white oppression as he saw it in Panama.

"El negro Santander," one of the short stories Enrique Gil Gilbert published in the volume *Yunga* (1938), has as its protagonist Santander, a black Jamaican typical of the many who have come to Ecuador to work on the railroad constructed between Guayaquil and Quito. The story dwells on his problems and his awareness of being black in a white world. The miseries, hardships, and injustices suffered by the exploited black and Indian workers are the results of the eagerness of the North American company to economize at their expense.

Gil Gilbert shows how the blacks were crowded into cattle cars, and together with the Indians, were considered inferior animals by their white bosses. The impossible working conditions, such as lack of water and inadequate rest periods, are catalogued. As a result of these conditions, many workers collapsed and were left to die. The risk of death by accident was high. The author tells how this imported labor force was brutally repressed whenever rebellion was attempted.

Santander is eventually driven mad by this treatment. He manages to kill a foreman and escape into the jungle. His freedom is short-lived, however, for as the story ends, the enemy is closing in on him. The story ends with the following line: "Everybody hates blacks, but blacks are poor, good people."[53] "El negro Santander," largely because of the creation and forceful characterization of the black protagonist, is deserving of the praise it has received as a work of art.

And Gonzalo Ramón in *Tierra baldía* (1958) has given us a more recent example of the exploitation of black people in Ecuador, again in the province of Esmeraldas, this time in the jungles of the Quinindé region. The immediate problems of the blacks are brought out in the following discussion:

> "What we have is enough, and we don't plant more because we don't have any help. They don't consider us worth it."
>
> "It's just that you people don't have any ambition and that's because you are uneducated. You are satisfied with too little. You take over a little piece of land and you don't even bother to take title to it. . . . You don't have the same problem as the Indian. . . . Your problem is to get them to give you ownership of those lands you work; you have to have schools; you have to get financial help from the banks. You have to demand better educational and health facilities. March on the capital and demand those things.[54]

An outspoken protest against the miserable working conditions in the backlands, jungles, and mountains of Esmeraldas, Ramón's novel depicts the colored workers in this area as forgotten men as far as the essentials of life are concerned, authentic underdogs left to live in misery, poverty, and grief, with no defenders to protect their rights as human beings.

Finally, a word about Juan Montalvo, the Ecuadorian essayist, as his curious ambivalence in his defense of blacks is almost as famous as that of Rubén Darío. Montalvo attacked racial discrimination in the United States, opposed slavery on religious and moral grounds, objected to political discrimination against blacks, praised highly those who fought for the abolition of slavery, expressed righteous indignation at a priest's refusal to bury his black servant, and, in general, presented himself as a defender of blacks, arguing that all South America had black or Indian blood. Yet, according to Kessel Schwartz,[55] whose work on Montalvo summarizes these details, most of Montalvo's remarks favorable to blacks are patronizing or paternalistic in tone. What is more, Schwartz assures us, Montalvo believed that black people had no civilization and were innately inferior beings both mentally and morally, whose only chance for progress lay in taking on white blood. Montalvo believed, further, that blacks were cowardly and that their women were sexually attractive to apes.

The literature of social protest in Latin America concerned specifically with black people focuses on the handicap of color. This concern is not limited to the nineteenth-century antislavery novel or to the proletarian novel of the twenties and thirties. Literary defenders of black people continue, in the interest of racial equality, to press for their fair treatment, even though now racist practices are not as blatantly discriminatory as the "black list" in Venezuelan oil country, the Gold Roll-Silver Roll system in the Canal Zone in Panama, the earlier discriminatory practices of pre-Castro Cuba, or of the banana, mining, or cacao companies in Central and South America.

Consistent with the continuing interest in the larger questions of equality, justice, and liberty, Kessel Schwartz recently pointed out that even the "new novelists" continue to try old themes of the social narrative using new techniques to promote old beliefs:

> It must be understood, however, that the "old" novel has never disappeared. The social novel continued to emphasize special themes such as the Indian, the Chaco War, anti-imperialism, the Mexican Revolution, political corruption, and rural and city problems—didactic themes repeated *ad nauseam* to try to enable the Spanish American to realize and interpret his circumstances and thus act upon it and perhaps transform it. . . . Although the novelists indulge in a variety of technical experiments and exhibit existential traits, they are definitely "engagés" . . . in Spanish America, the optimistic note of serving man and gaining human justice continues, and for many of the novelists the *praxis,* the *quehacer,* the project of all mankind, must be to strive to effect justice and liberty in this world.[56]

This perennial interest in social protest, as we shall see in the next chapter, is a significant aspect of the socio-negristic narrative as it links nonblack literary defenders of blacks in Latin America to Afro-Latin-American writers who take a similar social revolutionary stance against injustice.

I have identified and given several examples of the socio-negristic narrative that uses the black as social symbol because future research on black themes in Latin-American literature must take into account this link between nonblack literary defenders of the black and Afro-Latin-American writers. More research on this link is important, especially since closer reading of many of these socio-negristic novels could bear out, as in the case of some nineteenth-century antislavery novels, that "racism derives from a sense of group supremacy and is not nullified by simply pleading justice for the oppressed."[57] Moreover, it remains to be seen whether a genuinely social literature—to paraphrase Richard A. Prêto-Rodas[58] on Jorge de Lima, and Addison Gayle Jr.—requires, as a *sine qua non* for the literary portrayal of the black in the fullest sense, that the author be nonwhite.

At any rate, some of the literature of social protest on black themes is proletarian in nature complete with strikes, massacres, class conflict, even group solidarity, in which the struggle is against exploitation and oppression by the privileged few, as committed black and white writers alike in Latin America at times realize that some white people too are in the same economic boat as black people. But, some of them realize, nevertheless, that it is *because* of the black man's color that he is in that boat in the first place, regardless of the white man's excuse. An old black character in a Puerto Rican short story summed it up rather aptly when he said: *"Mi jijo, malo es ser pobre y negro. . . ."*[59] It is bad enough to be poor, or to be white and poor, but—he said—to be poor and black. . . ! Or in similar words of Dr. Ralph Abernathy on racism and being black: "I don't care where it is, you've got trouble. And if you're black *and* poor, you've got twice as much trouble."[60] Recently on television, the widow of Malcolm X made a statement which seems relevant. She said, in effect, "Some people are trying to call this a class thing. But the truth is we are suffering because we are black."

Fifty years after he made his famous statement regarding the problem of the color-line in the twentieth century, W. E. B. Dubois wrote, in 1953, that the color-line is still a great problem of this century. He went on:

> But today I see more clearly than yesterday that back of the problem of race and color lies a greater problem which both obscures and implements it: and that is the fact that so many civilized persons are willing to live in comfort even if the price of

this is poverty, ignorance and disease of the majority of their fellowmen; that to maintain this privilege men have waged war until today war tends to become universal and continuous, and the excuse for this war continues largely to be color and race.[61]

Regardless of the ''class thing,'' color is important and relevant to the plight of the black man in Latin America. Despite the optimism expressed in the title of the following chapter ''consciousness of color is not likely to disappear unless color itself disappears, or unless men lose their eyesight.''[62] This recent statement by Charles Silberman might well prove to be just as prophetic and applicable as the earlier one made by W. E. B. Dubois, in 1903, when applied to the problem of color and race in Latin America.

Black Song Without Color: The Black Experience and the Negritude of Synthesis in Afro-Latin-American Literature

> *Negritude is what one race brings to the common rendezvous where all will strive for the new world of the poet's vision.*
>
> *C. L. R. James*

Demystification and the White Aesthetic Rejected: The Developing Concept of Negritude in Latin America

Thus far we have seen black people faced with, among other facts of the black experience, amalgamation, insults, discrimination, stereotyping, and a somatic distance that governs their lives. The effects of racism and the white aesthetic on the black have made him very conscious of his color, and the reactions of black writers in some instances reflect this preoccupation. Indeed, racism and the white aesthetic are rejected by black writers in Latin America who deal at length with the black experience in much of their work. Black consciousness, however, does not prevent a broader view of man, or of man's inhumanity to man, from becoming a literary concern.

Back in the forties it was generally felt that the black writer in Latin America did not dwell on the black man's fate; that, unlike his North American brother, the Afro-Latin-American writer was too seduced by song and dance to concern himself with civil rights, justice, and freedom, that he was more interested in musical rhythms and in imitating the white man than in establishing bonds of racial solidarity with his black brothers around the world.[1] This impression of black literature in Latin America has not changed much over the years as it is still generally believed that negritude as a literary phenomenon is neither deeply felt[2] nor fully developed in that part of the world.[3] It is also thought in some quarters that Nicolás Guillén, "the great black poet of Cuba"[4] is not, strictly speaking, a poet of negritude.[5]

If, however, one of the basic premises of negritude is the recognition of being black and the acceptance of this fact, and if the movement represented " 'literature engagée' at its most eloquent,"[6] adherents to the doctrine in Latin America are numerous as many black writers there affirm their acceptance not only through expressions of black pride and rejection of white racism but also through calls for liberation, racial solidarity, and identification with black people around the world. Furthermore, many black writers in Latin America have cleared the initial hurdle of recognizing their self-worth and have moved into protest literature that not only focuses on the mistreatment of blacks but also goes beyond race in an effort to achieve, if not an antiracist society of universal brotherhood, at least the solidarity of all oppressed peoples regardless of color. Indeed, the developing concept of negritude as applied to Latin America will have to be seen in a higher form if we are to recognize the totality and true significance of the term and if we are to understand the genuine desire for brotherhood that blacks in Latin America feel toward whites, despite racist obstacles associated with the somatic distance.

Mestizaje, which was loosely defined in Chapter One as being the process of ethnic and cultural fusion, is an indisputable fact of the black experience in Latin America. This process, while often understood, as we have seen, to mean the physical, spiritual, and cultural rape of black people, has helped, nevertheless, in the creation of an atmosphere that fosters patriotism and cultural nationalism rather than separatism and black nationalism. Black writers in Latin America realize that the process of ethnic and cultural fusion has depleted their ranks. They believe, nevertheless, that despite racist obstacles the atmosphere created by the process allows for the development of a negritude as a justification of blackness but within the context of the mixed composition of the Latin-American nations. It is upon this integrative and conciliatory concept of negritude that we must build when we discuss negritude and the black experience in Latin America.

Of the many possible phases and notions of negritude[7]—some of which, for example, focus on political implications, on counteracculturation, on the black man's drive toward a reunification of his African heritage, on an emotional function that is exclusively black— the notion that best describes negritude in Latin America is the one that reflects a quest for an antiracist, possibly universal culture, "the culminating point of the dream of every serious advocate of Negritude,"[8] a universal brotherhood in which the black man will establish solidarity with all mankind.

Accordingly, although the desire to "return to Africa" is not strong, we can find not only antecedents to negritude in Latin America, as G. R. Coulthard[9] has demonstrated, but also the crystallization of the ultimate logical extreme—following the theories of Sartre, and later of Césaire, Fanon, and Senghor—to which negritude can be developed. Nowhere, to use Sartre's words, is the "synthesis or realization of the human in a society without races"[10] more desired than among blacks in Latin America. Nowhere does the black man assert his solidarity with the oppressed of all colors more than in Latin America. Nowhere is Fanon's assertion, in effect, that "there is no 'black' culture and that the 'black people' are fast disappearing"[11] more true than in Latin America. Nowhere is the concept more in a process of metamorphosis from a form of racialism to a "postulation of brotherhood"[12]—to use Césaire's words—than in Latin America. In short, nowhere is the negritude of synthesis as the opposite of racialism more significantly close to the concept supported by Senghor, the poet and the theorist of synthesis, than in Latin America. We shall see also, however, that despite this core conception of negritude, black consciousness and the clash of cultures originally posited by negritude, though softened by *mestizaje* in Latin America, are vividly evident in much of the literature by Afro-Latin-American writers who reject and condemn white racism and its by-products, while simultaneously reaffirming the black past and asserting the black present.

Controlled Literature: Black Consciousness and Early Black Writing from José Manuel Valdés to the Modernist Verse of Gaspar Octavio Hernańdez

Certainly not all of the literature by writers of African descent in Latin America deals with white racism, black awareness, social commentary, protest, color consciousness, racial pride, solidarity, injustice, and oppression. There are other themes, particularly in past centuries when black writers "crammed full of white morality, white culture, white education and white prejudices"[13] tried, sometimes unsuccessfully, to disguise their color. It is possible to read some of their literature "never finding a trace of the black man's sensuous and colorful imagination or the echo of the hatreds and aspirations of an oppressed people.''[14] In reading such colorless literature, however, I have often wondered which writers in Latin America tell us more about the pressures of white racism and slave societies: those who in the interest of survival or of getting their work published make concessions to the white standard by writing an "escapist" literature that caters more to racist demands for "white writing" than to the black experience; or those who, in coming to terms with these pressures, reject the white standard, fomenting instead a black consciousness in their works, which, more often than not, expresses as well a real desire for universal harmony among the races, even if aligned along class lines.

I concluded long ago that both categories of Afro-Latin-American writers tell us something about the black experience in Latin America even when, or especially when, that experience is rarely mentioned. This occurred, moreover, even in the carefully controlled literature of earlier times, when the Afro-Peruvian José Manuel Valdés (1767-1844), the first black poet to publish in Spanish America, was decrying his blackness, when the popular poet José Vasconcelos, "El Negrito Poeta," around the middle of the eighteenth century was reminding his listeners that, although black, he was born in Mexico:

> Aunque soy de raza *Conga,*
> Yo no he nacido africano
> Soy de nación *mejicano*
> Y nacido en *Almolonga,*[15]

> Although I am African,
> I was not born in Africa
> I am Mexican
> and I was born in Almolonga

It was occurring while Juan Francisco Manzano (1797-1854) and other slave poets in Cuba were ignoring their African heritage, when their free compatriot, Gabriel de la Concepción Valdés, "Plácido," (1809-44) was dissimulating, when Candelario Obeso (1849-84) in Colombia was courting white affection and finally committing suicide when it—some say—was denied him, and when Gaspar Octavio Hernández (1893-1918) in Panama was obsessed with whiteness. If we look closely enough we can discover that, despite their best efforts, black consciousness did find its way into their literary expression inadvertently in some cases and with reckless abandon in others: José Manuel Valdés was aware of his color and made some allusion to it in

his poetry; José Vasconcelos recognized his color and often defended
his blackness and that of others in his popular verse; Juan Francisco
Manzano, whose work, though filled with the tears, melancholy, and
prolonged suffering of a *"negro bueno"* which his self-admitted image
of a passive *"manso-cordero"* helped to perpetuate, did, on a couple
of occasions, manage enough pride to assert his individuality; Plácido,
suspected of a leadership role in a black conspiracy to either free the
slaves or to establish a black republic in Cuba independent of Spain,
was executed partly because of his "revolutionary" verse, partly
because of his ties with the black community, and largely because he
was "colored"; Candelario Obeso, who, in his *Cantos populares de
mi tierra* (1880), expressed a natural but quiet black dignity of a kind
that fills the reader with appreciation of the poet's ability to capture the
feelings of his people in various moods and situations, also wrote in
prose: "I am delighted to be black and my ugliness is a joy to me. . . .
Mankind will be born anew in my race."[16] And finally, though the
modernist verse of Gaspar Octavio Hernández is obsessed with
whiteness and tinged with the melancholic depression of a black who
yearns to be white, this strongly patriotic poet, in whose verse any
references to blackness are virtually nonexistent, did defend his race
with laudatory prose for blacks who, in his estimation, deserved it.[17]
Had he not met death at an early age, it is possible that blackness
would have become a constant in his verse as well.

"Our Race" and Black Literary Expression in Uruguay

PILAR BARRIOS

We do not have to look closely to discover evidence of black
consciousness in the literary expression of Afro-Latin-American
writers who began publishing after the death of Gaspar Octavio
Hernández. The Uruguayan poet, Pilar Barrios (1889), for example,
even though he was fond—like Gaspar Octavio Hernández—of
modernist verse and escapist allusions, did not share the Panamanian's
cult of whiteness. Barrios, like many of the Afro-Latin-American
writers who were to achieve literary success in his country and
elsewhere, first in the pages of *Nuestra Raza,* a black journal published
until 1948 in Montevideo, and later in book form in *Piel negra*
(Montevideo: Editorial Nuestra Raza, 1947), dwells on

> el intenso dolor de una raza
> que ha sufrido el mayor vilipendio
> ("Mis versos," *Piel negra,* p. 21)

the intense pain of a race
that has suffered every vilification imaginable

Although he sings of his

Raza negra, noble raza;
raza humilde, sana y fuerte
("La leyenda maldita," *Piel negra,* p. 55)

Black race, noble race;
humble race, healthy and strong

in much of his poetry, where titles such as "Tema racial," "Raza negra," "Piel negra," and "Hombre negro" leave little doubt about his preoccupation with the black experience, Barrios, like many black writers who rose to prominence in this century, continues to identify in *Mis cantos* (Montevideo: Editorial Comité Amigos del Poeta, 1949), his second book of poems, with black *"anhelos, ansias e inquietudes"*[18] while expressing at the same time his solidarity or fraternal bond with other races:

Yo quiero al Criollo y al Indio
porque en su suelo nací,
el negro me bulle adentro
y Africa la siento aquí
*   *   *
Pero también amo a España
porque, nieto de gallego
sangre de ella llevo en mí
*   *   *
Recoged todos mi canto
que a todos os dirigí
("Canto de la sangre," *Mis cantos,* no pagination)

I love the Creole and the Indian
because I was born in their land,
blackness stirs inside me
and I feel Africa in my heart
*   *   *
But I love Spain as well
because, grandson of a Galician,
I carry her blood in me

> Everyone take in my song
> which I dedicate to you

In "Frente a la hora que pasa" Barrios exhorts mankind to unite:

> Y así, hombro con hombro, junto al hombre blanco
>   *   *   *
> corramos en busca de nuestros derechos
> que nos corresponden como hombre y humanos.
> Basta de prejuicios, odios y reacciones;
> que gane a las almas y a los corazones
> un soplo de humana solidaridad.
>   (*Mis cantos,* no pagination)

> And like this, shoulder to shoulder, beside the white man
>   *   *   *
> let us go in search of the rights
> that we are entitled to as men and as human beings.
> Enough of prejudices, hates and reactions;
> let a breath of human solidarity
> win over hearts and souls.

This exhortation he repeats with little variation in "Fraternidad" and again more pointedly in "Hermano blanco . . .":

> Hermano blanco, ven e iremos juntos
> en hermanada asociación de ideas,
> llevando el verbo humano y solidario
> por todos los caminos de la tierra.

> White brother, come and we will go together
> our thoughts joined in fraternal association,
> carrying the human word in solidarity
> along all the roads of the world.

The poem ends on a note of urgency:

> ¡Hermano blanco! Iniciemos la cruzada
> de conjunción de espíritus de almas
> hasta hacer que el humano sentimiento
> triunfe sobre los odios y las armas.
>   (*Mis cantos,* no pagination)

> White brother! Let us begin the crusade

to unite spirits and souls
so that human feelings can
triumph over weapons and hate.

VIRGINIA BRINDIS DE SALAS

Virginia Brindis de Salas, a compatriot and contemporary of Barrios
and one of the few black female writers in Latin America, has done
much to foster black pride in her people, particularly in Uruguay. But
her poetry, like that of Barrios, often is directed toward all the

Hijos del suelo americano
blancos y negros hermanados

Sons of the American land
whites and blacks joined in brotherhood

to quote from the first poem, "A la ribera americana," of her first
book, *Pregón de Marimorena* (Montevideo n.p., 1974, p. 17), a poem
that contains a symbolic and significant reference to "a flag/of a single
color". Perhaps more so than Barrios, Brindis de Salas brandishes
strong words on behalf of the masses whose social redemption she has
taken to heart. Although well aware of her African origin and of her
responsibility to remind others of theirs, the black poetess,
nevertheless, echoing the claim to the American birthright made earlier
by José Vasconcelos (El Negrito Poeta) and Pilar Barrios, can write
with equal conviction:

Pueblo americano
yo soy tuya,
nací en tí.
    ("¡Aleluya!" *Pregón de Marimorena,* p. 58)

American people
I belong to you,
I was born here.

Her verse, which ranges from reminiscences of Africa to identification
with America, sings of freedom as in her second book of poems, *Cien
cárceles de amor* (Montevideo, 1949), she encourages blacks to forget

Los buques negreros, aquellas sentinas oscuras
del barco, horrores, el hambre;

azotes sufridos, olvídalo todo;
que lentamente viene, la ansiada libertad!
  ("Negro: siempre triste," p. 31)

The slave ships, those dark bilges
of the vessel, horrors, hunger;
whippings endured, forget it all;
your ardently desired liberty is slowly coming!

Black liberation, black pride, and the suffering of black people are repeatedly emphasized in her poetry, and the poetess presents a strong image to her white counterpart:

Yo negra,
tu blanca, mujer americana:
la misma sopa
habremos de comer
        *   *   *

y la misma ropa
y has de beber tu vino
en igual copa.
  ("¡Aleluya!" *Pregón de Marimorena,* p. 59)

I am black,
you are white, American woman:
the same soup
we will have to eat
        *   *   *

and the same clothing
and you will have to drink your wine
from the same cup.

The poetry of Virginia Brindis de Salas is very much in the mainstream of the literature by Latin-American writers of African descent because of her forceful presentation of the black experience in America; for her awareness of her African heritage invoked in allusions, African-sounding words and rhythms in Spanish, and direct references; and largely because of the revolutionary impact that her verses, such as the following, have made on black readers:

Cristo negro manoseado
por la audacia y por la fuerza,
dejarás tu mansedumbre
de cordero y tu vergüenza

Y fuerza contra la fuerza
                    *   *   *
quita la hiel y tu miedo
                    *   *   *
Sangre y llaga mucho enseñan.
    ("Cristo negro," *Pregón de Marimorena,* p. 27)

Black Christ worked over
by outrages and by force,
you will put your lamb-like meekness
and your shame behind you

And meeting force with force
                    *   *   *
put your fear aside
                    *   *   *
Blood and pain are very educational.

Though imbued with revolutionary zeal, her tender moments of
maternal affection provide an effective change of pace:

Quiero la cabecita
besar del niño negro
y darle así mi tierno
calor.
    ("Prez para los niños sin canto," *Pregón
    de Marimorena,* p. 26)

I love to kiss the tiny
head of the black child
and give him in this way
my tender warmth.

The black song of Virginia Brindis de Salas, while capable of such
tender sentiments, is, nevertheless, among the most virile expressions
of the black experience in Latin America.

Black Pride and Universal Justice: Adalberto Ortiz and
Afro-Latin-American Literature in Ecuador

ADALBERTO ORTIZ

Afro-Latin-American writers in Ecuador are perhaps even more
forceful than their Uruguayan counterparts in their presentation of the

black experience as well as in their adherence to the conciliatory and integrative concept of negritude. *Juyungo,* for example, the first novel of the mulatto poet, novelist, and diplomat, Adalberto Ortiz (1914-   ), which won first prize in 1942 as the best Ecuadorian novel of that year, is one of the best expressions of the black experience and the negritude of synthesis in Latin America. This novel, with the subtitle "Historia de un negro, una isla y otros negros," has been recently rediscovered and reissued. Enrique Anderson Imbert, with reason, has called it one of the best Spanish-American novels of this century.[19] Ortiz continues to write and has published several books of poems and stories; his second novel, *El espejo y la ventana,* awarded the National Prize for literature in 1964, was later published in 1967.

"Juyungo," a pejorative term, meaning monkey, devil, or evil, taken from the Cayapa Indian language in Ecuador, is applied insultingly to blacks. Ortiz's novel shows the effects of racism and prejudice on mulattoes and on a proud black man who hated to be scorned and insulted and who did not hesitate to strike back at the prejudices, resentments, and hatreds he encountered due to his black skin. Asención Lastre, the black protagonist, was a leader and a fighter, a proud man who rejected his slave heritage. He retaliated and killed without a moment's hesitation, thus taking vengeance on two men responsible for the death of his son and the resultant insanity of his wife. Throughout his life Asención simply wanted to live in dignity. His whole life was spent in search of the racial equality and social justice that would have guaranteed him that dignity.

Although Asención hated white people who considered him inferior and who discriminated against, abused, and exploited him, he saw that he could love white people and hate blacks, especially when the latter tried to take advantage of their own people. In spite of his tremendous race pride, Asención realized the important thing was to live like a man and to be man enough to face up to life with dignity and courage, recognizing injustice wherever it existed and in whatever form. He came to exhibit less bitterness and more tolerance in the final pages and to transfer his original hatred of whites to hatred of injustice. He killed, perhaps not just to kill whites, but for justice. He even fought for justice in his country's behalf. In the last scenes, Asención was a true patriot, joining with his fellow Ecuadorians to fight the Peruvian invasion, illustrating once more that the novel, while characterized by black pride and traditional hatred for white people, is concerned, nevertheless, with the larger question of universal justice for all men and the suffering of all mankind, regardless of color.

While dealing primarily with blacks and their relationships with whites and Indians in Ecuador, *Juyungo* merits accolades because of its artistic worth and because of the stylistic beauty of some of the passages depicting national scenery and the customs of black people in Ecuador. The novel is particularly significant, however, because the author through Asención Lastre presents a strong image of black pride and self-respect for black people. Much like other writers of African descent in Latin America, Ortiz, whose black protagonist is a "real race man," *"el más negro de los negros,"*[20] *"un negro-negro"*[21] who strikes us as being "black inside and out," nevertheless sees self-discovery of race as a first step toward the acquisition of a social conscience. Like his fellow black writers, Ortiz carries his protest beyond race, beyond the traditional hatred for whites, proposing in his work, often proletarian in type, social revolution, where necessary, in the interest of universal justice for all men.

Juyungo, however, though underlying the importance of class consciousness ("class more than race"[22]), never loses sight of the black man. Ortiz's poetry, too, in *Tierra, son y tambor: Cantares negros y mulatos* (Mexico City: Ediciones La Cigarra, 1945), is very consistent in this regard. Despite some personal uncertainty mentioned by Ortiz in a recent edition, the author continues as intensely as any other writer of African descent in Latin America to sing in his verse of Africa, to evoke his African heritage, and to recall his black past during slavery and before. For example, "Contribución," his opening poem, and one of his better efforts, sets the tone for much of his verse as it sings of:

> Africa, Africa, Africa,
> tierra grande, verde y sol, . . .
>
> Africa, Africa, Africa,
> big, green, sunny land, . . . (p. 23)

In this anthology piece Ortiz, from the first verse *"Africa, Africa, Africa"* down to *"América"* in the next to the last line, rhymes dactylic words throughout the poem in alternating patterns with words with accented final syllables as he sings in highly rhythmic phrasing of the African contribution to America. In "Casi color" Ortiz, himself a mulatto, sides, as in *Juyungo,* with the black man. In clear, unadulterated verse, he writes simply: "I want to be more black than white" (p. 55). And in his blackness he proclaims his racial solidarity with Africa and with blacks in other places:

He vivido en Congo
y he soñado en Harlem:
he amado en Calidonia
   (p. 56)

I have lived in the Congo
and I have dreamed of Harlem:
I have loved in Calidonia

ending his poem by reinforcing his preference in a litany of blackness:

Para olvidarme de todo
quiero ser negro.
Negro como la noche preñada del día,
Negro como un diamante carioca.
Negro para el azul.
Negro con sangre-sangre.
   (p. 56)

In order to forget about everything
I want to be black.
Black as the night pregnant with day,
Black as a carioca diamond.
Blue-black.
Black with real blood.

In "Antojo" Ortiz builds an impressive case against the white man, developing in poetic form a gradual awareness of the white man's deceptive ways, shattering, in effect, the white wish of a black girl:

Er blanco te coge, negra,
como una curiosidá
y cuando meno lo piensas
te va dejando botáa.
Er blanco te v'empreñá,
Er blanco te va a pateá.
   (p. 46).

The white man will take you, black woman,
as a curiosity
and when you least expect it
he will cast you off
The white man will impregnate you,
The white man will kick you around.

This advice well taken, the black girl, like Ortiz, makes her choice:

> Sólo quiero negro,
> mi negro quiero. (p. 46)

> I only love blackness
> I love my black man.

Although a firm believer in the ideology summed up in the phrase from *Juyungo,* ''class more than race,'' Ortiz characteristically asks in ''Yo no sé'':

> ¿Po qué será,
> me pregunto yo,
> que casi todo lo negro
> tan pobre son
> como yo soy? (p. 47)

> Why is it,
> I ask myself,
> that almost all blacks
> are as poor
> as I am?

It is in ''Breve historia nuestra,'' the opening poem to his collection, that Ortiz, after tracing the black man's plight and trajectory from freedom in Africa to slavery and servitude in the New World, sounds a note of warning based on the collective strength of his race. He proclaims optimistically:

> Ya no somos millares,
> somos millones.
>   *   *   **
>
> que soñamos bajo todas las palmeras
> que somos hombres,
> hombres, sí, libres.
>
> Eramos millares . . . .
> somos millones. . . . (p. 22)

> We are no longer thousands,
> we are millions.
>   *   *   **
>
> who dream beneath the palms
> that we are men,
> men, yes, free.

> We were thousands. . . .
> we are millions. . . .

Other poems that pointedly focus with pride and dignity on the black man and black folklore in his collection include "Romance de la llamarada," "Son de trópico," "Son del monte," "La tunda, tunda que entunda," "La tunda para el negrito," "Jolgorio," "Qué tendrá la Soledá," the powerful and rhythmic "Sinfonía bárbara," and his more recent, equally rhythmic "Negritud con bembosidades,"[23] one of two new poems the poet added to a later edition of his poetry. This poem once again establishes his solidarity with black people around the world, in Nigeria, in Panama, in Cameroon, in Puerto Rico, in the Congo.

NELSON ESTUPIÑÁN BASS

Another Ecuadorian writer who, like Adalberto Ortiz, expresses the experience primarily of the predominantly black inhabitants of the province of Esmeraldas is Nelson Estupiñán Bass (1915-   ). Though better known for his novels he is also a poet, and his aptly titled *Canto negro por la luz: Poemas para negros y blancos* (Esmeraldas, Ecuador: Ediciones del Núcleo Provincial de Esmeraldas de la Casa de la Cultura Ecuatoriana, 1954) contains several compositions such as "Canción del niño del incendio" that assert black pride:

> Algunos creen insultarme
> gritándome mi color,
> mas yo mismo lo pregono
> con orgullo frente al sol:
> Negro he sido, negro soy,
> negro vengo negro voy,
> negro bien negro nací,
> negro negro he de vivir,
> y como negro morir. (p. 50)

> Some believe they insult me
> by throwing my color in my face,
> but I myself proclaim it
> proudly with my head held high:
> Black I have been, black I am,
> I am black coming and going,
> I was born very black and

> black I must live,
> and a black I must die.

The introductory strophe repeated at the end of the poem stands out in this collection of predominantly free verse for its smooth-flowing rhythmic quality that suggests the ingredients for a "catchy" tune but one whose affirmation of blackness is just as meaningful as the medium of expression. Characteristically—for Estupiñán Bass, too, sings a song of universal brotherhood—this same poem raises the following hope:

> En los tiempos que vendrán
> cuando caigan las barreras
> del odio de los adultos,
> las barreras de colores
> de los niños se hundirán. (p. 52)

> In the times which are coming
> when the barriers
> of hate put up by adults fall,
> the barriers of colors
> that divide children will collapse.

In such poems as "Venganza" and "Rabia," with their suggestive titles, Estupiñán Bass vents his rage, and, in a moment of reflection, consoles himself as best he can with these words spoken to his *"compañeros negros"*:

> hermanos de color y lucha,
> me horrorizo y me alegro al mismo tiempo
> cuando pienso en el estallido de nuestra rabia.
>   ("Rabia," p. 46)

> brothers in color and in strife
> I am horrified and happy at the same time
> when I think about the moment when our rage explodes.

Though noted for his free verse, Estupiñán Bass demonstrates in "Lola Matamba" and "Negra bullanguera" a rare virtuosity with African-sounding words and rhythms associated with black poetry. His central message, however, is peace and the brotherhood of man, a message he even sends to the Cayapa Indian in the poem "Mensaje negro para el indio Cayapa." The poet believes that the black man has a special responsibility to make his voice heard by all who despise him because he believes that his mission of peace and brotherhood can ill afford to be ignored. His ''canto negro por la luz,'' hinted throughout the collection, is fully explored in the poem from which the book takes its title. He begins:

> Hombres blancos, rojos, mestizos, amarillos,
> para todos vosotros abro mis palabras como brazos,
> fraternales,
> a pesar de ser negras. (p. 80)

> White men, red men, mestizoes, and yellow men,
> I open my words like arms to all of you,
> fraternally,
> in spite of being black.

He continues, wondering whether

> tal vez parezca un absurdo
> que una voz negra cante en favor de la luz, (p. 80)

> perhaps it seems absurd
> that a black voice sings in favor of the light.

but he ends his poem with this good counsel:

> Miradme:
> yo mismo soy ahora
> una blanca bandera
> a pesar de ser negro. (p. 82)

> Look at me:
> I myself am now
> a white flag
> in spite of being black.

The tolerant attitude of Estupiñán Bass toward race relations is implied in his recent novel, *El último río* (1967), which, though charged with intense racial hatred, does settle into a more sober recognition of the simple fact that all men are equal. *El último río* takes a unique and humorous route toward the larger question of universal brotherhood. Unlike the racial situation developed in such novels as *Roquedal* and *El negro que tenía el alma blanca,* whose white authors are serious but whose black protagonists are unconvincing, even absurd, the novel of Estupiñán Bass becomes a parody of the bizarre extremes to which the delusions of whiteness can drive a black man to overcome his blackness. His approach provokes intended laughter. The reader immediately recognizes an obvious satire on the cult of whiteness shared by some black people, as well as a criticism of racism and color prejudice in Ecuador, evils which have weighed so heavily on the mind of the black protagonist that his only salvation as a human being was in the whiteness he so desperately sought while simultaneously rejecting his own people as unfit for civilized contact. In his efforts to overcome his blackness he stopped just short of painting himself white.

Pastrana, the black protagonist, since childhood had been very conscious of the handicap of his color. His acute color consciousness became a driving force in his life to acquire wealth, power, and position—in other words, whiteness. As he rose to the top he became more and more convinced that white people were superior and that blacks were stupid animals, definitely an inferior race. Black people should be sterilized, he felt, so as not to give birth to more of these animals. His dislike for his own people reached its highest expression when he became governor of the predominantly black province of Esmeraldas and immediately set machinery rolling to import white people into the province to cross-breed black people out of existence. His obsession reached farcical proportions when he fired all black people from his administration, painted his office white, dressed himself in white, and generally thought of himself as white, indeed, convinced himself that he *was* white.

Pastrana eventually came to his senses, especially when his fourth white mistress told him in a fit of jealousy that no matter what he did he would still be black. Quite predictably Pastrana began to realize the folly of his ways and to take pride in his race. His hatred took on a different color and his desire now was to dominate the white race. What followed was a complete reversal. He rescinded his cross-breeding orders, destroyed his white-washed office and everything white in it, and incurred the enmity of white people who had been anxious to support his persecution of blacks. And these white people, of course, demanded his impeachment.

El último río explores a wide variety of racial feelings in Ecuador. While criticizing white racism and the cult-of-whiteness tendency among black people, the author adds another dimension to his novel: the problem of greed that can drive a black man to enrich himself at the expense of his own people. Pastrana eventually loses his hatred for white people, and a final message becomes clear: all men are equal and must love one another if we are to get along in this world.

The following passage with its mellow reminiscences from the novel, while summarizing the psychological evolution of the black protagonist obsessed with race and color consciousness, serves at the same time to illustrate the balanced view toward race relations expressed in much of the literature by writers of African descent in Latin America:

> Now his rancor for both blacks and whites had faded; he smiled contentedly when he evoked those times in which he abhorred first one race and then the other; it pleased him to review what had been because it confirmed that only ashes remained of the aberrations that time was scattering further and further away from him. Now he did not consider his race unworthy, stupid, or barbarous; he no longer considered it responsible for all the ills that have been and are yet to be; but neither did he believe it superior, better than whites. White people were no better; they were not on a higher plane, nor were they models; he saw them now as no different from mestizos and blacks. For him, now in his seventies, color did not confer distinction; men were equal, and all, even the bad ones, had the same right to life.[24]

ANTONIO PRECIADO

Antonio Preciado, who belongs to the younger generation of black writers in Latin America today, deserves mention here as he is another Ecuadorian writer who gives poetic expression to the black experience. *Tal como somos* (Quito: Ediciones Siglo Veinte, n.d.), his second book of poems, is his most significant publication to date since it contains his prize-winning compositions, "Este hombre y su planeta" (1965) and "Siete veces la vida" (1967), both written when the author was a university student. Preciado's poetry is human poetry; his poems at times are intimate personal experiences, but the range of his preoccupations includes expression of his black identity as well as a fraternal identification, for example, with the Indian exploited in the mines of Bolivia, or with the peasants in the rice fields of Vietnam. Though recognizing his African roots and heritage, Antonio Preciado is developing a quiet but persuasive poetic spirit expressed in technically accomplished verse that does not rely heavily on the African sound and rhythm for poetic effect. Preciado is following in the footsteps of older writers of African descent in Ecuador in particular and in Latin America in general, but with a voice that is distinctively his own.

Integration, Black Life, and the Afro-Venezuelan Literature of Juan Pablo Sojo

Juan Pablo Sojo (1908-48), the Afro-Venezuelan essayist, poet, novelist, author of short fiction, pioneer in black theatre in Venezuela and expert on Afro-Venezuelan folklore, though proud of his color, recognized, perhaps more than any other black writer in Latin America, the fact of *mestizaje* in the black experience to be paramount, particularly in Venezuela where the black contribution is a strong factor not only biologically but artistically and economically as well.

Although believing there is less prejudice in Latin America than in the United States, Sojo recognizes, nevertheless, that it does exist despite widespread racial fusion. It is his opinion, expressed in *Temas y apuntes afro-venezolanos* primarily, that the prejudice that does exist is aesthetic in nature and is based on color and physical features. This anti-African prejudice, Sojo believes, is partly responsible for the fact that blacks in Barlovento, his native region, are not always favorably treated.

His novel, *Nochebuena negra* (1930, 1943), the best known of his several works on Afro-Venezuelan themes, deals with the *pobres negros* of Barlovento. Imbued with an atmosphere of sensuality, folklore, and violence the novel does not overlook the social condition of the blacks in that region who are often exploited by outsiders who come there to enrich themselves at the expense of black labor. In depicting this world of black life, Sojo relies heavily on a realistic and at times poetic interpretation of black legends, superstitions, and witchcraft.

The Popular and Revolutionary Black Poetry of Nicomedes Santa Cruz, the Afro-Peruvian "Decimista"

The black experience and the negritude of integration and conciliation are expressed in Peru largely in the verse of Nicomedes

Santa Cruz (1925-   ). Born into a family whose artistic talents range
from poetry, music, and theater to bullfighting, this Afro-Peruvian
decimista is a popular poet dedicated to the preservation and
cultivation of black culture, folklore, and music in his country. As with
the poetry of the Ecuadorian Nelson Estupiñán Bass, the Cuban
Nicolás Guillén, and Puerto Rico's leading black poet Victorio Llanes
Allende, and other Afro-Latin-American poets, much of the "black
rhythms" of Nicomedes Santa Cruz have been set to music. There are
several recordings in circulation of the poet reciting his verse and
interpreting Afro-Peruvian music. To date Santa Cruz has written
several thousand *décimas* and other poems, many of them collected
and published in the anthology *Décimas y poemas* (Lima: Campodónico Ediciones, 1971).

In the introduction to his anthology, the poet comments on the
critical reception met by some of his poems published in 1964 in
Cumanana that deal with the black problem in Africa and America. He
notes that critics foresaw a *"nuevo Nicomedes"* (p. 15) in his
departure from folklore in a series of serious poems that dealt with the
harsher side of the black experience. He writes: "It was the first time
that a Peruvian touched on the vital problems of Africa and
Afroamerica—and a black poet no less. 'Muerte en el ring,' 'La
noche,' 'Juan Bemba,' '¡Ay mamá!' 'Formigas pretas,' 'Congo
Libre,' 'Johanesburgo,' 'Sudáfrica,' 'De igual a igual' and 'Llanto
negro,' were the ten poems that provoked such judgments and
predictions" (p. 16). He continues: "Closing this collection of poems
(Cumanana) was a song that came to me in Feira de Santana, a
peaceful town in Bahía. I called it 'América Latina' and (the same as
'Talara' of my *Décimas*) more than closing another stage, announced
what is now my larger design which is continental and integrationist in
scope by making a fraternal appeal to:

> Indoblanquinegros
> Blanquinegrindios
> y negrindoblancos
>
> Indianwhiteblacks
> Whiteblackindians
> and blackindianwhites

to close ranks against imperialism in defense of our inalienable
rights. . . ." (p. 16)

While following in the tradition of Nicolás Guillén in his wider continental and universal concern, Santa Cruz is fast becoming recognized at home and abroad as an authentic poet of negritude and the black experience who does not hesitate to protest against racism encountered in his homeland and around the world. His black pride is evident in poems such as "De ser como soy, me alegro." And in "Desde la negra retinta" he develops further what can be interpreted as racial pride and identification with blackness:

> En cuanto a lo que me toca,
> de ser como soy me alegro:
> Ojos pardos, cutis negro,
> rizo el pelo y gruesa boca.
> El ser así no me apoca
> ni me vuelve mentecato. (p. 64)

> As far as I am concerned,
> I am happy to be just as I am:
> Brown eyes, black skin,
> curly hair and thick mouth.
> Being like this does not make me feel small
> nor does it make me a fool.

Despite his firm identification with blackness, his song is one of protest that is decidedly revolutionary, antiimperialist, and always on the side of the proletariat:

> Yo soy revolucionario
> porque habiendo quien me escucha
> pongo mi voz en la lucha
> al lado del proletario. ("¡Patria o muerte!", p. 28)

> I am a revolutionary
> because having someone to listen to me
> I add my voice to the fight
> on the side of the proletarian.

Nicomedes Santa Cruz is a complete poet, a black poet, but whose "canción de protesta" is for all people regardless of color. He can write:

> Africa, tierra sin frío,
> Madre de mi obscuridad, ("Congo libre," p. 318)

> Africa, land without cold,
> Mother of my blackness,

establishing a firm identification with the mother country:

> Africa, izwe lethu
> (Africa, nuestra tierra)
> debe sernos devuelta
>
> Lo grito en matabele
> en aymara, en swahili
> en kechwa y en zulú.
> Lo grito en castellano
> yo, tu hermano, mi hermano:
> Sudáfrica y Perú. ("Sudáfrica," p. 324)

> Africa, our land
> you must be returned to us
>
> I shout it in Matabele
> in Aymara, in Swahili
> in Kechwa and in Zulu.
> I shout it in Castilian
> I, your brother, my brother:
> South Africa and Peru.

His "canción de protesta," however, is at the same time

> para la Sierra
> donde el comunero
> no es el dueño de la tierra.
> * * *
> para el Obrero
> que se juega entero
> por la lucha sindical.
>
> Campesino del Perú
> Proletario del Perú
> Pueblo pobre del Perú
> canta mi canción.[25]

> for the mountains
> where the common man
> is not owner of the land.
> * * *
> for the worker

who participates fully
in union struggles.

Farmers of Peru
Laborers of Peru
Poor people of Peru
sing my song.

Nicomedes Santa Cruz is an optimistic poet who has faith not only in black people in Peru, Africa, and elsewhere, but also in his "Peruvian homeland" that "is headed toward integration." (p. 264) His "fraternal affection," (p. 264) in short, is directed toward all, as comfort and encouragement to those who have suffered injustices and as warning and wisdom to those who perpetuate them. In "Sanos deseos" he writes:

Quisiera extender los brazos
hacia norte, sur y oriente
para estrechar a mi gente
en un gigantesco abrazo. (p. 309)

I would like to stretch my arms
towards the north, south and east
to enfold my people
in a gigantic embrace.

His wish becomes a fervent plea that

Comprendieran que el Perú
es nación negrindoblanca. (p. 309)

they should understand that Peru
is a negroindianwhite nation.

He concludes almost apologetically;

Si soy duro en lo que digo
lo hago con fraterno amor:

If I am harsh in what I say
I do it out of fraternal affection:

In the poetry of Nicomedes Santa Cruz the larger questions of universal brotherhood, social revolution, and universal justice consistently complement his equally determined racial identification with black people and their culture at home and abroad. His poetry is truly continental in scope. Manifestations of continentalism appear throughout his collection. It is in "América latina," excerpted below, as Santa Cruz himself recognizes, where he best develops this broad level of geographical and political consciousness despite racial and social differences:

"América latina"
*   *   *

He aquí mis vecinos
He aquí mis hermanos
*   *   *

Nací cerca de Cuzco
Admiro a Puebla
Me inspira el ron de las Antillas
Canto con voz argentina
Creo en Santa Rosa de Lima
Y en los Orishás de Bahía
*   *   *

hundo mi brazo izquierdo en el Pacífico
y sumerjo mi diestra en el Atlántico
*   *   *

y así me aferro a nuestro Continente
en un abrazo latinoamericano. (pp. 371-73)

"Latin America"
*   *   *

My neighbors are here
My brothers are here
*   *   *

I was born near Cuzco
I admire Puebla
I am inspired by rum from the Antilles
I sing with the voice of the Argentine
I believe in St. Rosa of Lima
and in the Orishás of Bahía
*   *   *

I immerse my left arm in the Pacific
and submerge my right in the Atlantic
*   *   *

And in this way I bind myself to our continent
in a Latin American embrace.

It is on this note in this appropriately titled poem, the last in the
volume, that the Afro-Peruvian poet significantly has chosen to end his
first "complete" anthology of verse. For those of us who have heard
recordings of the poet reciting his poems or performing from his vast
collection of Afro-Peruvian folklore, it is advisable to add that
Nicomedes Santa Cruz must be heard not only for what he has to say
about, among other things, the black experience, but also to appreciate
and experience firsthand the poet's authentic talent for transmitting in
oral concert his popular poetry back to the people who inspire it.

Afro-Colombian Literature of Commitment

JORGE ARTEL

The black pride and the racial identification with blackness of the
Peruvian Nicomedes Santa Cruz are found in the poetry of Jorge Artel
(1909-   ), Colombian poet, novelist, journalist, scholar, and
diplomat, who dedicated his book of poems, *Tambores en la noche*
(Cartagena: Editora Bolívar, 1940), to *"Mis abuelos, los negros."*
From the opening pages of this volume, reissued in 1956 in Mexico by
the University of Guanajuato, he establishes in "Negro soy" his racial
identification with blackness:

> Negro soy desde hace muchos siglos
> Poeta de mi raza, heredé su dolor.
>
> I have been black for many centuries
> Poet of my race, I have inherited its pain.

Mindful of the poetic game white poets play with blacks and their
culture, Artel declares from the outset:

> La angustia humana que exalto
> no es decorativa joya
> para turistas.
> Yo no canto un dolor de exportación.
>
> The human anguish that I extol
> is not a decorative jewel
> for tourists.
> I do not sing a grief for exportation.

The last line of this poem is significant because Artel, who is just as fond of depicting in his verse the black dance ("Dancing," "Danza mulata," "La cumbia," etc.), black sensuality ("Sensualidad negra"), black rhythms imitating the sound of the drum ("Tambores en la noche," etc.) as is the white onlooker, nevertheless is careful to avoid duplicating the image of the black as a picturesque song and dance man so much in vogue with the white poetic negrists, especially during the thirties and forties in Cuba and elsewhere. Artel is strongly opposed to this image, and he repeats his concern that black poetry should dwell on the black man's suffering, largely absent from the "black poetry" of his white counterparts. In "Poema sin odios ni temores" he directs his concern to his people as a reminder:

> No lleva nuestro verso cascabeles de "clown"
> ni -acróbata turístico-
> plasma piruetas en el circo
> para solaz de blancos. (p. 145)

> Our verse does not carry clown's bells
> nor -touristic acrobatics-
> does it twirl about in the circus
> for the enjoyment of whites.

Rather, in this same poem he counsels his black brothers in the Caribbean, in Panama, in Colombia, in Mexico, "wherever you may be," that

> nosotros tenemos que encontrarnos
>   *   *   *
> somos una conciencia en América
>   *   *   *
> somos -sin odios ni temores-
> una conciencia en América! (p. 145)

> we have to find ourselves
>   *   *   *
> we are a conscience in America
>   *   *   *
> We are -without hate and fears-
> a conscience in America!

More than just a conscience, it is a constant presence because of the process of *"mestizaje"* and also because of the black contribution to the New World in many ways, even though now some of these contributions, like the black rhythms that have undergone change over the years, are "disguised as white."

What Artel does export is his genuine feelings of racial pride and solidarity with oppressed black people in other parts of the world. Widely traveled, Artel has lectured at Princeton and Columbia and now lives in Panama. He has had a firsthand view of the black experience from Harlem to Barlovento and has reflected his observations in poems whose titles are taken from the names of predominantly black areas such as these. The black man's suffering in the United States particularly is a thematic constant in his verse. In "El mismo hierro" he remembers the resigned indifference of his black brothers in waiting rooms. He remembers his black brothers in the United states where just looking at a white woman would get them hanged. And reviewing poetically what was recent history in the United States, Artel writes:

> He visto perseguirlos como fieras,
> lincharlos,
> sin que importe su afiebrada queja
> ni su muerte en los pantanos. (p. 105)

> I have seen them hunted down like wild animals,
> lynched,
> with no importance given to their frantic cries
> nor to their deaths in the marshes.

In reading the black poetry of Jorge Artel we are struck by the poet's complete identification not only with the black past but with the black present as well because to Artel the experience for black people has always been the same, namely, characterized by suffering. And it is through recognition of and identification with this suffering that Artel, Colombian poet, establishes rapport with his race. This affinity is best summed up in the following lines from "Encuentro":

> Yo soy el que te busca tras la huella sangrante
>   *   *   *
> hoy en nuestro dolor sin limites te encuentro. (p. 105)

> I am the one who seeks you, following your trail of blood
>   *   *   *
> today in our infinite pain I find you.

Jorge Artel's poetry is a constant attack on the injustices committed against black people and a permanent and consistent forum for the expression of the black experience in the Americas. Though prepared to identify with America, this identification must be on black terms, for it is America in the black poetry of Artel that must admit, however reluctantly, the black presence and influence.

ARNOLDO PALACIOS

Even more poignant than Artel's black poetry is the account of the black experience in Colombia narrated by Arnoldo Palacios in his "naturalistic" novel *Las estrellas son negras* (1949, reprinted in 1971 in Bogotá, by Editorial Revista Colombiana), where he shows us in the harshest tone what it is like to be poor and black in that country. Born under "a black star . . . Black like me!" (p. 97), Irra, the black protagonist, is extremely color-conscious and sensitive to the plight of blacks. The novel is characterized by an acute preoccupation with this problem, particularly in the Chocó region of Colombia, where the action takes place. Though highly conscious of his race and the anguish, suffering, poverty, and misery that fill the lives of blacks, Palacios, like many other black writers in Latin America, recognizes that there are poor white people in the world also, carrying his concern in effect beyond race to the more general question of economic misery in the world. Palacios leaves little doubt, however, that the problems of the black man are compounded because of his color.

MANUEL ZAPATA OLIVELLA

Manuel Zapata Olivella (1920-) is one of the best-known black writers in Colombia, if not in the whole of Latin America. His work, like that of many of his black contemporaries, focuses to a great extent on the black experience and is deeply committed to recording the plight of his people as well as to being an instrument of social change. Novelist, social anthropologist, and musicologist, Manuel Zapata Olivella, the founder, director, and publisher of the literary monthly *Letras nacionales* (Bogotá), also holds a degree in medicine and is a practicing psychiatrist. He has traveled widely in Europe and the Americas where he has held several visiting professorships, most recently at the University of Kansas, the University of Toronto, and Howard University in Washington, D.C.

He is the author of several novels, plays, and stories, many of them dealing with the black experience in Colombia, but with an awareness of racial problems in other parts of the world. *Corral de negros* (Cuba: Casa de las Américas, 1963), for example, while dealing with the black slums of Chambacú, near Cartagena, recalls the civil-rights activists in the United States as the author dramatizes civil disobedience, political involvement, and revolution, if necessary, to bring about a better way of life for black people in Colombia. The social, racial, and humanitarian sensibilities of the author are seen in *Tierra mojada* (Madrid: Editorial Bullón, 1947), his first novel, thought by the ''master'' himself, as Zapata Olivella calls Ciro Alegría, who read it in manuscript form, to be one of the early contributions to the black novel in Spanish America, comparable to the poetry of Nicolás Guillén.

Though concerned with the plight of blacks and with the expression of his own African heritage, Manuel Zapata Olivella, like other Afro-Latin-American writers of this century, expresses a concern for the future of men of all colors who are victims of oppression, as evidenced in *Tierra mojada,* whose affinities with Alegría's *El mundo es ancho y ajeno* are obvious, especially the general theme of man's inhumanity to man. In this novel Zapata Olivella depicts the hardships of the Afro-Indo-Hispano rice growers of the Sinú Peninsula near Cartagena, and in other novels such as *Detrás del rostro* (Madrid: Aguilar, 1963), he aligns himself with the social outcasts in his country. It is in *Corral de negros,* however, where he best provides insights into the black experience in Colombia.

Máximo, perhaps the most important character in this novel, was a leader in the black community and had been jailed fourteen times for protest activities on behalf of his people. He refused to go to the Korean war; he would rather die than kill others with whom he had no quarrel. Máximo felt that black people should resist oppression; he wanted to instill pride in his people by showing them their obligation to rebel against their slave inheritance. Máximo was killed in a demonstration march demanding more jobs, schools, and homes for black people in Colombia. Perhaps more than any other character in modern Latin-American fiction, Máximo, in fact, is reminiscent of the revolutionary spirit that characterizes not only the black people in the United States today but civil-rights activists in the Third World in general.

Three Afro-Cuban Poets: Regino Pedroso, Marcelino Arozarena, and Nicolás Guillén

REGINO PEDROSO

Black themes have always been a constant in Colombian literature, and such black writers as Jorge Artel, Arnoldo Palacios, and Manuel Zapata Olivella, even Hugo Salazar Valdés and Juan Zapata Olivella, continue to be a force on the twentieth-century Colombian literary scene comparable to the well-known Cubans of African descent: Regino Pedroso, Marcelino Arozarena, and Nicolás Guillén. Regino Pedroso (1897-   ), who is partly of Chinese ancestry as well, is not, strictly speaking, a poet of the black experience in that his literary preoccupation with the plight of the black man largely is limited to one poem, "Hermano negro," one of the most quoted and anthologized poems written in Latin America on any subject. Though Pedroso has come to be known as a proletarian poet on the strength of several volumes of social poetry, his universal negritude and understanding of the black experience overshadow in "Hermano negro" his wider concern for oppressed people regardless of color. In this poem the poet's identification with his black brother is complete:

> Negro, hermano negro,
> tú estás en mí: ¡habla!
> Negro, hermano negro,
> Yo estoy en tí: ¡canta!
> tu voz está en mi voz,
> tu angustia está en mi voz,
> tu sangre está en mi voz . . .
> ¡también yo soy tu raza! . . .
>> (*Poemas* [La Habana: Ediciones
>> Unión, 1966], p. 98)

> Blackman, black brother,
> you are in me: speak!
> Blackman, black brother,
> I am in you: sing!
> your voice is in my voice,
> your anguish is in my voice,
> your blood is in my voice . . .
> I am of your race too!

Even though he recognizes that slavery, economic exploitation, hunger, racial prejudice, and bigotry have not succeeded in suppressing the black man's gift of song, dance, and rhythm, even when that song is one of sorrow, the poet is not satisfied with this joyful reaction of blacks to their anguish: he wants black people to realize that while he is laughing, singing, and dancing he is being taken advantage of; he wants the black man to develop social consciousness by realizing that he is

> bajo el prejuicio de la raza,
> hombre explotado. (p. 100)

> underneath this racial prejudice,
> an exploited man.

But most of all he wants his black brother in Cuba to

silencia un poco tus maracas.
Y aprende aquí
y mira allí
y escucha allá, en Scottsboro, en Scottsboro, en Scottsboro. (p. 100)

silence a little your maracas.
And learn here
and look there
and listen to what's going on in Scottsboro . . .

This is an idea he repeats for emphasis throughout the remainder of the poem and most emphatically in the final verse. After asking rhetorically:

¿No somos más que negros?
¿No somos más que jácara?
¿No somos más que rumba, lujurias negras y comparsas?
¿No somos más que mueca y color,
mueca y color? (p. 100)

Are we not more than blacks?
Are we not more than merry ballads?
Are we not more than rhumba, black lusts and masquerades?
Are we not more than grimace and color,
grimace and color?

Pedroso addresses himself to black people in Haiti, in Jamaica, in New York, in Havana, and arriving at the culminating message to which he has been building, he calls for a different reaction to the black experience. Using, as other black poets have done, the Scottsboro case as a rallying point for turning black attention to more serious affairs of race in the world, Pedroso advises black people:

> Da al mundo con tu angustia rebelde,
> tu humana voz . . .
> ¡y apaga un poco tus maracas! (p. 101)

> Give to the world with your rebel anguish,
> your human voice . . .
> and soften a little your maracas!

This verse, perhaps more than any other in the literature by writers of African descent in Latin America, has softened the drum beat enough so that the rebellious voice of black people can be heard both individually and along class lines in concert with the oppressed of other colors.

MARCELINO AROZARENA

The title of this chapter, "Black Song Without Color," is taken from the title that the Afro-Cuban Marcelino Arozarena (1912-   ) gave not only to one of his first poems written thirty years ago, but also to the only collection of verse he has published. *Canción negra sin color* (La Habana: Cuadernos Unión, 1966) contains poems Arozarena had written and published over the last thirty-five years. These poems, largely on the black experience, are remarkably consistent in their characteristic expressions of the poet's pride in his blackness and in his African heritage. This slim volume is an enlightening document not only of the black experience but also of the view a black poet takes on social revolution and the universal brotherhood of man.

In "Evohé," a poem reminiscent of Pedroso's "Hermano negro," even in its reference to the Scottsboro case, Arozarena, like Pedroso, counsels his black brothers to take a more serious attitude toward life, to stop dancing, singing, and smiling for the tourists, and to contemplate the significance of the injustices perpetrated against black people around the world. In this context Scottsboro, he suggested at that time, is more meaningful to the black experience than African gods such as Ogún:

> ¡Evohé!
>   suelta el bongó,
> no seas risa de turistas en rumbática secuencia:
>   *   *   *
> piensa un poco en SCOTTSBORO y no en Ogún. (p. 19)

Evohé!
  let the bongo go,
don't be the laughing stock of tourists with your interminable dancing:
*   *   *
think a little about SCOTTSBORO and not about Ogún.

In "Justicia," a short poem, the poet predicts a day of reckoning that will leave little doubt that all men are equal:

> Vendrán los tiempos
> de las reivindicaciones
> y, entonces,
> *   *   *
> Todos seremos iguales. (pp. 15-16)

> The time of vindication will come
> and, then,
> *   *   *
> We will all be equal.

It is this message of equality that characterizes Arozarena's "black song without color."

Arozarena is well-grounded in African and Afro-Cuban culture and rhythms, and such poems as "Caridá," "Liturgia etiópica," "Carnaval de Santiago," "Ensayando la comparsa del Maja," "Cumbele macumbele," "Bongó," "Amalia," "La conga," as well as the vocabulary and bibliography he provides, reveal this vast knowledge. Despite the strong African flavor of much of his verse, however, in poems like "Canción negra sin color," "Justicia," "Evohé," "Negramaticantillana," "La canción de las zafras," "Cubandalusía," and especially in "Ya vamos viendo," Arozarena reveals himself to be a poet explicitly concerned with larger questions of man such as those raised earlier by José Martí, who had written that *"Hombre es más que blanco, más que mulato, más que negro . . ."* ("Man is more than white, more than mulatto, more than black . . ."), words Arozarena used in 1960 as a lead-in to his poems where, in reference to one of Martí's poems, he writes:

> —sé que cubano es más—
> *   *   *
> ¡¡Humano ha de ser más!! (p. 46)

> —I know that a Cuban is more—
> *   *   *
> A human being has to be more!

Even a cradle song becomes serious with Arozarena. Mindful of Emilio Ballagas's "Canto para dormir a un negrito" and Guillén's "Canto para despertar a un negrito," Arozarena develops in his "Canto para impulsar a un negrito" (p. 34-39) a series of rhythms that, though pleasing to the ears of the young, convey more than beautiful and clever sounds. His cradle song, while playful in form, imparts a message of inspiration to the young black who one day will have to wake up to the realities of the black experience.

The introductory quotation to his collection of verse—which he titles "Solidaridad con Martín Fierro"—is taken from José Hernández's poem, *Martín Fierro,* and is designed to establish his solidarity with the Argentine poet who also sings *"opinando/que es mi modo de cantar"* (p. 9). It is from the very beginning of his literary career with "Canción negra sin color" that Arozarena sings his black song in *"la voz de todos"* (p. 11), a voice that tries to communicate to the world the essence of the black experience as the poet knows it. Arozarena, who proudly proclaims, *"SOMOS, aunque no quieran saber que SOMOS"* (p. 11), is a black poet, a defender of the black man and of the exploited worker.

NICOLÁS GUILLÉN

Finally, negritude in Latin America understood in a higher form of cultural and racial *mestizaje* perhaps is best illustrated in the poetry, testimony, and ideology of Nicolás Guillén, Cuba's national poet, who for many years has preached the synthesis or the realization of the universal man in an antiracist society where brotherhood rather than narrow racialism is sought.

Although he is Latin America's most eloquent spokesman for racial and cultural synthesis, social revolution, and universal justice, Guillén in the late twenties, even before the word negritude was coined, was urging blacks, in "Pequeña oda a un negro boxeador cubano," to flaunt their "black power" in the faces of envious whites and to talk to them "in real black talk"[26] Now a septuagenarian, Guillen has always been a leading exponent of the poetry of negritude as a reaction against white supremacy. In the thirties he was already treating the black woman with respect in such poems as "Mujer nueva," where he sees her:

> Coronada de palmas
> como uno diosa recién llegada.[27]

> Crowned with palms
> like a goddess recently arrived.

His poetry at that time was aimed at establishing a sense of decency, pride, and respect among blacks, and in poems such as ''Sabas'' and those in *Motivos de son* his approach, largely one of realism, derision, and shock therapy, was designed to focus attention on the black experience while decrying, sometimes with compassion, sometimes with sharp words, the penchant of some blacks to ape white ways and the inability of others to walk with dignity, to be proud of their color even in hard times. In ''Sabas'' he exhorts the black:

> Coge tu pan, pero no lo pidas;
> >   *   *   *
> Plántate en medio de la puerta,
> pero no con la mano abierta.[28]
>
> Take your bread, but don't beg for it;
> >   *   *   *
> Stand firm in the middle of the doorway,
> but not with your hand out.

In the 1970s Guillén is still the poet who, for example, defends the right of Martin Luther King to a ''black soul'' in the poem ''Qué color,'' a soul that is ''black as coal''[29] rather than the white one the Russian poet Yevtushenko would assign him. Simultaneously, however, this poet of black self-assertion characteristically reminds black people not to forget John Brown ''who was not Black and who defended you *fusil* in hand.''[30]

Despite poetic statements such as ''I am a black man,''[31] Guillén had managed throughout his life to transcend black racialism. While never denying his African past the poet of the negritude of synthesis proclaims himself to be a ''Cuban Yoruba,''[32] and in this way establishes his national Cuban identity, his identity as an Afro-American whose humanist values make him a universal man free in his color but in close solidarity with his brothers of all colors, particularly the oppressed. The popular poetry of Guillén, consistently social, revolutionary, and intensely human, is a poetry of *mestizaje*, integration, and racial equality. Throughout his life Guillén has composed poems that drive home his messages of black pride, of the mixture of races and cultures in Cuba, of the necessity of black and white to join hands. In countless poems such as ''Son número 6,''

"Balada de los dos abuelos," "Dos niños," "La muralla," "El apellido," "La canción del bongó," Guillén is just as much the poet of the negritude of synthesis as he is, often simultaneously, the poet of the negritude of racial affirmation. It is the larger vision, however, augmented greatly by his realization of the inevitable and undeniable fact of *mestizaje,* by the poet's identification with the white proletariat, and by the principles of a revolution based on a social rather than a racial conscience that Guillén, in the eyes of most observers, has seemed to evolve from a perspective of race to one of class. This is understandable in a country that proclaims itself unique in having created an atmosphere in which, we are to believe, strict racial identities are no longer recognized to be as important as the greater goal of a nonracial society ideally characterized by racial and cultural synthesis.

It is in this sense of synthesis, tolerance, and racial affirmation that Nicolás Guillén, for half a century, has set the pace for much of the literature by writers of African descent in Latin America. His vision, whether black or mestizo, has provided a standard to offset the white aesthetic and the models of whiteness against which black writers, artists, and intellectuals have had to react in Latin America. Their reactions, while confronting manifestations of white racism, have generally had as a final goal the ultimate achievement of a higher synthesis that is beyond racialisms of any color.

Quince Duncan and "Foreign" Black Literature in Costa Rica

The higher synthesis mentioned above, particularly on a practical level, is a characteristic of the literature of Quince Duncan, one of Central America's best-known black writers and perhaps the most recent black writer in Latin America to achieve recognition outside his country. Born in San José, Duncan, who is a fourth-generation black Costa Rican of Jamaican ancestry is that country's first black writer in this century to succeed in bringing the hopes, life styles, and problems of his people to the attention of a wider audience. This he has done not only through creative literature but in articles and essays as well.

It is unfortunate that black literary expression in Central America, particularly in Costa Rica and the Canal Zone, like the black population itself, is looked upon too often as "foreign" in that despite the early arrival of black slaves during the colonial period the great majority of blacks in the area are of West Indian heritage, descendants of pioneer laborers primarily brought over in more recent times to work on railroad construction, in the banana plantations, and to help in the building of the Panama Canal. These black descendants who have grown roots in their new environment which their labor has helped to construct, have been neglected, however, and their contributions minimized. Duncan deals with this problem of neglect as well as with the problem of identity, and his work is hailed by the Costa Rican national press as the product of a writer who is giving voice to a part of the country's ethnic mosaic that has not always been favorably treated.

A writer since the age of fourteen and a student winner of several literary prizes in his country Duncan, in addition to articles in various journals and magazines, published *El pozo y una carta* in 1969, *Bronce* and *Una canción en la madrugada* in 1970, his first novel, *Hombres Curtidos*, in 1971, and his most recent novel, *Los cuatro espejos*, in 1972, and, in collaboration with the historian Carlos Meléndez, *El negro en Costa Rica* in that same year. Duncan is an active participant on the Costa Rican literary scene where he also serves on editorial boards and directs literary magazines. He is a regular contributor as well to black cultural groups in the form of speeches and courses given on black culture and literature.

El negro en Costa Rica is the publication that breaks new ground. Duncan's contribution to the volume deals with the contemporary scene; his personal involvement with this recent history and his sensitive powers of observation help make this book a valuable source reference for future studies on the black in Costa Rica. It is especially significant because he identifies "the prejudice of having no prejudice" in Costa Rica and points out the desire of blacks there to develop their own ways but within the context of Costa Rican nationality, with the same rights and privileges as the country's whites. Blacks too, he holds, are members, too long marginal, of the larger Costa Rican society.

Duncan points toward integration in the larger Costa Rican society but on black terms as he insists, for example, that black culture be taught in schools to help correct the myth that only whites have a history. Duncan rejects the white aesthetic, the myth of white superiority. He hopes that other blacks, too, will rid themselves of the influence of the white aesthetic and begin to think of themselves in positive terms.

In his stories we have subtle and sometimes blunt allusions to the problems he discusses in his essays as well as the same insights into black life and customs. The Anglo-Caribbean background is reflected through the portrayal of black customs as well as through the use of the English language in words and idioms used by characters most often in exclamatory expressions provoked by undesirable conditions, frustrations, and resentments. In *Los cuatro espejos* we see through the eyes of Charles the Pastor the author's skepticism and impatience with black superstitions and other black practices that contribute to their own oppression and that, to the author, represent a danger equal to the concept of white superiority manifest in antiblack prejudices, especially against blacks from Limón who quite often have to confront the old myths of the black past.

Universal Song: Afro-Latin-American Literature and the Negritude of Synthesis.

Blacks in Latin America, secure in their self-worth and proud of their contributions in areas other than the emotionally charged rhythm of the dance, are prepared to move in the direction of the "human color, universal and one" of which Unamuno, I believe, has spoken. Although Senghor's position that emotion is "Negro" and reason exclusively "white" is untenable in Latin America, his hope for a "Civilization of the Universal," a dynamic synthesis of the cultural values of all civilizations, and his characterization of negritude as democracy quickened by the sense of communion and brotherhood between men nevertheless are valid in that part of the world.

In sum, black writers, artists, and intellectuals in Latin America have long pressed for equal acceptance of the African cultural heritage. Even when identifying with this heritage, however, there is little desire among the black intellectual community for a spiritual or physical return to Mother Africa. Rather, like Nicolás Guillén, Afro-Latin-American writers see themselves as an inextricable part of the American scene. From the earliest black figures in Latin-American literary history, such as José Vasconcelos (El Negrito Poeta) whose racial identification is strongly evident but who is firmly fixed in the Mexican nation, and Juan Manuel Manzano, the slave poet who longed for integration into Cuban society, to many of the Afro-Latin-American writers in the twentieth century, some of them mentioned in this chapter, black literary expression in Latin America, while focusing to a large extent on the black experience and the heritage of suffering, has at the same time emphasized the role and place of black people in the development and destiny of the New World.

Though blackness is still a handicap and though the target of resentment often is the white oppressor, black spokesmen in Latin America in the manner of Nicolás Guillén are proud of their African heritage but at the same time are prepared to identify with the downtrodden of other colors. The racial struggle, in short, is often interpreted as part of a social revolutionary struggle, not just against the white oppressor but against any oppression, injustice, and unnecessary suffering of humanity. In much of the literature by writers of African descent in Latin America man's inhumanity to man becomes the keynote. The question becomes good versus evil, justice versus injustice, with self-consciousness of race momentarily taking a back seat.

Mestizaje in Latin America has done much to validate the prediction of Sartre who, realizing that some black poets transcended race, had stated that the black struggle and negritude as the exaltation of blackness would give way to the proletarian struggle, suggesting, in effect, that the black song of black poets was destined to be one without color. Much like for Césaire, for Nicolás Guillén, and to a large extent for most Afro-Spanish-American writers, "beyond the black-skinned men of his race it is the battle of the world proletariat that is his song."[33]

In earlier times, because of the pressures of white racism, black men for the most part sang a colorless song, a "white" song controlled by the white aesthetic and for white approval. The black man in Latin America, though acutely aware that these pressures continue to exist, still sings a song without color but for very different reasons. His song now is a universal song, but, like that of Nicolás Guillén, it is one that is, nevertheless, fully black.

6

A Summation, with Conclusions

Credibility and a Summation of Terms

We have seen black themes in Latin-American literature written from white perspectives from the false tears of the antislavery romantics in the nineteenth century to the picturesque stereotypes of the false black poetry craze of the 1930s and 1940s; from the false black images in twentieth-century narrative fiction to the social revolutionary stance taken by some of the literary defenders of blacks in this same century. We have seen the concomitant development or metamorphosis of black writing from the controlled literary expression of black consciousness in the eighteenth and nineteenth centuries to the same social revolutionary stance of committed black writers in this century who, like Aimé Césaire, first became aware of their race only to carry their protest beyond race.

We have touched on some of the terms used to describe the heightened interest in the black in this century whose discovery takes different forms and is manifested in literature in different ways. And in this regard we should point out that the German scholar Janheinz Jahn[1] for several years now has been developing his theory of Neo-African literature which he defines as literature in any European language showing African stylistic features, content, or patterns of expression—Africanisms—written either by writers of African descent or by white writers.

Neo-African literature as defined by Jahn takes two significant forms in Latin America: Indigenism (not to be confused with *indigenismo*) and Negrism. The first, he holds, finds expression in prose, the second in poetry. Jahn uses *Ecué-Yamba-O,* the first novel of Alejo Carpentier, to illustrate the description of black folklore in prose. Limiting his Latin-American examples of Indigenism to this novel of Carpentier, Jahn moves on to Haiti, leaving the erroneous impression that such prose is scarce outside this French-speaking black republic.

We have seen that the Puerto Rican poet Luis Palés Matos provides a classic example of the second form: Poetic Negrism. A third sub-species of Neo-African literature according to Jahn is negritude, which he largely sees as a French language movement but which I believe to be developing in a higher form in the literary expression of several Afro-Latin-American writers, among them Nicolás Guillén, whom Jahn associates with Negrism. Guillén's conscientious efforts to move beyond the superficial, we have seen, sets him apart from Negrism, which unlike the negritude movement, served no revolutionary purpose.

Perhaps there is some common ground, some overlapping between negritude and what we have called the socio-negristic narrative in Latin America in that protest against racial discrimination, even the revolutionary element, is present, unlike in poetic negrism, which remained basically a white intellectual movement even though relying to a great extent on African stylistic features. Socio-negristic prose dealt with the social problems of the black in his struggle against prejudice and social degradation, and in some cases the artistic re-creation of black life was achieved as in Carpentier's *Ecué Yamba O,* which, though thoroughly folkloric (indigenistic), does not ignore the social side. The socio-negristic narrative, unlike poetic Negrism, was committed to the black but largely in a proletarian way. We have seen too that indigenism, to use Jahn's term, the socio-negristic narrative, poetic Negrism, and negritude in Latin America are all concerned with the African element but within the immediate locale.

However admirable this concern, we have seen that the literary image of blacks in indigenistic prose and negristic poetry in Latin America is often unfavorable. Despite the artistic achievement of some of this literature on black themes, the credibility of some of the white writers suffers because they project images of black people that are unrealistic when we consider the viewpoint they take toward black psychology. Many authors perpetuate stereotypes and myths when they seriously project, for example, singular images of black slaves as repugnant, docile, contented, and faithful, or when they characterize the black man tied to a simian past from which there is no escape, or when they adopt the one-dimensional image of the black woman as an amoral, uninhibited, sexual animal. That these and other images not too dissimilar to nineteenth-century racist beliefs are still being perpetuated in the twentieth century suggests that antiblack feelings and the degradation of black people in Latin-American literature have not changed much since such "classics" from the past century as *Sab, Cecilia Valdés,* and *María.*

Many of these novelists, as we have pointed out, are well-intentioned. But the caricatures and stereotypes remain. And generalizations, such as the inferiority of all black people, are advanced concerning the whole, based all too often on the interpretation of one individual. Many of these authors assume that blacks are inferior and expect their black characters to assume the same. Such assumptions could be expected in the nineteenth century when writers were just products of their times. Since then, however, the behavioral sciences have proven that races are not inherently superior or inferior. Some twentieth-century Latin-American writers who still exercise a nineteenth-century mentality on race apparently have not been convinced.

Many Latin-American authors have moved toward racial equality and have attempted to correct these misconceptions. But it would be misleading to infer that the image of blacks, even in twentieth-century Latin-American literature, is overwhelmingly positive. It has been said many times in the United States—most recently by Addison Gayle, Jr.[2]— that white writers are unable to portray the black authentically, that black truths can come only from black writers. Although there has been no research done on this question in Latin America, certain facts of the black experience, nevertheless, are clear. It is clear that many false tears were shed for the black man in the nineteenth-century antislavery novel. It is clear that most white practitioners of poetic Negrism were more interested in the exotic and primitive than in the man. And it is also clear that in modern Latin America there are authors and fictional characters who consider themselves superior to black people, subscribing in effect to Enrique López Albújar's theory that white people harbor ingrained reflexes of repulsion toward blacks conditioned, it would seem, by the somatic distance and by racist attitudes kept alive by a deeply rooted tendency to associate the black man with a past of slavery, servitude, and inferiority. Even in Latin America, apparently, "there will always be a world—a white world—between you and me. . . . The other's total inability to liquidate the past once and for all."[3]

The White Aesthetic and the Paradox of Color

The approach to blackness and to the problem of color in Latin America is, nevertheless, paradoxical. Since paradox deals with the unexpected, the contradictory, what better word to characterize the racial situation south of the border, where the realities of the black experience, contrary to expectation, often belie the myth that that area is a veritable paragon of enlightened relations among the races. We have seen that some nineteenth-century abolitionist writers were antiblack as well as antislavery. We have seen the black "discovered" in the late nineteenth century despite the racist climate of opinion prevalent at that time. And this discovery, which, paradoxically, was led by racist whites, did much, nevertheless, to reinstate the black as a literary subject, although not always with results in his favor. We have seen racism and color prejudice condemned by some authors and, on occasion, perpetuated by these same authors.

We have seen that miscegenation in Latin America brings black and white together, while working, at the same time, toward the gradual extinction of the black man, a process applauded by many. We have seen how the extreme race consciousness of some black and mulatto writers does not prevent their carrying their protests beyond race. And some writers with black blood even, paradoxically, share and perpetuate white racist opinions about black people. Enrique López Albújar in Peru, for example, though calling for interracial sex between whites and mulattoes, portrays the black slave as docile and contented; and Ramón Díaz Sánchez in Venezuela condemns the black man to extinction while favoring the mulatto. We have seen, too, the cases of Rubén Darío and Juan Montalvo to be exemplary of this paradoxical or ambivalent approach to color in Latin America where racist contradictions range from an open admission of black blood by one person to a corresponding rejection of the black man often by that same person.

Even Simón Bolívar, the Liberator, offers a fascinating example of ambivalent attitudes toward the problem of color in Latin America. Though influenced by military and political considerations Bolívar had a sincere abolitionist attitude based on humanitarian impulses. He believed further that the historical fact of miscegenation formed the very basis for the Spanish-American people's national existence. And he retained special affection for his "mother" Hipólita, the black woman who raised him in childhood.[4] But toward the end of his life, Mörner[5] tells us, Bolívar harbored contempt mixed with fear in regard to colored people, speaking of men of dark skin with noticeable disdain and distrust.

Such contradictory attitudes toward color are legion in the Hispanic world, where the tradition of caricature and the heritage of white racial consciousness run parallel to early and recent defenses of blacks. In her studies of the presence of Africa in Hispanic culture, Martha K. Cobb[6] explored the paradoxical tug of war surrounding the concept of the black personality in Spanish literature and history by tracing the increasingly more pronounced depiction of Africans as primitives, savages, and slaves; a depiction occasioned in part by the triumph of Christianity, the expulsion of the Moors from Spain in 1492, and the importation of slaves from Africa into Spain and the Americas. She traces the complete reversal of fortune of the black man's image by showing how the caricatures, myths, and stereotypes multiplied with the disappearance from Western consciousness of such blacks who had set their own standards of culture as the "erudite Ethiopians, fierce Moorish warriors, Black kings, knights, and saints, the mysterious Prester John . . ."[7] She observes that the advent of the Renaissance and the age of discovery and exploration led to the rejection of the African of the Medieval world who was destined to be replaced by a different image that must satisfy the economic needs demanded by the new age.[8] Tracing the literary reflection of these changes which revealed a duality in the concept of blackness, Professor Cobb demonstrates this paradoxical approach to blackness with illustrations, for example, from Quevedo whose "Bodas de negros" exaggerates, ridicules, and burlesques the blackness of a wedding party. On the other hand, in his "La hora de todos," she points out, Quevedo expresses compassion for black slaves in their unfortunate condition.[9]

Such were the paradoxical approaches toward blackness that were clearly carried over into the New World, and which were to be continued by Rubén Darío, by Juan Montalvo, and by a host of Latin-American writers. This ambivalent attitude toward blackness was complicated also by a further paradox of prejudice that fostered a double standard, one for the Indian and another for the black. Juan Montalvo's racist views toward blacks at times were devastating. He was, however paradoxically, an ardent defender of the Indian. The Peruvian José Carlos Mariátegui, like Montalvo, was also both a defender of the Indian and a racist toward blacks and Orientals. These two defenders of the Indian join a long Hispanic tradition of ambivalent racial attitudes toward the Indian and the black in the New World dating in part, some would conjecture, from Las Casas, the supreme defender of the Indian who held similar views toward Indians and blacks throughout much of his lifetime.

The ambivalent attitude in general can be seen against the

background surveyed in a "provocative little book" by Henri Baudet, who in *Paradise on Earth: Some Thoughts on European Images of Non-European Man* traces a broad fundamental ambivalence in the Europeans' feelings toward non-Western people from the birth of Europe in the "Mediterranean era" down to the present century. These feelings of the European, Baudet believes, are characterized by a feeling of superiority and hostility to the "barbarians" on the one hand and feelings of modesty, inferiority, and guilt on the other. When comparing himself unfavorably to certain non-European types, Baudet believes that the European discovers in them qualities which he very much admires and finds lacking in himself and his own civilization.[10] "Paradoxically, at the same time that Europe was conquering the world Europeans were peopling that world with noble savages and/or sages of superior insight and wisdom."[11] The point Baudet makes is that the Noble Indian, *le bon nègre,* and the Noble Oriental, though all exploited at one time or another by Europeans, have all been clothed again at one time or another with attributes which man had supposedly possessed in Paradise before the Fall: natural goodness, innocence, and physical beauty, freedom from the wickedness and suffering of "civilization".[12]

The double standard reflected in the attitudes toward Indians and blacks in particular, as well as similar attitudes toward blacks in general in Latin America are also commonplace in the United States, as Winthrop D. Jordan has shown in *White Over Black: American Attitudes Toward the Negro 1550-1812.* Professor Jordan uses Thomas Jefferson as the supreme example of the paradoxical attitude toward blacks. The most enlightened spirit of his time, Thomas Jefferson combined his heartfelt hostility to slavery with a deep conviction that blacks were inferior to whites. And, in discussing the double standard that allows the relative aesthetic acceptance of the Indian in the United States, Jordan concludes that "the Negroe's appearance remained a barrier to acceptance as the noble type".[13] This aesthetic difference between Indians and blacks in the United States as well as in Latin America is deeply rooted, as we have seen, in archetypal images of color that rate blackness the farthest distance away on the somatic scale.

This antiblack aesthetic, which affects even the well-off black in Latin America, has made the man on the black end of the color spectrum distant not only from white people but from mulattoes as well. Consequently, the image we get of the black man and of the mulatto in Latin-American literature almost always seem to revert back to the white aesthetic, the ultimate source of racial conflict whether between blacks and whites, mulattoes and whites, or mulattoes and blacks. A large percentage of the literature on black themes in Latin America is an exercise in self-flattery by white writers who emphasize in their writings how important they think it is to be white, or to have white intelligence—to see everything, in short, in their own image. Even some black people in Latin America have manifested a racial death-wish by wanting to be white and, like the mulatto who generally thinks he is white, have adopted the habits of white people; they measure themselves by these standards, by the white concept of beauty and values. This yearning after whiteness, which some say is always present in racist societies, is very much present in Latin America and in Latin-American literature.

This legacy from slavery, when black people identified whiteness with freedom, serves not only as an indication of tendencies toward self-hatred on the part of black people but more importantly as an additional confirmation of the existence and influence of the pressures of white racism in Spanish America. ''It has not been the black people who have created their own social and psychological degradation''—Calvin Hernton once wrote—''It has been the morality of the white world which has alienated black people from the beauty and the dignity of their blackness, their *ethos,* from life, liberty, and the pursuit of happiness.''[14] The somatic distance which carries with it the ennoblement of the mulatto *vis-à-vis* the black in Latin America, is responsible for much of this alienation of the black man. Small wonder that some black people emulate whiteness and become victims of what John Killens has called the ''Great Brainwash,''[15] the belief that the closer one is to white the better off one is in the eyes of The Man, the white man, that is.

Even in Latin America the obsession with color, which the literature reflects, makes people want to move as far from the black end of the color spectrum as possible. Even in Latin America it is considered denigrating to marry someone darker than oneself.[16] Even in Latin America the tendencies toward self-hatred coupled with the cult of whiteness have bred a mentality on race not too unlike the one that dominated in the United States before the advent of black pride and black power. In Latin America people with dark skin often, it seems, prefer to hint at Indian rather than African ancestry.[17] Even though the mulatto might be the wave of the future for some Latin-American writers, even though the mulatto woman conveys for some writers the essence of Latin-American civilization itself, even though having black blood does not disqualify a person from high public office, even though interracial marriages are not out of the question, in Latin America it is still not good racial and social policy to have *too much* black blood; or, put another way, it is quite all right to have some black blood in Latin America, as long as it does not show.

The need, then, for demystification, but demystification in a double sense, namely, a rejection of the white racial mystique associated with the white aesthetic and a rejection of the more mystical aspects of negritude in favor of a more realistic emphasis on the racial, cultural, and historical realities of the black experience, past, present, and future in the New World. A rejection, in short, of the concepts of ''chosen races'', of racial mysticisms of all colors.

We may conclude, then, by saying that despite the white aesthetic with its unfortunate racist ramifications, the ultimate paradox of color in Latin America can be seen in this development of negritude away from or beyond a narrow racialism anchored in black pride and toward a negritude of synthesis, a metamorphosis that while using race and race pride as a point of departure, leads toward a society in which all such racialisms, paradoxically or ideally, can ultimately be put aside as unnecessary.

Notes

Introduction

1. Richard L. Jackson, "An Underdeveloped Area," *Hispania* 48 (1965): 870

2. Juan Comas, "Latin America," in *Research on Race Relations* (Paris: UNESCO, 1966). A modified version of this study is included in his recently published *Antropología de los pueblos iberoamericanos* (Barcelona: Editorial Labor, S.A., 1974).

3. *Race Mixture in the History of Latin America* (Boston: Little, Brown and Co., 1967).

4. *The Two Variants in Caribbean Race Relations: A Contribution to the Sociology of Segmented Societies*, translated by Eva M. Hooykaas from the Dutch (London: Oxford University Press, 1967), pp. 120, 121. Also see Hoetink's "The Dominican Republic in the Nineteenth Century: Some Notes on Stratification, Immigration and Race," in Magnus Mörner, ed., *Race and Class in Latin America* (New York: Columbia University Press, 1970), pp. 96-121, and Hoetink's "National Identity, Culture, and Race in the Caribbean," in John Q. Cambell, ed., *Racial Tensions and National Identity* (Nashville: Vanderbilt University Press, 1972), pp. 17-44. For other recent comparative studies see Michael Banton, *Race Relations* (London: Tavistock, 1967); John Hope Franklin, ed., *Color and Race,* (Boston: Houghton Mifflin, 1968); Melvin M. Turnin, ed., *Comparative Perspectives on Race Relations,* (Boston: Little, Brown, 1969); Carl Degler, *Neither Black nor White: Slavery and Race Relations in Brazil and the United States* (New York: MacMillan, 1971); Marvin Harris, *Patterns of Race in the Americas* (New York: Walker and Co., 1964); Mörner, ed., *Race and Class in Latin America,* Pierre Van den Berghe, *Race and Racism, A Comparative Perspective* (New York: Wiley and Son, 1967).

5. Hoetink, *The Two Variants in Caribbean Race Relations,* p. 153.

6. "Cultural Strangulation: Black Literature and the White Aesthetic," in Addison Gayle, Jr., ed., *The Black Aesthetic,* (New York: Doubleday, 1971), p. 40.

7. "Historical Research on Race Relations in Latin America during the National Period," in Mörner, *Race and Class in Latin America,* p. 225.

8. *MIA Newsletter,* February, 1974, p. 2. Even as recent a history of Latin American literature as Rudolf Grossmann, *Historia y problemas de la literatura latinoamericana* (Madrid: Revista de Occidente, 1972), contains blatantly racist opinions which quite justifiably have been singled out and blasted by Roberto Fernández Retamar in "Algunos problemas teóricos de la literatura hispanoamericana," *Casa de las Américas,* no. 89 (1975): 134-135.

9. "Estereótipos de negros através de Literatura Brasileira," *Boletin de Sociologia* (São Paulo), No. 3 (1953): 9-27.

10. *O negro na ficção brasileiro* (Rio de Janeiro: Edições Tempo Brasileiro, 1965) and "Negro Themes and Characters in Brazilian Literature," *African Forum* 2 (Spring 1967): 20-34.

11. *Negritude as a Theme in the Poetry of the Portuguese-Speaking World* (Gainesville: University of Florida Press, 1970).

12. "Abolitionism in Brazil: Anti-Slavery and Anti-Slave," *Luso-Brazilian Review* (Winter 1972): 30-36.

13. *Black Skin, White Masks* (New York: Grove Press, Inc., 1967), p. 188.

14. There are numerous studies and anthologies of "black poetry," from the early essays written in the thirties and forties by E. Ballagas, R. Guirao, F. Ortiz, J. Juan Arróm, etc., some reprinted by Oscar Fernández de la Vega and Alberto N. Pamies in their *Iniciación a la poesía afroamericana* (Miami: Ediciones Universal, 1973), the lead-off volume in their welcome new series "Colección Ebano y Canela," to the important work by G. R. Coulthard in the fifties and

sixties, *Raza y color en la literatura antillana* (Seville: Universidad de Sevilla, 1958), *Race and Colour in Caribbean Literature* (London: Oxford University Press, 1962), "Antecedentes de la negritud en la literatura hispanoamericana," *Mundo Nuevo,* No. 11 (May 1967), pp. 73-77. A recent rash of publications include, in addition to the abovementioned *Iniciación a la poesía afroamericana,* Wilfred Cartey, *Black Images* (New York: Teachers College Press, 1970), Rosa E. Valdés-Cruz, *La poesía negroide en América* (New York: Las Américas Publishing Co., 1970), Ildefonso Pereda Valdés, *Lo negro y lo mulato en la poesía cubana* (Uruguay: Ediciones Ciudadela, 1970), Hortensia Ruiz del Vizo, *Black Poetry of the Americas (A Bilingual Anthology)* (Miami: Ediciones Universal, 1972); Enrique Noble, *Literatura afro-hispanoamericana: Poesía y prosa de ficción* (Toronto: Xerox College Publishing, 1973), and Mónica Mansour, *La poesía negrista* (Mexico, D. F.: Ediciones Era, 1973). Some of these recent works deal in part with "black poetry" outside of the Caribbean as well. Several articles and doctoral dissertations are beginning to appear on black themes and Afro-Spanish-American authors on the mainland, the following studies among them: Barry Amis, "The Negro in the Colombian Novel," (Ph.D. diss., Michigan State University, 1970); Antonio F. Anillo, "La novelística comprometida de Manuel Zapata Olivella," (Ph.D. diss., George Washington University, 1972); Richard Paul Doerr, "La magia como dinámica de evasión en la novelística de Manuel Zapata Olivella," (Ph.D. diss., University of Colorado, 1973); Martha L. Canfield, "Los precursores de la poesía negra," *Razón y Fábula,* No. 21 (Sept.-Oct. 1970): 13-26; Martha K. Cobb, "Africa in Latin America, Customs, Culture, and Literature," *Black World* 21, No. 10 (Aug. 1972): 4-19. Sister Rose Teresa Amor in "Afro-Cuban Folktales as Incorporated into the Literary Tradition of Cuba," (Ph.D. diss., Columbia University, 1969), studied the literary value of black folktales, myths, and legends that black slaves brought to Cuba from Africa. She correctly observed that, in view of current interest in the black heritage, Afro-Cuban folktales collected largely by Lydia Cabrera, Rómulo Lachatañaré, and Ramón Guirao (and, I would add, similar material in Ecuador, Colombia, Venezuela, and the Río de la Plata area, for example) offer much material for future study and analysis. Since then, two recent studies have appeared: Hilda Perera, *Idapo: El sincretismo en los cuentos de Lydia Cabrera* (Miami: Ediciones Universal, 1971), and Rosa Valdés-Cruz, *Lo ancestral africano en la narrativa de Lydia Cabrera* (Barcelona: Editorial Vosgos, S. A., 1974). Also see Stanley Cyrus, *El cuento negrista sudamericano. Antología* (Quito: Editorial Casa de la Cultura Ecuatoriana, 1973).

Chapter 1

1. Martha K. Cobb, "Africa in Latin America: Customs, Culture, Literature," *Black World* 21, No. 10 (Aug. 1972): 6.

2. Abdias do Nascimento, *Cadernos Brasileiros* 10, No. 47 (May-June 1968): 5; and "The Negro Theatre in Brazil," *African Forum* 2 (Spring 1967): 44.

3. Abdias do Nascimento, "Afro-Brazilian Culture," *Black Images* 1, Nos. 3 and 4 (Autumn and Winter 1972): 42.

4. Hoetink, "The Dominican Republic in the Nineteenth Century," p. 117.

5. Ibid.

6. His principal work is *De Instauranda Aethiopum Salute: El mundo de la esclavitud negra en América* (Seville, 1927), reprinted by the Empresa Nacional in Bogotá, Colombia, in 1956.

7. "No nos queda más que un remedio: blanquear, blanquear, y entonces, hacernos respetar." See Fernando Ortiz, "José Antonio Saco y sus ideas," *Revista Bimestre Cubana* 2 (1929): 40-45.

8. Hoetink, *The Two Variants in Caribbean Race Relations,* p. 186.

9. Ibid., pp. 186-87.

10. Richard Pattee, "Latin America Shows Us Up," *Negro Digest* 2 (1944): 70.

11. Juan Comas, "Latin America," p. 150.

12. H. Hoetink, *Slavery and Race Relations in the Americas* (New York: Harper and Row, 1973), p. 114.

13. Barry Reckord, *Does Fidel Eat More than Your Father? Conversations in Cuba* (New York: The New American Library, 1971), pp. 118-19.

14. David Brian Davis, *The Problem of Slavery in Western Culture* (Ithaca, New York: Cornell University Press, 1966), p. 275.

15. Hoetink, *Slavery and Race Relations in America,* p. 156.

16. Roger Bastide, "Variations on Négritude," in Albert H. Berrian and Richard A. Long, eds., *Négritude: Essays and Studies* (Hampton, Virginia: Hampton Institute Press, 1967), p. 71.

17. Reported by H. Hoetink in *The Two Variants in Caribbean Race Relationships,* p. 171.

18. Ibid.

19. Gil Green, *Revolution Cuban Style* (New York: International Publishers, 1970), pp. 90-94.

20. Oracy Nogueira, "Skin Color and Social Class," in Vera Rubin, ed., *Plantation Systems in the New World* (Washington, D.C.: Pan American Union, 1959), pp. 164-79. "Nogueira's distinction has little relevance in the case of people with darker skins. The prejudice against the 'pure' Negro in Brazil as well as in the United States is a prejudice of origin and of mark." H. Hoetink, *The Two Variants in Caribbean Race Relations,* p. 53.

21. Juan Comas, "Latin America," p. 150.

22. H. Hoetink, *Slavery and Race Relations in the Americas,* p. 114.

23. Magnus Mörner, *Race Mixture in the History of Latin America* (Boston: Little, Brown and Co., 1967), pp. 72-73.

24. See his two books, *The Two Variants in Caribbean Race Relations* and *Slavery and Race Relations in the Americas.*

25. Nogueira, "Skin Color and Social Class," p. 171.

26. Ibid., p. 177.

27. Ann Cook, "Black Pride—Some Contradictions," *Negro Digest* 19 (February 1970): 36-42, 59-63.

28. Ibid., p. 40.

29. Ibid., p. 41.

30. This play is available in the MacMillan Modern Spanish American Literature Series.

31. Stuart Schwartz, "Cities of Empire: Mexico and Bahia in the Sixteenth Century," *Journal of Inter-American Studies* 11 (1969): 628, quoted in Frederick P. Bowser, "Colonial Spanish America," in *Neither Slave nor Free: The Freedman of African Descent in the Slave Societies of the New World,* with an introduction by David W. Cohen and Jack P. Greene (Baltimore and London: The Johns Hopkins University Press, 1972), p. 56.

32. Bowser, "Colonial Spanish America" p. 58.

33. Ibid., p. 55. There are increasing signs that light-skinned blacks are identifying more closely with their darker brothers in Latin America. These signs have been recognized by Antonio Olliz Boyd, "The Concept of Black Esthetics as seen in Selected Works of Three Latin American Writers: Machado de Assis, Nicolás Guillén and Adalberto Ortiz." Ph.D. diss., Stanford University, 1974; Cleveland Donald Jr., "Equality in Brazil: Confronting Reality" *Black World* 22, No. 1 (November 1972): 23-34, and Carlos Miguel Suárez Rodillo, "El negro y su encuentro de si mismo a través del teatro," *Cuadernos Hispanoamericanos,* no. 271 (January 1973): 34-49. Ironically, these signs appear at the same time as the following curious and perhaps serious suggestion made by Ronald Mirando of Los Angeles, California, who advises light-skinned blacks in the U.S. to "arabize" or "latinize" their names and identify with mixed bloods in Latin America and the Arab countries. He reasons:

> Mestizoes and near-whites could never develop a sense of shame or have negative identity problems in Latin-American countries because these groups comprise the numerical majority of the population. Wide-scale miscegenation in the Latin and also Arab countries and Pakistan has resulted in a mixed-blood and near-white numerical majority.

The *mestizo* occupies a dignified and respected social, economic and political position. No social-race-caste system exists in Latin America as in the United States. Mestizoes enjoy social flexibility in intermingling and intermarrying with both blacks and whites and among themselves.

To achieve a more positive identity, the U.S. light-skinned "black" should consider identifying with the predominantly mixed-blood (biologically speaking) Latin-American and Arab countries. To strengthen this identification, the light-skinned U.S. "black" should learn to speak Spanish, Portuguese or Arabic. Extensive travel and knowledge of the culture, customs, etc. of the Latin and Arab countries and perhaps "Hispanizing" or "Arabizing" our names would further strengthen this positive identity.

The U.S. light-skinned "black" should observe other mixed-blood groups in this country, such as the Puerto Ricans, Chicanos, Hawaiians, Arabs, Portuguese, Cape Verdians, etc., and see the pride they have in their color and "mixed" racial ancestry. The light-skinned "black" can never achieve a healthy self-respect by identifying with "white" Europe and America or "black" Africa and the "black" non-Hispanic Caribbean. (*Ebony,* May 1975, pp. 10, 12)

This modern identity problem is further compounded by the words of Carmelo Romero of Chicago who asks:

. . . why is it that many of us when in the States are unwilling to publicly admit that we are Black? My answer is that many of us are afraid of being identified with Afro-Americans and don't want to be subject to the same type of disrespect and hatred. Many of my Black Puerto Rican brothers and sisters fail to realize that no matter how light our skin or how many languages we speak, whites see us as niggers.

Some Afro-Puerto Ricans are bewildered by America's racist practices, implying that Puerto Rico is free of racism. Not true. The caste system that developed on the island during slavery relegated "pure" Blacks to menial roles, mulattoes to overseer roles and left the major control of the island's life to whites and octoroons. The remainders of that system are still evident.

                                           *   *   *

African-Latino identity is becoming an important issue as more of us become involved in shaping our communities here and at home. African-Latinos should closely watch the policies of the various Latino organizations to make sure the groups don't exhibit any anti-African tendencies. As African people, our responsibilities are to Africa and her people, no matter where in the world we are found. (*Essence,* October 1975, p. 76)

34. C. Eric Lincoln, *Sounds of the Struggle* (New York: William Morrow and Co., Inc., 1970), p. 212.

35. Ibid.

36. "Black is Beautiful, but How About Light Blacks?" *Jet,* June 1, 1972, pp. 30-31.

37. "The Pleasure and Problem of the 'Pretty' Black Man," *Ebony* 29, No. 11 (Sept. 1974): 138.

38. See Carlos Meléndez and Quince Duncan, *El negro en Costa Rica* (San José, Editorial Costa Rica, 1972).

39. Mörner, *Race Mixture in the History of Latin America,* p. 20.

40. Ildefonso Pereda Valdés, *El negro en el Uruguay* (Montevideo: Revista del Instituto Histórico y Geográfico del Uruguay, 1965), pp. 203, 205.

41. See Thomas Blair, "Mouvements afro-brasiliens de libération de la période esclavagiste à nos jours," *Présence Africaine* 19 (1945): 96-101. Also see Florestan Fernandes's chapter on black civil rights and social movements in Brazil in *The Negro in Brazilian Society* (New York: Columbia University Press, 1969), pp. 187-233.

42. *Veja,* January 13, 1971, cited in Anani Dzidzienyo, *The Position of Blacks in Brazilian Society* (London: Minority Rights Group Report No. 7, 1971), p. 18.

43. Frederic M. Litto, "Some Notes on Brazil's Black Theatre," in Lloyd W. Brown, ed., *The Black Writer in Africa and the Americas* (Los Angeles: Hennessey and Ingalls, Inc., 1973), p. 215.

44. Abdias do Nascimento, "The Negro Theatre in Brazil," *African Forum* 2 (Spring 1967): 44.

45. Roger Bastide, "Variations on Négritude," p. 73.

46. Abdias do Nascimento, *Dramas para Negros, Prólogo para brancos* (Rio de Janeiro: Teatro Experimental do Negro, 1961), p. 21. Quoted by Richard A. Prêto-Rodas, in "The Development of Négritude in the Poetry of the Portuguese Speaking World," Edward D. Terry, ed., *Artists and Writers in the Evolution of Latin America* (University, Alabama: University of Alabama Press, 1969), p. 59.

47. Abdias do Nascimento, "The Negro Theatre in Brazil," p. 43.

48. In Lee Lockwood, *Conversations with Eldridge Cleaver, Algiers* (New York: Dell Publishing Co., 1970), p. 19; Eldridge Cleaver, "Fidel Castro's African Gambit," *Newsweek*, May 3, 1976, p. 13.

49. Abdias do Nascimento, "Afro-Brazilian Culture," p. 42.

50. Pepe Carril, *Shango de Ima: A Yoruba Mystery Play*, English adaptation by Susan Sherman, introduction by Jerome Rothenberg and Edward James (Garden City, New York: Doubleday and Co., Inc., 1970), p. 28.

51. Ibid., italics in the original.

52. Haberly, "Abolitionism in Brazil," p. 45.

53. A phrase used by Anani Dzidzienyo in *The Position of Blacks in Brazilian Society*, p. 5.

54. "Afro-Brazilian Culture," p. 42.

55. Carlos Meléndez and Quince Duncan, *El negro en Costa Rica*, p. 125.

56. Samuel Betances, "The Prejudice of Having no Prejudice," Part I, in *The Rican, A Journal of Contemporary Puerto Rican Thought*, No. 2 (Winter 1972): 41-54 and Part II in No. 3 (Spring 1972): 22-37.

57. For a discussion primarily of the historical example of the explosion of black identity set in motion by the Haitian Revolution that began in 1794, contrasted with the recent experience of the Duvalier regime, and of the positive example of the Cuban Revolution, see René Depestre, "Problemas de la identidad del hombre negro en las literaturas antillanas," *Diez años de la Revista Casa de las Américas 1960-1970*, No. 31 (July-August 1965): 51-59.

Chapter 2

1. Gertrudis Gómez de Avellaneda, *Sab* (La Habana: Editorial Nacional de Cuba, 1963), p. 18.

2. Ibid., pp. 65-66.

3. Raymond S. Sayers, *The Negro in Brazilian Literature* (New York: Hispanic Institute in the United States, 1956), p. 27.

4. Aphra Behn, *Oroonoko or, the Royal Slave* (New York: W. W. Norton and Company, 1973), p. 8.

5. Henri Baudet, *Paradise on Earth: Some Thoughts on European Images of Non-European Man* (New Haven: Yale University Press, 1965), p. 30.

6. Reported in José A. Fernández de Castro, *Tema negro en la literatura cubana* (La Habana: El Mirador, 1943), p. 40. Also see Gertrudis Gómez de Avellaneda, *Sab*, prólogo y notas de Mary Cruz (La Habana: Instituto Cubano del Libro, 1973), p. 43.

7. Cirilo Villaverde, *Cecilia Valdés o la loma del ángel* (New York: Las Américas Publishing Co., 1964), p. 96.

8. For a discussion of the characteristics of "resignación y mansedumbre cristianas," which Anselmo y Suárez attributes to Francisco, see his letter reproduced in Anselmo Suárez y Romero,

Francisco: el Ingenio o las Delicias del Campo (Miami: Mnemosyne Publishing Co., 1969), p. 14.

9. Reported in *Homenaje a S. Zavala: Estudios históricos americanos* (Mexico, D. F., 1953), p. 260.

10. Jorge Isaacs, *María* (Buenos Aires: Editorial Sopena, 1938), p. 117.

11. Concha Melélendez, "El arte de Jorge Isaacs en *María*," in her *Figuración de Puerto Rico* (San Juan: Instituto de Cultura Puertorriqueña, 1958), p. 115.

Chapter 3

1. Mörner, "Historical Research on Race Relations," p. 224.

2. Reported in Mörner, *Race Mixture in the History of Latin America*, p. 141.

3. *In Quest of Identity* (Chapel Hill: University of North Carolina Press, 1967), pp. 12-33.

4. Mörner, *Race Mixture in the History of Latin America*, pp. 139-42.

5. Ibid., p. 142, and idem, *Race and Class in Latin America*, p. 225.

6. See, for example, Gastón Baquero, *Darío, Cernuda, y otros temas poéticos* (Madrid: Editora Nacional, 1969), p. 215.

7. *The Modern Culture of Latin America: Society and the Artist* (London: Pall Mall Press, 1967), p. 103.

8. See Seymour Menton, "In Search of a Nation," *Hispania* 38 (December 1955): 432-42.

9. Mónica Mansour (*La poesía negrista*, Mexico, D. F.: Ediciones Era, 1973) has written: "Nevertheless, it is interesting to point out that even Martí—perhaps without realizing it—reflects in his writings traditional prejudices against blacks, even though he attributes these characteristics to historical reasons. He says, for example, that the free black will be able to overcome the primitive characteristics that they have inherited from African savages." She points out that despite his great concern for human rights, "Martí refers to blacks through the eyes of western civilization; that is, from the outside. He insists on equality between the races; nevertheless, he accepts the traditional stereotypes of the black as child-like and primitive." (pp. 108-9)

10. "The Historical Background of Race Relations in the Caribbean," *Miscelánea de estudios dedicados a Fernando Ortiz* 3 (Havana: Ucor, García, S.A., 1957): 1580.

11. Quoted in Franz Fanon, *Black Skin, White Masks* (New York: Grove Press, Inc., 1967), p. 199.

12. Phrase used by Gastón Baquero, *Darío, Cernuda, y otros temas poéticos:* "All of those studies on drums that nobody plays any more, on religions that people no longer practice, only lead to perpetual Africanization of the Hispanic American black." (p. 213)

13. Mörner, *Race and Class in Latin America*, p. 227. See also in ibid., O. Ianni, "Research on Race Relations in Brazil," p. 258.

14. Baquero, *Dario, Cernuda, y otros temas poéticos,* p. 213.

15. See Cartey, *Black Images,* p. 130.

16. Ibid.

17. There are several studies and anthologies available on the black in the literature of Spain in the Golden Age and before. See the titles in note 14 in the Introduction, especially Cartey's chapter: "Ethnic Preludes," in *Black Images*, pp. 1-38. Also see, for example, Alma C. Allan, "Literary Relations between Spain and Africa: An Introductory Statement," *Journal of Negro History* 50 (April 1965): 97-105; E. Ballagas, *Mapa de la poesía negra americana* (Buenos Aires: Editorial Pleamar, 1946); Horacio Jorge Becco, *El tema del negro en cantos, bailes y villancicos de los siglos XVI y XVII* (Buenos Aires: Editorial Ollantay, 1951); John Brooks, "Slavery and the Slave in the Works of Lope de Vega," *Romanic Review* 19, No. 3 (1928): 232-43; Juan R. Castellano, "El negro esclavo en el entremés del Siglo de Oro," *Hispania* 44, No. 1 (March 1961): 55-65; Américo Castro, "Los esclavos libres de Lope de Vega," *Revista de Filología*

Española (Madrid) 6 (1919): 308-309; Edmund de Chasca, "The Phonology of the Speech of the Negroes in Early Spanish Drama," *Hispanic Review* 14 (1946): 322-39; A. V. Ebersole, " 'Black is Beautiful' in Seventeenth Century Spain," *Romance Notes* 12, No. 2 (Spring 1971): 387-91; Howard M. Jason, "The Negro in Spanish Literature to the End of Siglo de Oro," *College Language Association Journal* 9, No. 2 (December 1965): 121-31; Rafael Marquina, "The Negro in the Spanish Theatre before Lope de Vega," *Phylon* 4 (1943): 147-52; Luis Monguió, "El negro en algunos poetas españoles y americanos anteriores a 1800," *Estudios sobre literatura hispanoamericana y española* (Mexico, D. F., 1958): 43-57, and in *Revista Iberoamericana* 44, No. 22 (July/December 1957): 245-59; Luis Morales Oliver, *Africa en la literatura española,* 3 vols., Madrid: Consejo Superior de Investigaciones Científicas, 1957); Fernando Ortiz, "The Negro in the Spanish Theatre," *Phylon* 4 (1943): 144-47; Ildefonso Pereda Valdés, "Contribución al estudio del tema del negro en la literatura castellana hasta fines de la Edad de Oro," *El negro rioplatense y otros ensayos* (Montevideo: Claudio García y Cía., 1937); Margaret Sampson, "Africa in Medieval Spanish Literature: Its Appearance in *El Caballero Cifar,*" *Negro History Bulletin* 32 (December 1969): 14-19; J. Sanz y Díaz, *Lira negra: Selecciones españolas y afroamericanas* (Madrid: Aguilar, 1962); Raymond S. Sayers, "Introduction: The Negro in the Literature of the Iberian Peninsula," in his book in the United States, *The Negro in Brazilian Literature* (New York: Hispanic Institute, 1956), pp. 15-32; F. Weber de Kuriat, "Sobre el negro como tipo cómico en el teatro español del siglo XVI," *Romance Philology* 17, No. 63 (Nov. 1963): 380-91; William E. Wilson, "Some Notes on Slavery during the Golden Age," *Hispanic Review* 7 (1939): 171-74; and Carter G. Woodson, "Attitudes of the Iberian Peninsula," *The Journal of Negro History* 20, No. 2 (April 1935): 190-243.

18. *The Devil, the Gargoyle and the Buffoon: The Negro as Metaphor in Western Literature* (Port Washington, New York: Kennikat Press, 1969).

19. Ibid., p. 78.

20. Fernando Ortiz, "Más acerca de la poesía mulata. Escorzos para su estudio," *Revista Bimestre Cubana* 37, No. 1 (January-February 1936): 23-39.

21. "La lengua de la poesía afrocubana," *Español actual,* No. 7 (May 1, 1967): 1-3. Also see his book: *Estudio sobre el español de Cuba* (New York: Las Américas Publishing Co., 1971), p. 67. Mónica Mansour (*La poesía negrista,* México: Ediciones Era, 1973), reinforces her point, namely, that José Martí "condemns the imitation of the dialect or badly pronounced Spanish of the black," by quoting (p. 109) the following relevant passage from F. Fanon:

> Yes, the black must be a "good Negro"; once this is established, the rest comes easy! To have him speaking in dialect is to tie him to an image, imprisoning him in it, making him a permanent victim of an *appearance* for which he is not responsible." *Peau noire, masques blancs* (Paris: Ed. Seuil, 1952), p. 47

22. Reprinted in Angel Rosenblat, *Lengua literaria y lengua popular en América* (Caracas: Universidad Central de Venezuela, 1969), p. 67.

23. "El hombre blanco en la poesía negra," *Lotería* 4, No. 44 (June 1959): 139.

24. Bernardo Arias Trujillo, *Risaralda* (Medellín: Editorial Bedout, 1960), pp. 38-40.

25. Enriqueta, "la gran negra," of Zalamea Borda's *Cuatro años a bordo de mí mismo* (Bogotá: Organización Continental de los Festivales del Libro, n.d.), for example, takes center stage:

> Her eyes shine from the light and from too much drink. She begins to move her body, imperceptibly, from her head to her waist. . . . Movement runs through her body from her naked round shoulders to her firm belly; . . . Her hips move like waves under control, . . . (p. 100)

There is a black dance in *Juyungo,* and in Xavier Icaza's *Panchito Chapopote,* Porfiriata appears periodically throughout the story to dance his *rumba.* Asturias in *Los ojos de los enterrados* (Buenos Aires: Losada, 1961) has joined the sensual portrayal of black dance: "Chombo, the black Panamanian, and a black woman with a whining voice with slow, silent movement not so much to dance as to rub against each other, to rub against each other . . . The black woman laughed . . . For a while she danced not on her feet but with her breasts on the chest of the black man." (p. 275) And special note should also be taken of Tomás Carrasquilla's description of the Mapale dance in *La Marquesa de Yolombó* (in *Obras completas* [Medellín: Bedout, 1958]):

> The hips shake in a convulsive movement; breasts tremble as though they were gelatin. Mouths pant; bodies twist, glistening with sweat; eyes, rings, and necklaces glitter. Bodies come together in a spasmodic embrace; . . . It is a fragment of that Africa far away, that they carry in their blood and that their eyes have never seen. (pp. 65-66)

26. *¡¡Oh, mío Yemayá!!* (Manzanillo, Cuba: Editorial "El Arte," 1938), p. xxix. In Tomás Carrasquilla's *La Marquesa de Yolombó,* voodoo and witchcraft taught the Marquesa by a black servant brought about her downfall. Witchcraft appears in the form of a love potion in Ordóñez Argüello's *Ebano.* In *Luna verde* by Joaquín Beleño C., a black attributes his rejection by a white girl to witchcraft, and in *Gamboa Road Gang,* by the same author, witchcraft is thought responsible for the headaches and nightmares suffered by a white girl who had denounced an innocent black man. *Cumboto* by Ramón Díaz Sánchez is fully represented with black superstition, witchcraft, and magical rituals. Gerardo Gallego's *El embrujo de Haití* deals with witchcraft, voodoo doctors, and spells cast for various reasons; there are also descriptions of voodoo rites, black rituals, and superstition in his *Beau Dondón conquista un mundo.* Among the stories of Manuel Díaz Rodríguez there is "Las ovejas y las rosas del padre Serafín," which includes a black man who was hanged because he was suspected of murder and of practicing witchcraft. And among other examples there is *Pobre negro* of Rómulo Gallegos, whose portrayal of black witchcraft, superstition, religious ceremonies, folktales, songs, and dances are well known. Set in Barlovento, blacks here, for example, wear amulets and charms to ward off evil spirits.

27. J. Pablo Sojo, *Temas y apuntes afro-venezolanos* (Caracas: Cuadernos Literarios de la Asociación de Escritores Venezolanos, 1943), p. 39.

28. Arturo Uslar Pietri, *Las lanzas coloradas* (Buenos Aires: Losada, 1949), pp. 85-86.

29. In John Henrick Clark, ed., *William Styron's Nat Turner: Ten Black Writers Respond* (Boston: Beacon Press, 1968), p. 34.

30. This exchange of correspondence is reprinted in E. López Albújar, *Matalaché* (Lima: Juan Mejía Baca and P. I. Villanueva, n.d.), pp. 7-12.

31. Chapter title in Claude Wauthier, *The Literature and Thought of Modern Africa* (New York: Frederick A. Praeger, 1967), p. 180.

32. And there are novels in which the black, motivated in part by a symbolic element of revenge, is irresistibly drawn to white women, as in Adalberto Ortiz's *Juyungo,* and in part, as Franz Fanon would describe it, by his desire to "whiten" himself at all costs, to become a white man by being worthy of white love and loved as a white man (Nelson Estupiñán Bass, *El último río;* Alberto Insúa, *El negro que tenía el alma blanca;* Enrique López Albújar, *Matalaché*). In Gil Gilbert's story, "El negro Santander," the blacks hated the white men who slept with black women although they themselves desired white women. And in Díaz Sánchez's *Mene,* a black dreams of seducing white girls, as do some blacks in Rómulo Gallegos's *Pobre negro,* who go to war for this very purpose. And there are novels in which black men, because of racist pressures, want white descendants, even if it means having them by default, through marriage with white widows already with white children (Manuel Zapata Olivella, *Tierra mojada;* Nelson Estupiñán Bass, *El último río*).

Many of these concepts of race identifiable with United States patterns form the basis of the interracial relationships in *Luna verde, Gamboa Road Gang,* and *Curundú* in Panama. Joaquín Beleño C., in these novels, has made three of the most ambitious attempts to work in as many of the standard clichés as possible, including, as I said in the text, the white woman who cries rape when her overtures are rejected by her black target. These novels and others show how the sexualization of racism, evident in Latin-American literature, is closely identified with the race problem in the United States. Many of the partners involved are white principals from the United States, who for a variety of reasons, have come to reside in Latin-American countries, where racial contact with local and foreign-born blacks is unavoidable.

Chapter 4

1. W. E. Dubois, *The Souls of Black Folk* (New York: Fawcett Publications, 1961), p. 23.

2. Juan Comas has reviewed some of this research undertaken during the last thirty years on the question of whether or not racial prejudice based on skin color does exist in Latin America. Some of the studies he reviews hold that prejudice in Latin America is social and economic, and not racial. Others, however, confirm that racism and color prejudice are real problems by showing that dark color, for example, is associated with low status in Mexico; that discrimination is based on a supposed racial inferiority in Central America; that despite the claim to racial justice on the part of Costa Ricans and Panamanians, a prejudice based on physical and biological characteristics does exist; that in Guatemala there is racial discrimination against blacks; that color is all-important in the Caribbean area, where a lighter color of skin is a great asset, or where, as one researcher put it, a white skin has high market value. Some of these studies show, further, that racial prejudice remains a solid factor in Martinique and Guadeloupe, where the social status of an individual is determined first by the color of his skin and second by his economic position; that in Cuba, *de facto* though not *de jure* segregation and discrimination in favor of the white group exist; that racial prejudice does exist in Brazil; that in Colombia race is a factor in the social and economic stratification of the country's population. See Juan Comas, "Latin America."

The following observation by Oracy Nogueira forms a fine link between conclusions reached, for example, by black Brazilians and by such independent scholarly research: "The tendency of the Brazilian intelligentsia to deny or underestimate prejudice as it exists in Brazil and the difficulty of most North American observers to perceive it, contrasts with the general impressions of the non-white Brazilian population. In the studies sponsored by UNESCO, one point which is noteworthy is the recognition of prejudice in Brazil. Thus, for the first time, the testimony of social scientists frankly admits and corroborates the contention of the non-white population of Brazil based on their own experience." "Skin Color and Social Class," p. 169.

3. Seymour L. Gross and John E. Hardy, eds., *Images of the Negro in American Literature* (Chicago: University of Chicago Press, 1966), p. 1. Also see Mario J. Valdés, "The Literary Social Symbol for an Interrelated Study of Mexico," *Journal of Inter-American Studies* 7, No. 3 (July, 1965): 386: "Literature and the study of literature can give a working hypothesis for the area under examination as plausible generalizations to be co-ordinated and tested against the information gathered by the social scientist, thus integrating into a whole of knowledge."

4. Despite the heritage of white racial consciousness in the Hispanic world, liberal sentiment and humanitarian impulses toward blacks, paradoxically, led to voices of protest as early as the sixteenth century, if not against slavery, at least against some of its uglier aspects. It is likely that the first voices to rise in protest against black slavery were Spanish, even though this early humanitarianism did not succeed in abolishing the institution. We can, however, recognize as legitimate early defenders of the black in Spanish and Portuguese America those persons, largely churchmen, who carried their fervor of reform to the black. The subject of the early Spanish and Portuguese defenders of the black in America has not been sufficiently stressed in the area's historiography.

5. Mario J. Valdés defines the term "social symbol" as a "term used to indicate the fictional characters and sometimes the actions, objects, setting, and situations which, through their literary portrayal, become identified with a particular social phenomenon and thus carry the extraliterary burden of protest, or merely serve as the testimony of the existence of the

phenomenon.'' ''The Literary Social Symbol for an Interrelated Study of Mexico'' Valdés emphasizes in his fine article not just what gives rise to the protest but also the way the protest is incorporated into the novel. Distinguishing techniques usually fall under the headings of either implicit protest or explicit protest.

6. Alejo Carpentier, ¡*Ecué-Yamba O!* (Madrid: Editora España, 1933), p. 102.

7. García Calixto has the theory that Carpentier's attacks on Haitians and Jamaicans are more political than racial in that his preference for higher wages for Cuban workers including blacks was undercut by the government's decree that allowed importation of cheaper labor. García Calixto, who believes this to be Carpentier's basis for his repeated rejection of the novel as bad, says that Carpentier redeemed himself with the Haitians fifteen years later in *El reino de este mundo.* See ''El negro en la narrativa cubana,'' (Ph.D. diss., C.C.N.Y. 1973), p. 237.

8. For recent studies on these strongholds that runaway slaves developed into organized communites, see Roger Bastide, *African Civilizations in the New World* (New York: Harper and Row, 1972) and María del Carmen Borrego Pla, *Palenques de negros en Cartagena de Indias a fines del siglo XVII* (Seville: Escuela de Estudios Hispano-americanos de Sevilla, 1973). Also see Richard Price, ed., *Maroon Societies: Rebel Slave Communities in the Americas* (New York: Doubleday, 1973). Part one contains six studies devoted to rebel communities in Spanish America. He writes in the Introduction that ''maroons and their communities can be seen to hold a special significance for the study of slave societies. For while they were, from one perspective, the antithesis of all that slavery stood for, they were at the same time everywhere an embarrassingly visible part of these systems. Just as the very nature of plantation slavery implied violence and resistance, the wilderness setting of early New World plantations made *marronage* and the existence of organized maroon communities a ubiquitous reality. Throughout Afro-America, such communities stood out as an heroic challenge to white authority, and as the living proof of the existence of a slave consciousness that refused to be limited by the whites' conception or manipulation of it.'' p. 2.

9. Carpentier's *Los pasos perdidos* (1953), though not primarily concerned with black characters, does have a black writer, a black singer, a black guitar player, black cooks, black dancers, and a black dwarf; and Carpentier in this novel makes repeated references to America as a place where the great amalgam of races is taking place, a New World peopled primarily by Indians, blacks, and others. He pauses at one time to remark on the racial composition of a woman passerby whose ethnic appearance suggested Indian influence in the hair and cheekbones, Mediterranean influence in the brow and nose, black influence in the heavy shoulders and the breadth of hips. The black makes regular appearances in Carpentier's short stories, especially in his ''Los fugitivos'' (1946) which, again, takes slavery as a theme. In addition to this tale of a black slave in flight, Carpentier has written ''El camino de Santiago'' (1958), another story that includes a black runaway slave. And in ''El acoso'' (1957) the aged black wetnurse is important to the protagonist of the story. There are blacks in his ''Cuento de luna'' (1933) and in ''Oficio de tinieblas'' (1944). Carpentier has devoted considerable attention to the African sources for much of Cuban music in *La música en Cuba* (1946). Among the extensive bibliography on Carpentier is Pedro M. Barreda-Tomás, ''Dos visiones del negro, dos conceptos de la novela,'' *Hispania* 55, No. 1 (March 1972): 34-44. Also see Luis Quesada, ''Desarrollo evolutivo del elemento negro en tres de las primeras narraciones de Alejo Carpentier,'' in *Literatura de la emancipación hispanoamericana y otros ensayos. Memoria del XV Congreso del Instituto de Literatura Iberoamericana Sesión en Lima 9-14 de agosto de 1971, Lima* (Lima: Universidad Nacional Mayor de San Marcos, 1972), pp. 217-23.

10. Harry Ring, *How Cuba Uprooted Race Discrimination* (New York, 1961), p. 10.

11. Seymour Menton, ''La novela de la revolución cubana,'' *Cuadernos Hispanoamericanos* 10, No. 1 (January-February, 1964): 239.

12. Severo Sarduy, *Gestos* (Barcelona: Seix Barral, 1963), p. 12. The second novel of Sarduy, *De donde son los cantantes* (1967), again has blacks in prominent roles; they are especially

crucial to the author's concept of *"la cubanidad"* which includes Chinese and Spanish elements in addition to the black. As in Sarduy's *Gestos,* Guillermo Cabrera Infante presents the world of the black nightclub singer in his first novel, *Tres tristes tigres,* published four years after winning the 1964 Biblioteca Breve prize under the title, *Vista del amanecer en el trópico.* In *La novena estación* (1959) of José Becerra Ortega the chauffeur is a mulatto. In Humberto Arenal's *El sol a plomo* (1959), one of the young characters is a black.

13. G. R. Coulthard, *Race and Color in Caribbean Literature* (London: Oxford University Press, 1962), p. 118.

14. Coulthard discusses the emigration novel in Puerto Rico where in such novels as *Trópico en Manhattan* (1951) by Guillermo Cotto-Thorner, the Puerto Rican becomes an unhappy victim of racial discrimination in New York. The same theme is repeated in Manuel Manrique's *Island in Harlem* (1965), but the emphasis here is on the second-class citizenship experienced both by black Puerto Rican immigrants and Harlem-born blacks and their mutual identification based on the same struggle against police dogs, night sticks, beatings, police brutality, and other provocations. I understand that similar oppressive practices concerning the black are dealt with in *Isla en Manhattan* by René Marqués, which I have not been able to consult. Pedro Juan Soto deals with racial and social injustice, for example, in *Usmail* (1959), and *Terrazo,* a collection of short stories by Abelardo Díaz Alfaro, focuses in part on racism in Puerto Rico. For a recent study on black themes particularly in Puerto Rico, see Ben Coleman, "Black Themes in the Literature of the Caribbean," in *The Rican: A Journal of Contemporary Puerto Rican Thought,* No. 3 (Spring 1973): 48-54.

15. *El Periquillo Sarniento* (México, D. F.: Porrúa, 1963), p. 319. For a detailed study of Lizardi's attacks on white racism see Salvador Bueno, "El negro en *El Periquillo Sarniento:* anti-racismo de Lizardi," *Cuadernos Americanos* 182-83, No. 4 (July-August 1972): 124-39.

16. Noteworthy is the article by Joseph Sommers who, although the principal defender of Angustias as a *"criatura de la inspiración del autor,"* nevertheless, admits that many of Rojas González's ideas were suggested by other writers, that he was influenced by contemporary writers, and that he even borrowed directly from some of them ("La génesis literaria de Francisco Rojas Gonzáles," *Revista Iberoamericana* 29 [1963]: 306-9). More incriminating is the opinion of Seymour Menton who, because of the similarities between the lives of Angustias and doña Bárbara, has unsparingly termed the novel a Mexican *Doña Bárbara,* yet conceding that it does have its own literary merits (*"La negra Angustias,* una *Doña Bárbara* mexicana," *Revista Iberoamericana* 19 [1954]:229-308). And there are striking similarities, too, in the style, characterization, and structure of *La negra Angustias* and Mariano Azuela's *Los de abajo,* perhaps the greatest of the novels of the Mexican Revolution (Richard L. Jackson "Notas sobre *Los de abajo* y *La negra Angustias,"* *Annali* 8 [1966]:261-64).

17. In P. Amilcar Echeverría, ed., *Antología de prosistas guatemaltecos* (Guatemala: Editorial Universitaria, 1957), pp. 184-99.

18. Ibid., p. 185.

19. Reported in J. H. Ferguson, *Latin America: The Balance of Race Redressed* (London, 1961), p. 80.

20. *Viento fuerte* (Buenos Aires: Losada, 1962), pp. 137-38.

21. *El papa verde* (Buenos Aires: Losada, 1966), p. 80.

22. Ibid., p. 85; in this novel there are also black servants, dock workers, and baseball players, as well as blacks from Belize, from New Orleans, etc.

23. *Los ojos de los enterrados* (Buenos Aires: Losada, 1961), p. 213.

24. Ibid.

25. Ibid., p. 214.

26. Ibid., p. 215.

27. In addition to the story of Juambo there are other blacks and mulattoes in this novel, ranging from beggars and prostitutes to workers of all types. *Mulata de tal* (1963), while based on

Indian myths and viewpoints, carries this title because Asturias felt that the term *mulata* was better than *mestiza* or *zamba* in that it suggested a special grace of movement that was lacking in the other terms (see Luis Harss and Barbara Dohmann, *Into the Mainstream* [New York: Harper and Row, 1967], p. 96). There are blacks in *El Señor Presidente* (1947), in *Hombres de maíz* (1949), and in *Weekend in Guatemala* (1956).

28. Many inhabitants of the northern region of Belize are descendants of Mexicans who came down there to escape Indian uprisings in Yucatán a century ago. The novel *Hombres contra la muerte* (1947) by M. A. Espino, which deals with the difficult existence of the Indian, black, and mestizo lumber workers in the jungles of Belize, opens with a main character arriving in Belize from Mexico. The author repeatedly emphasizes that these workers, who provide wealth and comfort for others through their labor, are not as fortunate as those who reap the benefits. The black experience is treated in the short stories of Salarrué in El Salvador, and in Honduras, Ramón Amaya Amador has written *Prisión verde* (1950), the first novel in that country to deal with the United Fruit Company. Paca Navas Miralda sets her novel, *Barro* (1951), in banana country along the Atlantic coastal region of Honduras. Again, antiimperialist criticism is evident in her treatment of the United Fruit Company. In fact she gives the whole history of the Company from its early beginnings as the Bluefield Steamship Company. A recent book by Matías Funes, *Oro y miseria. Las minas del Rosario* (1966), follows the line of social protest by coming to the defense of the lower classes of Honduras. The novel is a condemnation of those responsible for the misfortunes of the black, mestizo, and Indian workers. There are blacks in Nicaragua including English-speaking immigrants from Belize and from the Caribbean islands. The black district of Bluefields is especially noteworthy in this regard, and the novel *Ebano* (1955) by Ordóñez Argüello, set in this district, though hardly favorable toward blacks, has some value because of its description of the area and of the situation of the banana workers. Blacks and their white antagonists are present in the stories of José Ramón Orozco and in the novel *Sangre en el trópico* (1930) by Hernán Robleto.

29. For a fuller treatment of the black presence in the work of Rubén Darío see René Durand, *La Négritude dans l'oeuvre poétique de Rubén Darío* (Dakar: L'Université de Dakar, 1970), and Richard L. Jackson, "La presencia negra en la obra de Rubén Darío," *Revista Iberoamericana* 33 (1967): 395-417.

30. *Mamita Yunai* (México, D. F.: Fondo de Cultura Popular, 1957), p. 14.

31. Hugo Lindo, II, ed., *Antología del cuento moderno centroamericano* (San Salvador: Universidad de El Salvador, 1950).

32. Avila Eneida has studied the theme of the banana companies in Central American fiction in a series of articles: "Las compañías bananeras en la novelística centroamericana," *Lotería* 5, No. 57 (August 1960); No. 58 (September 1960); and No. 59 (October 1960), and in an earlier doctoral dissertation at Tulane University (1959) with the same title. Miriam H. Thompson has written a doctoral dissertation dealing in part with the banana companies in Central American fiction: "Anti-Imperialism as Reflected in the Prose Fiction of Middle America," (Tulane University, 1955). Also see Carlos Meléndez, *El negro en Costa Rica* (San José: Editorial Costa Rica, 1972), particularly the article by Alvaro Sánchez M., "El negro en la literatura costarricense," pp. 161-75, which deals with the black theme in the Costa Rican literature of Carlos Luis Fallas, Joaquín Gutiérrez, and others.

33. John Biezanz, *The People of Panama* (New York: Columbia University Press, 1964), pp. 2, 12.

34. Joaquín Beleño C., *Luna verde* (Panama: Editora Panamá-América, 1951), p. 18.

35. Ibid., pp. 205-206.

36. Joaquín Beleño C., *Curundú* (Panama: R. de Panamá, 1963), p. 174. For a detailed study of racial segregation and other racial problems in the Zone and in Panama, especially in Beleño's work, see Mirna Miriam Pérez-Venero, "Raza, color y prejuicios en la novelística panameña contemporánea de tema canalero" (Ph. D. diss., Louisiana State University, 1973), and her later articles: "A Novelist's Erotic Racial Revenge," *Caribbean Review* 4, No. 4 (October-

November-December 1972): 24-27, and "El sistema de segregación racial en las novelas canaleras de Joaquín Beleño C.," *Lotería,* No. 188 (July 1971): 19-30. Also see Aristides Blanco, "Análisis de *Gamboa Road Gang:* novela de Joaquín Beleño" (M. A. thesis, University of Panama, 1963).

37. See Barry Amis, "The Negro in the Colombian Novel," (Ph. D. diss., Michigan State University, 1970).

38. Amis wrote that *Sol en Tambalimbú* (1949) by Diego Castrillón Arboleda and *Corral de negros* (1963) by Manuel Zapata Olivella represent the novel of social protest on black themes in Colombia. He concludes that, unlike *Corral de negros* by the Afro-Colombian Manuel Zapata Olivella, *Sol en Tambalimbú* seems to suggest that the Negro cannot overcome the alien social forces which confront him, presenting, in effect, a negative picture of blacks (p. 205).

39. Antonio Arango, *Oro y miseria* (Nicaragua: Editorial El Libro Manizales, 1942), p. 125.

40. In Mariano Picón Salas, *Antología de prosa venezolana* (Madrid-Caracas: Aguilar, 1965), pp. 929-39.

41. Juan Pablo Sojo, *Temas y apuntes afro-venezolanos* (Caracas: Cuadernos Literarios de la Asociación de Escritores Venezolanos, 1943), p. 39.

42. "In Search of a Nation," *Hispania* 38 (1955): 437.

43. "Día de recordación y otras reflexiones," *Bohemia* (June 1949), p. 438.

44. Rómulo Gallegos, *Obras completas,* Vol. 1 (Madrid: Aguilar, 1959), p. 1085.

45. Ibid., p. 638.

46. Ibid., p. 816.

47. Kessel Schwartz, *A New History of Spanish American Fiction,* Vol. 2 (Coral Gables, Florida: University of Miami Press, 1971), p. 127.

48. Ño Francia in Demetrio Aguilera Malta's *Don Goyo* (1933) is a natural rebel. Don Pío in *Nuestro pan* (1942) is a veteran of black uprisings in Esmeraldas. Independent and self-reliant, Don Pío remembers when white people captured blacks and made them work in their homes without pay. He remembered his mother, a victim of this practice who died resisting it. Jaramillo, a black character in Alfredo Pareja Díez Canseco's *Hombre sin tiempo* (1947), hated white people and exhibited an air of independence and self-assurance that led him to try to escape from prison, an attempt that left him with both legs broken and permanently crippled.

49. Unlike Reuben Siegel, "The Group of Guayaquil. A Study in Contemporary Ecuadorian Fiction," (Ph. D. diss., University of Wisconsin, 1951), Karl H. Heise discusses Adalberto Ortiz as the sixth member of this group in his doctoral dissertation, "Society and Artistic Techniques in the Novels of the 'Grupo de Guayaquil' " (Michigan State University, 1972).

50. *Baldomera* (Santiago, Chile: Editorial Ercilla, 1938), p. 11

51. *Las cruces sobre el agua* (1938), p. 56.

52. See William W. Megenney, "Problemas raciales y culturales en dos piezas de Demetrio Aguilera Malta," *Cuadernos Americanos* 176, No. 3 (May-June, 1971): 221-28.

53. "El negro Santander," in *Yunga* (Santiago, Chile: Zig-Zag, n.d.), p. 53.

54. *Tierra Baldía* (Quito: Casa de la Cultura Ecuatoriana, 1957), p. 135.

55. Kessel Schwartz, "Montalvo and the Negro," *Romance Notes* 9 (1964): pp. 29-32.

56. *A New History of Spanish American Fiction,* pp. 96, 104.

57. Eugene Perkins, "Benevolent Racism: the Oppressor as Messiah," *Black Books Bulletin* 3, No. 4 (Winter 1975), p. 14.

58. "The Black Presence and Two Brazilian Modernists: Jorge de Lima and José Luis do Rêgo," in Merlin H. Foster, ed., *Tradition and Renewal: Essays on Twentieth-Century Latin American Literature and Culture,* (Urbana: University of Illinois Press, 1975), pp. 100-101.

59. Abelardo Díaz Alfaro, "Bagazo," in *Terrazo* (San Juan, Puerto Rico: Imprenta Venezuela, 1947), p. 24.

60. "A Two-Continent Visit on Behalf of the Poor," *Ebony* (June 1970), p. 60.

61. W. E. B. Dubois, *The Souls of Black Folk* (New York: Fawcett Publications, 1961), p. XIV.

62. Charles Silberman, *Crisis in Black and White* (New York: Vintage Books, 1964), p. 166.

Chapter 5

1. For example, see Silverio Boj, "La poesía negra en Indoamérica," *Sustancia* 1 (1939-40): 591-608, and Jorge Montoya Toro, "Meridiano de la poesía negra," *Universidad de Antioquia,* No. 10 (April-July 1943): 171-80.

2. See Cartey, *Black Images,* p. 45.

3. See Prêto-Rodas, *Negritude as a Theme in the Poetry of the Portuguese Speaking World,* p. 10.

4. Gastón Figueira, "Dos poetas iberoamericanos de nuestro tiempo: I: Nicolás Guillén; II: Manuel del Cabral," *Revista Iberoamericana* 10 (1945): 108; reprinted in Cartey, *Black Images,* p. 117.

5. See Robert Márquez, "Introducción a Guillén," *Casa de las Américas,* No. 65-66 (1971): 136.

6. Michael Dash, "Towards a West Indian Literary Aesthetic—The Example of Aimé Césaire," *Black Images* 3, No. 1 (Spring 1974): 21.

7. Surveyed in Albert H. Berrian and Richard A. Long, eds., *Negritude: Essays and Studies* (Hampton, Virginia: Hampton Institute Press, 1967).

8. Ibid., p. xiii.

9. G. R. Coulthard, "Antecedentes de la negritud en la literatura hispanoamericana," *Mundo Nuevo,* No. 11 (May 1967): 73-77.

10. Jean Paul Sartre, "Orphée Noir," preface to *Anthologie de la nouvelle poésie nègre et malgache* (Paris: Presses Universitaires de France, 1948), p XI, quoted in Franz Fanon, *Black Skin, White Masks* (New York: Grove Press, 1967), p. 133.

11. See chapter "On National Culture" in Franz Fanon, *The Wretched of the Earth,* preface by Jean Paul Sartre, trans. Constance Farrington (New York: Grove Press, 1968), pp. 206-48.

12. In an interview printed in *Casa de las Américas,* No. 49 (June-August 1968), p. 125; quoted by G. R. Coulthard, "Negritude—Reality and Mystification," *Caribbean Studies* 10, No. 1 (1970): 51.

13. Quoted by León Damas in his *Poètes d'expression française. 1900-1945* (Paris: Editions du Seuil, 1947), pp. 12-13. Taken from a manifesto published in 1932 by Etienne Léro. This manifesto, as Norman R. Shapiro correctly observes, was to be one of the cornerstones of negritude. Quoted in *Negritude: Black Poetry from Africa and the Caribbean,* ed. and trans. from the French by Norman R. Shapiro (New York: October House, Inc., 1970), p. 7.

14. Ibid.

15. N. Leon, *El negrito poeta mexicano y sus populares versos* (Mexico, D. F.: Imprenta del Museo Nacional, 1912), p. 136. Written:

> Aunque soy de raza conga
> yo no he nacido africano,
> soy, de nación, mexicano
> y nacido en Almolonga.

in Rubén M. Campos, "La tradición del Negrito Poeta," *El folklore literario de México* (México, D. F.: Publicaciones de la Secretaría de Educación Pública, 1929), p. 97.

16. Candelario Obeso, *Cantos populares de mi tierra* (Colombia: Biblioteca Popular de Cultura Colombiana, 1959), pp. 51 and 52.

17. See, for example, his articles on Edmundo Botello and Federico Escobar in Gaspar Octavio Hernández, *Obras selectas* (Panamá: Imprenta Nacional, 1966), pp. 317-420.

18. *Piel Negra,* p. 38.

19. Enrique Anderson-Imbert, *Spanish American Literature, A History 1910-1963,* Vol. 2,

trans. by John V. Falconieri, 2nd ed., revised and updated by Elaine Malley (Detroit: Wayne State University Press, 1969), p. 728.

20. Adalberto Ortiz, *Juyungo* (Buenos Aires: Editorial Americalee, 1943), p. 248.

21. Ibid., p. 253.

22. Ibid., p. 82.

23. In Adalberto Ortiz, *El animal herido* (Quito: Editorial Casa de la Cultura Ecuatoriana, 1959), inserted between pages 52 and 53.

24. *El último río* (Quito: Editorial Casa de la Cultura Ecuatoriana, 1966), p. 335.

25. "Canción del hombre nuevo," published in *Casa de las Américas,* No. 45 (November-December 1967), p. 155.

26. Nicolás Guillén, *Antología mayor* (Havana: Ediciones Unión, 1965), p. 39.

27. Ibid., pp. 39-40.

28. Ibid., p. 79.

29. Nicolás Guillén, *Cuba, amor y revolución* (poemas) (Lima: Editorial Causachun, 1972), p. 100.

30. "Selected Poems of Nicolás Guillén," trans. Robert Márquez, *The Black Scholar* 3, No. 5 (January, 1972), 51.

31. *Guillén: Man-making Words. Selected Poems of Nicolás Guillén,* trans., annotated, with an introduction by Robert Márquez and David Arthur McMurray (Amherst: University of Massachusetts Press, 1972), p. 129.

32. Nicolás Guillén, *Antología mayor,* p. 129.

33. Quoted in Franz Fanon, *Black Skin, White Masks,* p. 133.

Chapter 6

1. See Janheinz Jahn, *Muntu: An Outline of the New African Culture* (New York: Grove Press, Inc., 1961), and *A History of Neo-African Literature: Writings in Two Continents* (London: Faber and Faber Ltd., 1968).

2. Addison Gayle, Jr., "Cultural Hegemony: The Southern White Writer and American Letters," in John A. Williams and Charles F. Harris, eds., *Amistad 1* (New York: Vintage Books, 1970), p. 22.

3. Franz Fanon, *Black Skin, White Masks* (New York: Grove Press, Inc., 1967), p. 122.

4. Mörner, *Race Mixture in the History of Latin America,* p. 88.

5. Ibid.

6. Martha K. Cobb, "An Inquiry into Race Concepts Through Spanish Literature," *Black World* 21, No. 4 (February 1972): 32-40.

7. Ibid., p. 39.

8. Ibid.

9. Ibid.

10. Franklin L. Baumer in Foreword to Baudet, *Paradise on Earth: Some Thoughts on European Images of Non-European Man,* p. v.

11. Ibid.

12. Ibid.

13. Winthrop D. Jordan, *White over Black: American Attitudes Towards the Negro 1550-1912* (Chapel Hill: University of North Carolina Press, 1968), p. 27.

14. Calvin Hernton, *White Paper for White Americans* (New York: Doubleday and Co., 1965), pp. 40-41.

15. John Killens, *Black Man's Burden* (New York: Pocket Books, 1969), p. 132.

16. Julian Pitt Rivers, "Race, Color, and Class in Central America and the Andes," in John Hope Franklin, ed., *Color and Race* (Boston: Beacon Press, 1968), p. 269.

17. Magnus Mörner, *Race Mixture in the History of Latin America,* p. 2.

A Selected Bibliography

This bibliography contains most of the titles cited in the footnotes mentioned in the text, or consulted in the preparation of this study. Dates and places of publication have been included where available.

A. Literary Works and Anthologies

Aguilera Malta, Demetrio. *Canal Zone*. Santiago de Chile: Editorial Ercilla, 1935.

————. *Dientes blancos*. México, D. F., 1959.

————. *Don Goyo*. Madrid: Editorial Cenit, 1933.

————. *Sangre azul*. Washington, D.C., 1948.

Alegría, Ciro. *El mundo es ancho y ajeno*. México, D. F.: Editorial Diana, S. A., 1963.

Amaya Amador, Ramón. *Prisión Verde*. México, D. F.: Editorial Latina, 1950.

Amilcar Echeverría, P., ed. *Antología de prosistas guatemaltecos*. Guatemala: Editorial Universitaria, 1957.

Arango, Antonio. *Oro y miseria*. Nicaragua: Editorial El Libro Manizales, 1942.

Arcocha, Juan. *Los muertos andan solos*. La Habana: Ediciones R., 1962.

Arenal Humberto. *El sol a plomo*. New York: Las Américas Publishing Co., 1959.

Arias Trujillo, Bernardo. *Risaralda* (1936). Medellín de Colombia: Editorial Bedout, 1960.

Arozarena, Marcelino. *Canción negra sin color*. Havana: Cuadernos Unión, 1966.

Arriví, Francisco. *Máscara puertorriqueña*. Río Piedras, Puerto Rico: Editorial Cultural, 1971.

Artel, Jorge. *Tambores en la noche*. Cartagena, Colombia: Editora Bolívar, 1940.

Asturias, Miguel Angel. *El papa verde*. Buenos Aires: Editorial Losada, 1954.

————. *El señor presidente*. Buenos Aires: Editorial Losada, 1952.

————. *Hombres de maíz*. Buenos Aires: Editorial Losada, 1949.

————. *Los ojos de los enterrados*. Buenos Aires: Editorial Losada, 1961.

————. *Mulata de Tal*. Buenos Aires: Editorial Losada, 1963.

————. *Viento fuerte*. Buenos Aires: Editorial Losada, 1955.

————. *Weekend in Guatemala*. Buenos Aires: Editorial Goyanarte, 1956.

Azuela, Mariano. *Los de abajo*. México, D. F.: Fondo de Cultura Económica, 1961.

Ballagas, Emilio. *Mapa de la poesía negra americana*. Buenos Aires: Editorial Pleamar, 1946.

Barnet, Miguel. *Biografía de un cimarrón*. Havana: Instituto de Etnología y Folklore, 1966.

Barrios, Pilar, *Mis cantos*. Montevideo: Editorial Comité Amigos del Poeta, 1949.

————. *Piel negra*. Montevideo: Editorial Nuestra raza, 1947.

Becco, Horacio Jorge. *El tema del negro en cantos, bailes y villancicos de los siglos XVI y XVII*. Buenos Aires: Editorial Ollantay, 1951.

Becerra Ortega, José. *La novena estación*. Havana: Imprenta "El Siglo XX", 1959.

Behn, Aphra. *Oroonoko, or The Royal Slave* (1688). New York: W. W. Norton and Company, 1973.

Beleño C., Joaquín. *Curundú*. Panamá: n.p., 1963.

———. *Gamboa Road Gang*. Panamá: Departamento de Bellas Artes y Publicaciones, 1960.

———. *Luna verde*. Panamá: Editora Panamá-América, 1951.

Blanco, Eduardo. "Manuelote." In *Tradiciones épicas y cuentos viejos*. Paris, 1879.

Bolívar Alvarez, Rafael. "La negra." *El Cojo Ilustrado* 6 (1897): 850.

Brindis de Salas, Virginia. *Cien cárceles de amor*. Montevideo. n.p., 1949.

———. *Pregón de Marimorena*. Montevideo: n.p., 1947.

Cabrera Infante, Guillermo. *Tres tristes tigres*. Barcelona: Seix Barral, 1968.

Carpentier, Alejo. *Ecué Yamba O*. Madrid: Editora España. 1933.

———. *El acoso*. Buenos Aires: Editorial Losada, 1956.

———. *El reino de este mundo*. México, D. F.: E.D.I.A.T.S.A., 1949.

———. *El siglo de las luces*. México, D. F.: Cia. General de Ediciones S.A., 1962.

———. *Los pasos perdidos*. México, D. F.: Cia. General de Ediciones, S.A., 1962.

Carrasquilla, Tomás. *La marquesa de Yolombó*. In *Obras completas*. Medellín de Colombia: Editorial Bedout, 1958.

Carril, Pepe. *Shango de Ima: A Yoruba Mystery play*. Garden City, New York: Doubleday and Co., Inc., 1970.

Castrillón Arboleda, Diego. *Sol en Tambalimbú*. Bogotá: Editorial Kelly, 1949.

Cotto-Thorner, Guillermo. *Trópico en Manhattan*. San Juan, Puerto Rico: Editorial Occidente, 1951.

Cruz, Sor Juana Inés de la. *Poesías completas*. México, D. F.: Ediciones Botas, 1941.

Cuadra, José de la. *Los Sangurimas*. In *Obras completas*. Quito: Casa de la Cultura Ecuatoriana, 1958.

Cyrus, Stanley. *El cuento negrista sudamericano. Antología*. Quito: Editorial Casa de la Cultura Ecuatoriana, 1973.

Damas, León. *Poètes d'expression française. 1900-1945*. Paris: Editions du Seuil, 1947.

Darío Rubén. *Obras completas*. 5 vols. Madrid: Aguado, 1950-1955.

Díaz Alfaro, Abelardo. *Terrazo*. San Juan, Puerto Rico: Imprenta Venezuela, 1947.

Díaz Rodríguez, Manuel. "Las ovejas y las rosas de Pedro Serafín." In *Peregrina*. Madrid, 1922.

Díaz Sánchez, Ramón. *Cumboto*. Santiago de Chile: Editorial Universitaria, 1967.

———. *Mene*. Buenos Aires: Editorial Universitaria de Buenos Aires, 1966.

Dobles, Fabián. "La mujer negra del río." In Hugo Lindo, ed., *Antología del cuento centroamericano*. San Salvador: Universidad de El Salvador, 1950.

Duncan, Quince. *Bronce*. San José, Costa Rica: Cuadernos de Arte Popular, 1970.

———. *El pozo y una carta*. San José, Costa Rica: Cuadernos de Arte Popular, 1969.

———. *Hombres curtidos*. Panamá: Cuadernos de Arte Popular, 1971.

———. *Una canción en la madrugada*. San José, Costa Rica: Editorial Costa Rica, 1970.

Espino, Miguel Angel. *Hombres contra la muerte*. México, D. F.: Editorial Costa Amic, 1947.

Estupiñán Bass, Nelson. *Canto negro por la luz*. Esmeraldas, Ecuador: Ediciones del Núcleo Provincial de Esmeraldas de la Casa de la Cultura Ecuatoriana, 1954.

———. *Cuando los guayacanes florecían*. Quito: Casa de la Cultura Ecuatoriana, 1954.

———. *El último río*. Quito: La Cultura Ecuatoriana, 1967.

———. *Senderos brillantes*. Quito: Casa de la Cultura Ecuatoriana, 1974.

Fallas, Carlos Luis. *Mamita Yunai* (1941). México, D. F.: Fondo de Cultura Popular, 1957.

Fernández de Lizardi, José Joaquín. *El periquillo sarniento* (1816). México, D. F.: Porrúa, 1963.

Franceschi, Víctor. *Carbones*. Panamá: Departamento de Bellas Artes y Publicaciones del Ministerio de Educación, 1956.

Funes, Matías. *Oro y miseria. Las minas de Rosario*. Honduras, 1966.

Gallegos, Gerardo. *Beau Dondon conquista el mundo*. Havana, 1942.

————. *Los ritos mágicos: El Vudú*. Madrid: Fomento Editorial, S.A.. 1973.

Gallegos, Rómulo. *Canaima*. Buenos Aires: Espasa Calpe, 1947.

————. *Cantaclaro*. Buenos Aires: Espasa Calpe, 1941.

————. *Doña Bárbara*. Buenos Aires: Espasa Calpe, 1947.

————. *Obras completas*. Madrid: Aguilar, 1959.

————. *Pobre negro*. Buenos Aires: Espasa Calpe, 1961.

Gallegos Lara, Joaquín. *Cuentos*. Quito: Casa de la Cultura Ecuatoriana, 1956.

Gilbert, Gil. *Nuestro pan*. Guayaquil: Vera y Cía., 1942.

————. "El negro Santander." In *Yunga*. Santiago de Chile: Zig-Zag, 1938.

Gómez de Avellaneda, Gertrudis. *Sab*. Havana: Editorial Nacional de Cuba, 1963. Also Havana: Instituto Cubano del Libro, 1973. Prologue and notes by Mary Cruz.

Gorostiza, Celestino. *El color de nuestra piel*. New York: The MacMillan Company, 1966.

Granados, Manuel. *Adire y el tiempo roto*. Havana: Casa de las Américas, 1967.

Guillén, Nicolás. *Antología Mayor*. Havana: Ediciones Unión, 1965.

————. *Cuba, amor y revolución*. Lima: Editorial Causachun, 1972.

————. *Man-making words. Selected Poems of Nicolás Guillén*. Trans., annotated, and with an introduction by Robert Márquez and David Arthur McMurray. Amherst: University of Massachusetts Press, 1972.

————. *Obra poética (1920-1972)*. Havana: Instituto Cubano del Libro, 1972.

————. *¡Patria o muerte! The Great Zoo and other Poems*. Edited and translated by Robert Márquez. New York and London: Monthly Review Press, 1972.

————. "Selected Poems of Nicolás Guillén." Trans. Robert Márquez. *The Black Scholar* 3, No. 5 (January 1972): 50-53.

————. *Tengo*. Trans. by Richard J. Carr, Old Mill Place, Detroit, Michigan: Broadside Press, 1974.

Hernández Cata, Alfonso. "La piel." In *Los frutos ácidos*. Buenos Aires, 1946.

Hernández, Gaspar Octavio. *Obras Selectas*. Panamá: Imprenta Nacional, 1966.

Hugo, Victor. *Bug-Jargal*. In *The Novels, Poems and Dramas of Victor Hugo*, Vol. 16. New York: P. F. Collier, N. D.

Icaza, Xavier. *Panchito Chapopote*. México, D. F.: Editorial 'Aloma,' 1961.

Insúa, Alberto. *El negro que tenía el alma blanca*. Madrid: Espasa Calpe, 1958.

————. *La Sombra de Peter Wald*. Espasa Calpe, 1942.

Isaacs, Jorge. *María*. Buenos Aires: Editorial Sopena, 1938.

Lachatañeré, Rómulo. *¡¡Oh, mío. Yemayá!!* Manzanillo, Cuba: Editorial "El arte," 1938.

Lajara, Sanz. *Los rompidos*. Buenos Aires: Editorial Americalee, 1963.

Lindo, Hugo, ed. *Antología del cuento moderno centroamericano*. San Salvador: Universidad de El Salvador, 1950.

López Albújar, Enrique. *Matalaché*. Lima: Juan Mejía Baca and P. L. Villanueva, 1934.

Macedo, María Rosa. *Ranchos de caña*. Lima: La Empresa Periodística, S.A. "La Prensa," 1941.

Manrique, Manuel. *Island in Harlem*. New York: The John Day Co., 1966.

Marqués, René. "Isla en Manhattan." In *Otro día nuestro*. Prólogo de Concha Meléndez. San Juan, Puerto Rico: Imprenta Venezuela, 1955.

Marrero Aristy, Ramón. *Over*. Ciudad Trujillo [Santo Domingo], R. D.: Imp. "La Opinión," 1939.

Meneses, Guillermo. *Canción de negros*. In *Cinco novelas*. Caracas: Monte Avila Editores, 1972.

————. *Tres cuentos venezolanos*. Caracas: Ediciones Elite, 1936.

Miralda, Paca Navas de. *Barro*. Guatemala: Editorial Ministerio de Educación Pública.

Morúa Delgado, Martín. *La Familia Unzúaza*. In *Obras Completas*, Vol. 2. Havana: Ediciones de la Comisión Nacional del Centenario de Martín Morúa Delgado, 1957.

————. *Sofía*. Havana: Instituto Cubano del Libro, 1972.

Noble, Enrique. *Literatura afro-hispanoamericana: Poesía y prosa de ficción*. Toronto: Xerox College Publishing, 1973.

Novás Calvo, Lino. *Pedro Blanco el negrero* (1932). Buenos Aires: Espasa Calpe, 1944.

Obeso, Candelario. *Cantos populares de mi tierra*. Bogotá: Biblioteca Popular de Cultura Colombiana, 1950.

Ordóñez Argüello, Alberto. *Ebano*. El Salvador: Dirección General de Bellas Artes, 1954.

Ortiz, Adalberto. *El animal herido*. Quito: Editorial Casa de la Cultura Ecuatoriana, 1959.

———. *El espejo y la ventana*, Guayaquil, Ecuador: Editorial Casa de la Cultura Ecuatoriana, Núcleo del Guayas, 1970.

———. *Juyungo*. Buenos Aires: Editorial Americalee, 1943.

———. *Tierra, son y tambor: Cantares negros y mulatos*. México, D. F.: Ediciones La Cigarra, 1945.

Palacios, Arnoldo. *Las estrellas son negras*. Bogotá: Editorial Revista Colombiana, 1971.

Palacios, Eustaquio. *El alférez real*. Medellín: Editorial Bedout, 1965.

Palés Matos, Luis. *Tuntún de pasa y grifería. Poemas afroantillanos* San Juan: Biblioteca de Autores Puertorriqueños, 1937.

Pareja Díez-Canseco, Alfredo. *Baldomera*. Santiago de Chile: Ediciones Ercilla, 1938.

———. *Hombres sin tiempo*. Buenos Aires: Losada, 1941.

Pedroso, Regino. *Poemas*. Havana: Ediciones Unión, 1966.

Picón Salas, Mariano, ed. *Antología de prosa venezolana*. Caracas: Ediciones Edine, 1957.

Preciado, Antonio. *Tal como somos*. Quito: Ediciones Siglo Veinte, n.d.

Ramón, Gonzalo. *Tierra baldía*. Quito: Casa de la Cultura Ecuatoriana, 1957.

Ramos, José Antonio. *Caniqui*. Havana: Consejo Nacional de Cultura, 1963.

Robleto, Hernán. *Sangre en el trópico*. Madrid, 1930.

Rojas González, Francisco. *La negra Angustias*. México, D. F.: Cia. General de Ediciones, 1955.

Rueda, Lope de. *Eufemia*. In J. Moreno Villa, ed., *Lope de Rueda*. Madrid: Espasa Calpe, S.A., 1958.

Ruiz del Vizo, Hortensia. *Black Poetry of the Americas (A Bilingual Anthology)*. Miami: Ediciones Universal, 1972.

———. *Poesía negra del Caribe y otras áreas*. Miami: Ediciones Universal, 1972.

Sandoval, Alonso de. *De Instauranda Aethiopum Salute: El mundo de la esclavitud negra en América*. Bogotá: Empresa Nacional, 1956.

Santa Cruz, Nicomedes. "Canción del hombre nuevo." *Casa de las Amércas*, núm. 45 (November-December 1967): 155.

———. *Décimas y poemas*. Lima: Campodónico Ediciones, 1971.

Sanz y Díaz, J. *Lira Negra: Selecciones españolas y afroamericanas*. Madrid: Aguilar, 1962.

Sarduy, Severo. *De donde son los cantantes*. México, D. F.: Joaquín Mortiz, 1967.

———. *Gestos*. Barcelona: Seix Barral, 1963.

Sartre, Jean Paul. "Orphée noir." In L. S. Senghor, ed., *Anthologie de la nouvelle poésie nègre et malgache de langue française*. Paris: Presses Universitaires de France, 1948.

Sinán, Rogelio. *La boina roja*. Panamá, 1961.

———. *Plenilunio* (1947). México, D. F.: Editorial Constancia, 1953.

Sojo, Juan Pablo. *Nochebuena negra*. Caracas: Ed. General Rafael Urdaneta, 1943.

Soler Puig, José. *Bertillón 166*. Havana: Casa de las Américas, 1960.

Soto, Pedro Juan. *Usmail* (1959). Río Piedras, Puerto Rico. Editorial Cultural, Inc., 1970.

Suárez Romero, Anselmo. *Francisco* (1839). Havana: Cuadernos de Cultura, 1947, and Miami's Mnemosyne Publishing Co., 1969.

Trillo Pays, Dionisio. *Pompeyo Amargo*. Montevideo: Claudio García, 1942.

Uslar Pietri, Arturo. *Las lanzas coloradas*. Buenos Aires: Losada, 1949.

Villaverde, Cirilo. *Cecilia Valdés*. New York: Las Américas Publishing Co., 1964.

Zalamea Borda, Eduardo. *4 años a bordo de mí mismo*. Bogotá: Compañía Gran Colombiana de Ediciones, S.A., 1934.

Zambrana, Antonio. *El negro Francisco*. Havana: Imprenta P. Fernández y Cía., 1951.

Zapata Olivella, Manuel. *Corral de negros*. Havana: Casa de las Américas, 1963.

———. *Detrás del rostro*. Madrid: Aguilar, 1963.

———. *Tierra mojada* (1947). Madrid: Editorial Bullón, 1964.

B. Critical Studies and References

Allan, Alma C. "Literary Relations between Spain and Africa: An Introductory Statement." *Journal of Negro History* 50 (April 1965): 97-105.

Amis, Barry. "The Negro in the Colombian Novel." Ph. D. dissertation, Michigan State University, 1970.

Anderson-Imbert, Enrique. *Spanish American Literature, A History* . 2 Volumes. Translated by John Falconiere. Detroit: Wayne State University Press, 1969.

Anillo, Antonio F. "La novelística comprometida de Manuel Zapata Olivella." Ph. D. dissertation, George Washington University, 1972.

"A Two-Continent Visit on Behalf of the Poor." *Ebony*. June 1970, pp. 54-64.

Banton, Michael. *Race Relations*. London: Tavistock, 1967.

Baquero, Gastón, *Darío, Cernuda, y otros temas poéticos*. Madrid: Editora Nacional, 1969.

Barreda-Tomás, Pedro M. "Dos visiones del negro, dos conceptos de la novela." *Hispania* 55, No. 1 (March 1972): 33-44.

Bastide, Roger. *African Civilizations in the New World*. New York: Harper and Row Publishers, 1972.

———. "Color, Racism, and Christianity." In John Hope Franklin, ed., *Color and Racism*. Boston: Beacon Press, 1968.

———. "Estereótipos de negros através da literatura Brasileira." *Boletím de Sociologia* (São Paulo), núm. 3 (1953): 9-27.

———. "Variations on Négritude." In Albert H. Berrian and Richard A. Long, eds., *Négritude: Essays and Studies*. Hampton, Virginia: Hampton Institute, 1967.

Baudet, Henri. *Paradise on Earth: Some Thoughts on European Images of Non-European Man*. New Haven and London: Yale University Press, 1965.

Beltrán, Carlos. *Brasil: tipos humanos y mestizaje*. Madrid: Ediciones Cultura Hispánica, 1970.

Berrian, Albert H. and Long, Richard A., eds. *Negritude: Essays and Studies*. Hampton, Virginia: Hampton Institute Press, 1967.

Betances, Samuel. "The Prejudice of Having no Prejudice. Part I." *The Rican, A Journal of Contemporary Puerto Rican Thought*, No. 2 (Winter 1972): 41-54.

———. "The Prejudice of Having no Prejudice. Part II." *The Rican, A Journal of Contemporary Puerto Rican Thought*, No. 3 (Spring 1972): 22-37.

Biesanz, John. *The People of Panama*. New York: Columbia University Press, 1964.

"Black is Beautiful, but How About Light Blacks." *Jet*. June 1972, pp. 30-31.

Blair, Thomas. "Mouvements Afro-bresiliens de Libération de la période esclavagiste à nos jours." *Présence Africaine* 53 (1965): 96-101.

Boj, Silverio. "La poesía negra en Indoamérica." *Sustancia* (1939-40): 591-608.

Borrego Pla, María del Carmen. *Palenques de negros en Cartagena de Indias a fines del siglo XVII*. Seville: Escuela de Estudios Hispano-americanos de Sevilla, 1973.

Bowser, Frederick P. "Colonial Spanish America." In David W. Cowen and Jack P. Green, eds., *Neither Slave nor Free: The Freedman of African Descent in the Slave Societies of the New World*. Baltimore and London: The Johns Hopkins University Press, 1972.

Boyd, Antonio Olliz. "The Concept of Black Esthetics as seen in Selected Works of Three Latin American Writers: Machado de Assis, Nicolás Guillén and Adalberto Ortiz." Ph. D. dissertation, Stanford University, 1975.

Brooks, John. "Slavery and the Slave in the Works of Lope de Vega." *Romanic Review* 19, No. 3 (1928): 232-43.

Brushwood, John. *Mexico in its Novel*. Austin: University of Texas Press, 1966.

Bueno, Salvador. *Historia de la literatura cubana*. Havana: Editora del Ministerio de Educación, 1963.

———. "El negro en *El Periquillo Sarniento:* anti-racismo de Lizardi." *Cuadernos Americanos,* No. 4 (July-August 1972), 124-39, 182-83.

———. "Review of *Caribbean Literature: An Anthology* by G. R. Coulthard." [London: University of London, 1966] *Casa de las Américas,* No. 1, 36-37 (1966): 186-89.

———. *Temas y personajes de la literatura cubana*. Havana: Ediciones Unión, 1964.

Calixto, García. "El negro en la narrativa cubana." Ph. D. dissertation, City College of New York, 1973.

Campos, Rubén M. "La tradición del Negrito Poeta." *El folklore literario de México*. México, D. F.: Publicaciones de la Secretaría de Educación Pública, 1929.

Canfield, Martha L. "Los precursores de la poesía negra." *Razón y fábula,* No. 21 (September-October, 1970): 13-26.

Carpentier, Alejo. *La música en Cuba*. México, D. F.: Fondo de Cultura Económica, 1946.

Cartey, Wilfred. *Black Images*. New York: Teachers College Press, 1970.

Castellano, Juan R. "El negro esclavo en el entremés del Siglo de Oro." *Hispania* 44, No. 1 (March 1961): 55-65.

Castro, Américo. "Los esclavos libres de Lope de Vega." *Revista de Filología Española* (Madrid) 6 (1919): 308-309.

Chasca, Edmund de. "The Phonology of the Speech of the Negroes in Early Spanish Drama." *Hispanic Review* 14 (1946): 322-39.

Clark, John Henrick, ed. *William Styron's Nat Turner: Ten Black Writers Respond*. Boston: Beacon Press, 1968.

Cleaver, Eldridge. "Fidel Castro's African Gambit." *Newsweek,* May 3, 1976, p. 13.

Clytus, John. *Black Man in Red Cuba*. Coral Gables: University of Miami Press, 1970.

Cobb, Martha K. "A Role for Spanish in the Humanities Program." *Hispania* 54, No. 2 (May 1971): 302-307.

———. "Africa in Latin America: Customs, Culture and Literature." *Black World* 21, No. 10 (August 1972): 4-19.

———. "An Appraisal of Latin American Slavery through Literature." *Journal of Negro History* 58 (1974): 460-69.

———. "An Inquiry into Race Concepts Through Spanish Literature." *Black World* 21, No. 4 (February 1972): 32-40.

———. "Martín Morúa Delgado." *Negro History Bulletin* 36 (1974): 12.

———. "Concepts of Blackness in the Poetry of Nicolás Guillén, Jacques Roumain and Langston Hughes." *CLA Journal* 18, No. 2 (1974): 262-72.

Codina, Iverna. "Adalberto Ortiz y la presencia del negro." In *América en la novela*. Buenos Aires: Ediciones Cruz del Sur, 1964.

Coleman, Ben. "Black Themes in the Literature of the Caribbean." *The Rican: A Journal of Contemporary Puerto Rican Thought,* No. 3 (Spring 1973): 48-54.

Comas, Juan. "Latin America." *Research on Race Relations*. Paris, UNESCO, 1966.

———. *Relaciones inter-raciales en América Latina: 1940-60*. México, D. F.: Universidad Nacional Autónoma de México, 1961.

Cometta Manzoni, Aida. "Trayectoria del negro en la poesía de América." *Nosotros* 44-45 (November/December 1939): 196-212.

Cook, Ann. "Black Pride—Some Contradictions." *Negro Digest* 19 (February 1970): 36-42, 59-63.

Coulthard, G. R. "Antecedentes de la negritud en la literatura hispanoamericana." *Mundo Nuevo,* No. 11 (May 1967): 73-77.

———. "Crisis o agotamiento de la negritud," pages 202-13. *Actas del tercer Congreso Internacional de Hispanistas*. México, D. F.: El Colegio de México, 1970.

———. ''Negritude—Reality and Mystification.'' *Caribbean Studies* 10, No. 1 (1970): 42-51.

———. ''Paralellisms and Divergencies between Negritude and Indigenismo.'' *Caribbean Studies* 8, No. 1 (April 1968): 31-55.

———. *Race and color in Caribbean Literature.* London: Oxford University Press, 1962.

———. *Raza y color en la literatura antillana.* Seville: Universidad de Sevilla, 1958.

Dash, Michael. ''Marvellous Realism— The Way out of Negritude.'' *Black Images* 3, No. 1 (Spring 1974): 80-95.

———. ''Towards a West Indian Literary Aesthetic— The Example of Aimé Césaire,'' *Black Images* 3, No. 1 (Spring 1974): 21-28.

Davis, David Brian. *The Problem of Slavery in Western Culture.* Ithaca, New York: Cornell University Press, 1966.

Degler, Carl. *Neither Black nor White: Slavery and Race Relations in Brazil and the United States.* New York: MacMillan, 1971.

Depestre, René. ''Les Métamorphoses de la négritude en Amérique.'' *Présence Africaine,* No. 75 (1970): 19-33.

———. ''Problemas de la identidad del hombre negro en las literaturas antillanas.'' *Diez años de la revista Casa de las Américas 1960-1970,* No. 31 (July-August 1970): 51-59.

Díaz-Rozzotto, Jaime. ''Ponencia sobre negritude e indigenismo—Ritmo y tiempo.'' *Cuadernos Americanos* 197 (November/December 1974): 31-42.

Doerr, Richard Paul. ''La magia como dinámica de evasión en la novelística de Manuel Zapata Olivella.'' Ph. D. dissertation, University of Colorado, 1973.

Donald, Cleveland, Jr. ''Equality in Brazil: Confronting Reality,'' *Black World* 22, No. 1 (November 1972): 23-34.

Drake, St. Clair. ''The Black Diaspora in Pan-African Perspective.'' *The Black Scholar* 7, No. 1 (September 1975): 2-14.

Dubois, W. E. B. *The Souls of Black Folk.* New York: Fawcett Publications, 1961.

Dunzo, Annette J. ''Blacks of Sub-Saharan African Origin in Spain: Image in the Theatre (1500-1700).'' Ph. D. dissertation, UCLA, 1974.

Durand, René. ''La figura del negro en el *Martín Fierro* de José Hernández.'' *El ensayo y la crítica literaria en Iberoamérica.* Toronto: University of Toronto, 1970.

———. *La Négritude dans l'oeuvre poétique de Rubén Darío.* Dakar: L'université de Dakar, 1970.

Dzidzienyo, Anani. *The Position of Blacks in Brazilian Society.* London: Minority Rights Group Report No. 7, 1971.

Ebersole, A. V. ''Black is Beautiful in Seventeenth Century Spain.'' *Romance Notes* 12, No. 2 (Spring 1971): 387-91.

Eneida, Avila. ''Las compañías bananeras en la novelística centroamericana.'' Ph. D. dissertation, Tulane University, 1959.

———. ''Las compañías bananeras en la novelística centroamericana.'' *Lotería* 5, No. 57 (August 1960); No. 58 (September 1960); No. 59 (October 1960).

Esquenazi-Mayo, Roberto. ''Impacto de Africa en la literatura hispanoamericana.'' In *Expression, Communication and Experience in Literature and Language.* London: The Modern Humanities Research Association, 1973.

Estupiñán Bass, Nelson. ''Apuntes sobre el negro de Esmeraldas en la literaria ecuatoriana.'' *Norte,* No. 53 (September/October 1967): 101-109.

Fairchild, Maxie Neale. *The Noble Savage: A Study in Romantic Naturalism.* New York: Russell and Russell, 1961.

Fanon, Franz. *Black Skin, White Masks.* Translated by Charles Lam Markmann New York: Grove Press, Inc., 1967.

———. *The Wretched of the Earth.* Translated by Constance Farrington, New York: Grove Press, 1968.

Ferguson, J. H. *Latin America: The Balance of Race Redressed.* London: Oxford University Press, 1961.

Fernández, Florestan. *The Negro in Brazilian Society*. Edited by Phyllis B. Eveleth. Translated by J. D. Skiles, A. Brunet and A. Rothwell. New York: Columbia University Press, 1969.

Fernández de Castro, José A. *Tema negro en la literatura cubana*. Havana: El Mirador, 1943.

Fernández de la Vega, Oscar, and Pamies, Alberto N. *Iniciación a la poesía afroamericana*. Miami: Ediciones Universal, 1973.

Figueira, Gastón. "Dos poetas iberoamericanos de nuestro tiempo: I: Nicolás Guillén; II: Manuel del Cabral." *Revista Iberoamericana* 10 (1945): 107-17.

Franco, Jean. *The Modern Culture of Latin America: Society and the Artist,* London: Pall Mall Press, 1967.

Franchesi, Victor. "El hombre blanco en la poesía negra." *Lotería* 4, No. 44 (June 1959): 134-39.

Franklin, John Hope, ed. *Color and Race*. Boston: Houghton Mifflin, 1968.

Gallegos, Rómulo. "Día de recordación y otras reflexiones." *Bohemia* (June 1949), p. 438.

Gallegos Lara, Joaquín. "Raza, poesía y novela de Adalberto Ortiz." Prologue to Adalberto Ortiz, *El animal herido*. Quito: Casa de la Cultura Ecuatoriana, 1959.

Gayle, Jr., Addison. "Cultural Hegemony: The Southern White Writer and American Letters." *Amistad I*. Edited by John A. Williams and Charles F. Harris. New York: Vintage Books, 1970.

————. "Cultural Strangulation: Black Literature and the White Aesthetic." In Addison Gayle, Jr., ed., *The Black Aesthetic*. New York: Doubleday, 1971.

Graf, Henning. "Africa en América—Algunos aspectos de la simbiosis literaria afroamericana." *Humanitas* (1974): 353-96.

Granda, Germán de. "Sobre el origen de la 'habla de negro' en la literatura peninsular del Siglo de Oro." *Prohemio* 2, No. 1 (April 1971): 97-109.

Green, Gil. *Revolution Cuban Style*. New York: International Publishers, 1970.

Gross, Seymour L., and Hardy, John Edward, eds. *Images of the Negro in American Literature*. Chicago: University of Chicago Press, 1966.

Haberly, David. "Abolitionism in Brazil: Anti-Slavery and Anti-Slave." *Luso-Brazilian Review* (Winter 1972): 30-45.

Hall, Gwendolyn Midlo. *Social Control in Slave Plantation Societies*. Baltimore: The Johns Hopkins Press, 1971.

————. "The Myth of Benevolent Spanish Slave Law." *Negro Digest* 19 (February 1970): 31-38.

Harris, Marvin. *Patterns of Race in the Americas*. New York: Walker and Co., 1964.

Harss, Luis, and Dohmann, Barbara. *Into the Mainstream*. New York: Harper and Row, 1967.

Heise, Karl H. "Society and Artistic Techniques in the Novels of the 'Grupo de Guayaquil.' " Ph. D. dissertation, Michigan State University, 1972.

Henry, Richard and Teresa C. Salas. "Nicomedes Santa Cruz y la poesía de su conciencia de negritud." *Cuadernos Americanos* 202 (September-October 1975): 189-99.

Hernton, Calvin. *Sex and Racism in America*. New York: Doubleday and Co., 1965.

————. *White Paper for White Americans*. New York: Doubleday and Co., 1966.

Hoetink, Harmannus. "National Identity, Culture and Race in the Caribbean." In John O. Campbell, ed., *Racial Tensions and National Identity*. Nashville: Vanderbilt University Press, 1972.

————. *Slavery and Race Relations in the Americas*. New York: Harper and Row, 1973.

————. "The Dominican Republic in the Nineteenth Century: Some Notes on Stratification, Immigration and Race." In Magnus Mörner, ed., *Race and Class in Latin America*. New York: Columbia University Press, 1970.

————. *The Two Variants in Caribbean Race Relations: A Contribution to the Sociology of Segmented Societies*. London: Oxford University Press, 1967.

Homenaje a Silvio Zavala: estudios históricos americanos. México, D. F.: El Colegio de México, 1953.

Ianni, O. "Research on Race Relations in Brazil." In Magnus Mörner, ed., *Race and Class in Latin America*. New York: Columbia University Press, 1970.

Instituto Panamericano de Geografía e Historia. *El mestizaje en la historia de Iberoamérica*. México, D. F.: Editorial Cultural, 1961.

Jackson, Richard L. "An Underdeveloped Area." *Hispania* 48 (1965): 870.

——. "Black Phobia and the White Aesthetic in Spanish American Literature." *Hispania* 58, No. 3 (September 1975): 467-80.

——. "La presencia negra en la obra de Rubén Darío." *Revista Iberoamericana* 33 (1967): 395-417.

——. "Mestizaje vs. Black Identity: The Color Crisis in Latin America." *Black World* 24, No. 9 (July 1975): 4-21.

——. "Miscegenation and Personal Choice in Two Contemporary Novels of Continental Spanish America." *Hispania* 50 (1967): 86-88.

——. "Notas sobre *Los de abajo* y *La Negra Angustias*." *Annali* 8 (1966): 261-64.

Jahn, Janheinz. *A History of Neo-African Literature: Writings in Two Continents*. London: Faber and Faber Ltd., 1968.

——. *Muntu: An Outline of the New African Culture*. New York: Grove Press, Inc., 1961.

Jason, Howard M. "The Negro in Spanish Literature to the End of Siglo de Oro." *College Language Association Journal* 9, No. 2 (December 1965): 121-31.

Johnson, Lemuel. *The Devil, the Gargoyle and the Buffoon: The Negro as Metaphor in Western Literature*. Port Washington, New York: Kennikat Press, 1969.

Jordan, Winthrop D. *White over Black: American Attitudes Towards the Negro 1550-1812*. Chapel Hill: University of North Carolina Press, 1968.

Killens, John. *Black Man's Burden*. New York: Pocket Books, 1969.

King, James Ferguson. "Negro History in Continental Spanish America." *Journal of Negro History* 29, No. 1 (1944): 7-23.

——. "The Negro in Continental Spanish America: A Select Bibliography." *The Hispanic American Historical Review* 24, No. 3 (1944): 547-59.

Knight, Franklin W. *The African Dimension in Latin American Societies*. New York: MacMillan Publishing Co., 1974.

Lastra, Pedro. "Notas sobre la narrativa de Alejo Carpentier." *Anales de la Universidad de Chile* 120 (1962): 94-101.

León, N. *El negrito poeta mexicano y sus populares versos*. México, D. F.: Imprenta del Museo Nacional, 1912.

Lincoln, C. Eric. *Sounds of the Struggle*. New York: William Morrow and Co. Inc., 1968.

Litto, Frederic M. "Some Notes on Brazil's Black Theatre." In Lloyd W. Brown, ed., *The Black Writer in Africa and the Americas*. Los Angeles: Hennessey and Ingalls, Inc., 1973.

Lockhart, James. *Spanish Peru, 1532-1560*. Madison: University of Wisconsin Press, 1968.

Lockwood, Lee. *Conversations with Eldridge Cleaver. Algiers*. New York: Dell Publishing Co., 1970.

Logan, Rayford W. "The Negro in Spanish America." *The Negro in the Americas*. Washington, D.C.: Howard University, 1940.

López Morales, Humberto, *Estudio sobre el español de Cuba*. New York: Las Americas Publishing Co., 1971.

——. "La lengua de la poesía afrocubana." *Español actual*, No. 7 (May 10, 1967): 1-3.

Loveluck, Juan. *La novela hispanoamericana*. Chile: Editorial Universitaria, 1966.

Lowenthal, David. "Race and Color in the West Indies." In John Hope Franklin, ed., *Color and Race*. Boston: Beacon Press, 1968.

Mansour, Mónica. *La poesía negrista*. México, D. F.: Ediciones Era, 1973.

Márquez, Robert, "Introducción a Guillén." *Casa de las Américas*, No. 65-66 (1971): 136-42.

Marquina, Rafael. "The Negro in the Spanish Theatre before Lope de Vega." *Phylon* 4 (1943): 147-52.

May, Charles Paul. *Central America: Lands Seeking Unity.* New York: Thomas Nelson and Sons, 1966.

✓ Megenney, Williams W. "Problemas raciales y culturales en dos piezas de Demetrio Aguilera Malta." *Cuadernos Americanos* 176, No. 3 (May-June 1971): 221-28.

Meléndez, Concha. "El arte de Jorge Isaacs en *María."* In her *Figuración de Puerto Rico.* San Juan: Instituto de Cultura Puertorriqueña, 1958.

———. "Sor Juana y los negros." *Signos de Iberoamérica.* México, D. F., 1936.

Meléndez, Carlos and Duncan, Quince. *El negro en Costa Rica.* San José: Editorial Costa Rica, 1972.

Menton, Seymour. *Historia crítica de la novela guatemalteca.* Guatemala: Editorial Universitaria, 1960.

———. "In Search of a Nation." *Hispania* 38 (December 1955): 432-42.

———. *"La negra Angustias, una* Doña Bárbara *mexicana." Revista Iberoamericana* 19 (1954): 229-308.

———. "La novela de la revolución cubana." *Cuadernos Americanos* 132, No. 1 (1964): 231-41.

Modern Language Association. *MLA Newsletter.* February 1974.

Monguió, Luis. "El negro en algunos poetas españoles y americanos anteriores a 1800." *Revista Iberoamericana* 44, No. 22 (July/December 1957): 245-59. Reprinted in *Estudios sobre literatura hispanoamericana y española.* México, D. F., 1958.

Montoya Toro, Jorge. "Meridiano de la poesía negra." *Universidad de Antioquia,* No. 10 (April-July 1943): 171-80.

Morales Oliver, Luis. *Africa en la literatura española.* 3 vols. Madrid: Consejo Superior de Investigaciones Científicas, 1957.

Moreno Fraginals, M. "El problema negro en la poesía cubana." *Cuadernos Hispanoamericanos,* No. 3 (1948): 519-30.

Mörner, Magnus, "Historical Research on Race Relations in Latin America during the National Period." In idem, ed., *Race and class in Latin America.* New York: Columbia University.

———. Ed. *Race and class in Latin America.* New York: Columbia University Press, 1970.

———. *Race Mixture in the History of Latin America.* Boston: Little, Brown and Co., 1967.

Morse, Richard. "Negro-White Relations in Latin America." *Reports and Speeches of the Ninth Yale Conference on the Teaching of the Social Sciences.* New Haven, April 3-4, 1964.

Nascimento, Abdias do. "Afro-Brazilian Culture." *Black Images* 1, Nos. 3 and 4 (autumn and winter, 1972): 41-46.

———. *Dramas para negros e prólogo para brancos.* Rio de Janeiro: Teatro Experimental do Negro, 1961.

———. "Testemunho." *Cadernos Brasileiros* 10, No. 47 (May-June 1968): 3-7.

———. "The Negro Theatre in Brazil." *African Forum* (1967): 35-53. Reprinted in S. Okechukwu Mezu, ed., *Modern Black Literature.* Buffalo, New York: Black Academy Press, 1971.

Nogueira, Oracy. "Skin Color and Social Class" [pp. 164-79] *Plantation Systems in the New World.* Washington: Pan American Union, 1959.

Ortiz, Adalberto. "La negritud en la cultura latinoamericana." *Expresiones culturales del Ecuador,* No. 1 (June 1972): 10-18.

Ortiz, Fernando. "José Antonio Saco y sus ideas." *Revista Bimestre Cubana* 2 (1929): 40-45.

———. "Más acerca de la poesía mulata. Escorzos para su estudio." *Revista Bimestre Cubana* 37, No. 1 (January-February 1936): 23-39.

———. "The Negro in the Spanish Theatre." *Phylon* 4 (1943): 144-47.

Ospina, Uriel. *Problemas y perspectivas de la novela americana.* Bogotá: Ediciones Tercer Mundo, 1964.

Pattee, Richard. "Latin America Shows Us Up." *Negro Digest* 2 (May 1944): 69-73.

Pereda Valdés, Ildefonso. "Contribución al estudio del tema del negro en la literatura castellana hasta fines de la Edad de Oro." *El negro rioplatense y otros ensayos.* Montevideo: Claudio García y Cía., 1937.

———. *El negro en el Uruguay.* Montevideo: Revista del Instituto Histórico y Geográfico del Uruguay, 1965.

———. *Lo negro y lo mulato en la poesía cubana.* Uruguay: Ediciones Ciudadela, 1970.

Perera, Hilda. *Idapo: El sincretismo en los cuentos de Lydia Cabrera.* Miami: Ediciones Universal, 1971.

Pérez-Venero, Mirna Miriam. "A Novelist's Erotic Racial Revenge" [pp. 24-27] *Caribbean Review* 4, No. 4 (October, November, December 1972).

———. "El sistema de segregación racial en las novelas canaleras de Joaquín Beleño C." *Lotería,* No. 188 (July 1971): 19-30.

———. "Raza, dolor y prejuicios en la novelística panameña contemporánea de tema canalero." Ph. D. Dissertation, Louisiana State University, 1973.

Pitt Rivers, Julian. "Race, Color, and Class in Central America and the Andes." In John Hope Franklin, ed., *Color and Race.* Boston: Beacon Press, 1968.

Portuondo, José Antonio. "El negro, héroe, bufón y persona en la literatura cubana colonial." *Unión* 7, No. 4 (December 1968): 30-36.

Prêto-Rodas, Richard A. *Negritude as a Theme in the Poetry of the Portuguese Speaking World.* Gainesville: University of Florida Press, 1970.

———. "The Development of Negritude in the Poetry of the Portuguese Speaking World." In Edward D. Terry, ed., *Artists and Writers in the Evolution of Latin America.* University, Alabama: University of Alabama Press, 1969.

Price, Richard, ed. *Maroon Societies: Rebel Slave Communities in the Americas.* New York: Doubleday, 1973.

Quesada, Luis. "Desarrollo evolutivo del elemento negro en tres de las primeras narraciones de Alejo Carpentier" [pp. 217-23]. *Literatura de la Emancipación hispanoamericana y otros ensayos. Memoria del XV Congreso del Instituto de Literatura Iberoamericana Sesión en Lima.* Lima: Universidad Nacional Mayor de San Marcos, 1972.

Rabassa, Gregory. "The Negro in Brazilian Fiction Since 1888." Ph. D. dissertation, Columbia University, 1954.

———. "Negro Themes and Characters in Brazilian Literature." *African Forum* 2 (Spring 1967): 20-34.

———. *O Negro na Ficçao Brasileira.* Rio de Janeiro: Ediçōes Tempo Brasileiro, 1965.

Ramos, Guerreiro. *Patologia social do "branco" brasileiro.* Rio de Janeiro, 1955.

Ratcliff, Dillwyn F. *Venezuelan Prose Fiction.* New York: Instituto de las Españas, 1933.

Reckord, Barry. *Does Fidel Eat More Than Your Father? Conversations in Cuba.* New York: The New American Library, 1971.

Recopilación de textos sobre Nicolás Guillén. Ed. by Nancy Morejón, Havana: Casa de las Américas, 1974.

Ribadeneira, Edmundo. "La presencia del negro." In *La moderna novela ecuatoriana.* Quito: Editorial Casa de la Cultura Ecuatoriana, 1958.

Richard, Renaud. *"Juyungo* de Adalberto Ortiz, ou de la haine raciale a la lutte contre l'injustice." *Bulletin Hispanique* 72 (1970): 152-70.

Ring, Harry. *How Cuba Uprooted Race Discrimination.* New York, 1961.

Rosenblat, Angel. *Lengua literaria y lengua popular en América.* Caracas: Universidad Central de Venezuela, 1969.

Sagrera, Martin. *Los racismos en América Latina.* Buenos Aires: Ediciones La Bastilla, 1974.

———. *Racismo y política en Puerto Rico.* Rio Piedras: Editorial Edil Inc., 1973.

Salas, Teresa C. and Richard Henry. "Nicomedes Santa Cruz y la poesía de su conciencia de negritud." *Cuadernos Americanos* 202 (September-October 1975): 182-99.

Sampson, Margaret. "Africa in Medieval Spanish Literature: Its Appearance in *El Caballero Cifar." Negro History Bulletin* 32 (December 1969): 14-19.

Sánchez, Luis Alberto. *El pueblo en la revolución americana*. Lima: P. L. Villanueva, 1971.

———. *Proceso y contenido de la novela hispanoamericana*. Madrid: Gredos, 1953.

Sánchez M., Alvaro. "El negro en la literatura costarricense." In Meléndez, Carlos and Duncan, Quince, *El negro en Costa Rica*. San José: Editorial Costa Rica, 1972.

Sayers, Raymond S. *The Negro in Brazilian Literature*. New York: Hispanic Institute in the United States, 1956.

Scheines, Gregorio. *Novelas rebeldes en América*. Buenos Aires: Editorial Americalee, 1960.

Schwartz, Kessel. *A New History of Spanish American Fiction*. 2 volumes Coral Gables, Florida: University of Miami Press, Vol 1, 1972; Vol 2, 1971.

———. "Montalvo and the Negro." *Romance Notes* 9 (1964): 29-32.

Schwartz, Stuart. "Cities of Empire: Mexico and Bahia in the Sixteenth Century." *Journal of Inter-American Studies* 11 (1969): 628.

Seeber, E. D. *Anti-Slavery Opinion in France during the Second Half of the Eighteenth Century*. Baltimore: Johns Hopkins University Press, 1937.

Shapiro, Norman R., Ed. and Translator. *Negritude: Black Poetry from Africa and the Caribbean*. New York: October House, Inc., 1970.

Siegel, Reuben. "The 'Group of Guayaquil.' A Study in Contemporary Ecuadorian Fiction." Ph. D. dissertation, University of Wisconsin, 1951.

Silberman, Charles. *Crisis in Black and White*. New York: Vintage Books, 1964.

Skidmore, Thomas. *Black into White. Race and Nationality in Brazilian Thought*. New York: Oxford University Press, 1974.

Sojo, Juan Pablo. *Temas y apuntes afro-venezolanos*. Caracas: Cuadernos Literarios de la Asociación de Escritores Venezolanos, 1943.

Solaún, Mauricio and Kronus, Sidney. *Discrimination without Violence: Miscegenation and Racial Conflict in Latin America*. New York: John Wiley and Sons, 1973.

Sommers, Joseph. "La génesis literaria de Francisco Rojas González." *Revista Iberoamericana* 29 (1963): 306-309.

Stabb, Martin. *In Quest of Identity*. Chapel Hill: University of North Carolina Press, 1967.

Stimson, Frederick S. *Cuba's Romantic Poet. The Story of Plácido*. Chapel Hill: The University of North Carolina Press, 1964.

Suárez Radillo, Carlos Miguel. "El negro y su encuentro de sí mismo a través del teatro." *Cuadernos Hispanoamericanos*, No. 271 (January 1973): 34-40.

Tannenbaum, Frank. *Slave and Citizen: The Negro in the Americas*. New York: Alfred A. Knopf, 1963.

"The Pleasure and Problem of the 'Pretty' Black Man." *Ebony,* September, 1974, pp. 132-43.

Thompson, Miriam. H. "Anti-Imperialism as Reflected in the Prose Fiction of Middle America." Ph. D. dissertation, Tulane University, 1955.

Torres-Rioseco, Arturo. "Social Poetry." *New World Literature*. Berkeley: University of California Press, 1949.

———. "Negro Verse." *The Epic of Latin American Literature*. Berkeley: University of California Press, 1959.

Tous, Adriana. *La poesía de Nicolás Guillén*. Madrid: Ediciones Cultura Hispánica, 1971.

Turnin, Melvin. Ed. *Comparative Perspectives on Race Relations*. Boston: Little, Brown, 1969.

Valdés, Mario J. "The Literary Social Symbol for an Interrelated Study of Mexico." *Journal of Inter-American Studies* 7, No. 3 (July 1965): 385-99.

Valdés-Cruz, Rosa E. *La poesía negroide en América*. New York: Las Américas Publishing Co., 1970.

———. *Lo ancestral africano en la narrativa de Lydia Cabrera*. Barcelona: Editorial Vosgos, S. A., 1974.

Van den Berghe, Pierre. *Race and Racism, a Comparative Perspective*. New York: John Wiley and Sons, 1967.

Wauthier, Claude. *The Literature and Thought of Modern Africa*. New York: Frederick A. Praeger, 1967.

Weber de Kuriat, F. "Sobre el negro como tipo cómico en el teatro español del siglo XVI." *Romance Philology* 17, No. 63 (November 1963): 380-91.

Williams, Eric. "The Historical Background of Race Relations in the Caribbean." In *Miscelánea de estudios dedicados a Fernando Ortiz,* Vol. 3. Havana: Ucor, Garcia, S. A., 1957.

Wilson, William E. "Some Notes on Slavery during the Golden Age." *Hispanic Review* 7 (1939): 171-74.

Woodson, Carter G. "Attitudes of the Iberian Peninsula." *The Journal of Negro History* 20, No. 2 (April 1935): 190-243.

Yáñez, Agustín. *El contenido social de la literatura iberoamericana*. México, D. F.: El Colegio de México, 1943.

Zea, Leopoldo. "Negritud e indigenismo." *Cuadernos Americanos* 197 (November/December 1974): 16-30.

Zenón Cruz, Isabelo. *Narcisco descubre su trasero (El negro en la cultura puertorriqueña),* Vol. I. Humacao, Puerto Rico: Editorial Furidi, 1974.

Index